STATE VIOLENCE IN NORTHERN IRELAND 1969–1997

RAYMOND MURRAY

MERCIER PRESS

MERCIER PRESS
PO Box 5, 5 French Church Street, Cork
16 Hume Street, Dublin 2

Trade enquiries to CMD DISTRIBUTION,
55a Spruce Avenue, Stillorgan Industrial Park, Blackrock, Dublin

© Raymond Murray, 1998

ISBN 185635 235 8

10 9 8 7 6 5 4 3 2

FOR
DENIS FAUL

Printed in Ireland by Colour Books Ltd.

CONTENTS

INTRODUCTION

December 1971 marked a watershed in my life. Political prisoners who had been ill-treated and tortured in Holywood Palace Barracks and Girdwood Park Barracks were imprisoned in Armagh Jail where I was chaplain. I saw the horrific marks on their bodies. I experienced the blatant cover-up of this illegal and immoral behaviour. Directly and indirectly, the army, police, doctors, civil administration and government were involved in this criminal action.

Pursuance of the grievances of those who suffered duress in interrogation centres, a never-ending story in the recent long war in Northern Ireland, led Denis Faul and myself into campaigning against other violations of human rights in Northern Ireland in subsequent years: corruption of law; lack of independence in the matter of inquiry into complaints; the abuse of emergency laws; harassment and intimidation of civilians by security forces; injuries and deaths caused by rubber and plastic bullets; collusion between British security forces, British intelligence and loyalist paramilitaries; unjust killings and murders by state security forces; excessive punishments in the prisons; cruel strip searching in prisons. In the 1970s only a few people actively helped to try and stop these violations of human rights: the Civil Rights Movement, the Association for Legal Justice, the National Council for Civil Liberties, Amnesty International and some concerned priests, doctors, surgeons and lawyers. In latter years the Committee for the Administration of Justice, Belfast, and the Pat Finucane Centre, Derry, have come to prominence as state watchers. Fr Brian Brady, Fr Denis Faul, Sister Sarah Clarke of London and myself worked individually and together from 1971. We were also connected with the Association for Legal Justice where a small number of valiant people worked day and night to take statements and record the plight of the oppressed. I recall them with respect and pride: Frances Murray, Clara Reilly, Anne Murray, Rita Mullen, Rosaleen Boyle, Margaret Gatt, Mary Thornberry, Seán McCann and Paddy Kelly. There was also a distinguished group of solicitors who gave advice and took up cases. Paddy McGrory heads the list, honourably followed by Oliver Kelly, Eilis McDermot, Pat Finucane, Peter Madden, Chris Napier, Pádraigín Drinan, Pat Marrinan, Ted Jones, Francis Keenan and Paschal O'Hare.

There are two kinds of histories, one fact and one semi-fiction. This is the conclusion of my experience in working for human rights. The history put out by the ruling class borders on fiction. Their official communiqués are published first and grab the headlines. They hold attention while a crisis lasts. It is an attempt to legitimise illegal actions by which they maintain their power over the powerless and the poor. It is tyranny's deceit.

The second history is the short and simple annals of the poor, the worm's eye view. It is often secret. It is the story of the injustice done to them in order to preserve the power and privilege of a few. When power is threatened, the 'lion' and the 'eagle' and the 'bear' will grab the nearest and crush them as an example to the rest. It matters not that they are innocent or guilty. What matters is that they are close at hand and are representative.

Can true history be written? Is it essentially the story of the ruling class? Is it the speeches of President Ronald Reagan and the memoirs of Mrs Margaret Thatcher? Is it not also the story of the unemployed in Birmingham and the deprived blacks in Atlantic City? Must the 'nobodies' remain statistics of birth, death and marriage? There are many 'hidden Irelands' but who has hidden them? The sufferings, the tensions, the spiritual striving for holiness of countless poor families, the injustices done to the underprivileged and the miraculous survival of their traditions in spite of the ever-present monster of power, these are true history. We should give the poor the dignity of their names.

Traditionally too much writing of the history of Ireland was based on state papers and the public judgements of governments and judges. Historical expression was reduced to a truculent embarrassment which silenced the cries for justice of the poor. When the state was wrong it hid the facts and stopped the truth being told. The writer of the introductory history to *Liber Munerum Publicorum Hiberniae 1152–1827* says, 'We may observe here once for all that Ireland of itself has no history, properly speaking'. No wonder Pádraic Pearse countered such attitudes in his tract, *The Spiritual Nation:*

> But the soul of the enslaved and broken nation may conceivably be a more splendid thing than the soul of the great free nation; and that is one reason why the enslavements of old and glorious nations that have taken

place so often in history are the most terrible things that have ever happened in the world.

Since we are commemorating in 1998 the bicentenary of the United Irishmen, we might recall the comment on the deprivation of justice by the United Irishman Arthur O'Connor in his address *To the Irish Nation:*

> But, why should I waste time in proving that government, in the hands of Irish administration, has been a system for supporting the few in oppressing the many, instead of yielding impartial protection? Has it not been by sowing, maintaining and fomenting division, that Irish administrations have governed Ireland? Look to the continuation of civil discord, of plunder and bloodshed, which has infested our island, since the Welch landed in 1165, to this instant, that these hell-hounds intituled Ancient Britons are butchering our disarmed people. Look in this century to the writings of wretchedness, of misery, of want and oppression, under the different shapes of White-boys, Right-boys, Hearts-of-oak men, Peep-o-day boys, and Steel-men. Yet where is there an instance on record, in which the Government or Legislature in Ireland have inquired into the causes of their constant unerring marks of oppression? No! A system of smothered war between the oppressors and the oppressed, could not bear inquiry, for it would bear redress. Redress means restoration of plunder and restoration of rights. Therefore sanguinary laws and military outrage, whose expences are endless, have been substituted for justice, whose expences are nothing.

Fr Denis Faul and I wrote similar words in *The Furrow,* April 1984:

> The killing of a man involves an obligation to make good the damage to his dependants; stealing means that the object stolen must be given back; if one has taken another's land (or another's country) one must return it as part of the reconciliation process; if one has deprived a person of his character one must restore it; if one has sent people to jail by false witness or by the use of force in extracting statements, then that evil work must be reversed and undone to achieve reconciliation; if one discriminates in the ordering of society, then that discrimination must be reversed to bring about reconciliation. Reconciliation involves the work of justice, of restoring to the other person what you have taken from him and paying for the injury done him, with a determination that that will not occur again.
>
> It involves giving back to people their dignity, self-respect, freedom, human rights, the right to worship and educate their children in their faith, to receive back the place that has been taken and the community/country that has been confiscated and oppressed.

The conflicts of the 1798 period are no different from those of today. I have witnessed the state in Northern Ireland kill, torture, bribe, and imprison people unjustly. Denis Faul and I tried to stop these violations of human rights by official complaints, by breaking the silence in the media, by publishing books, pamphlets and broadsheets, by noising the problems abroad. This book *State Violence in Northern Ireland, 1969–1997,* draws together pieces illustrative of the violations of human rights by the state in Northern Ireland. They were written fresh during those years. Most of them have already been published in books, pamphlets and magazines. People who have lived through this period in Northern Ireland will immediately recall the perspective they convey. I am sure they will help others understand the frustration of the 'nobodies' who did not get justice and whose voices were almost suppressed.

I wrote an essay in *Seanchas Ard Mhacha* in 1982 on the killing of a prisoner, Thomas Birch, a United Irishman, who was being brought under guard by the Dublin Militia from Glenane in south Armagh to Armagh Prison. When a rescue was threatened, one of the soldiers killed him. The wriggling of legal officials and military personnel to pervert justice in that case is mirrored true in this present book. Thomas Pelham, Chief Secretary in Dublin Castle, wrote to General Lake,

> I received your letter of the 25th and you may rest assured that every sort of attention shall be paid to the sergeant of the Dublin Militia who is to be tried in Armagh. I do not think that any mark of particular favour can be shown to him before his trial but if he is acquitted as I have no doubt he must be I can venture to say that the Lord Lieutenant will be glad to bestow some distinguished mark of favour upon him.

We witnessed such an attitude in Northern Ireland over these troubled years. People were assassinated by policy of the British government; witness the Gibraltar murders. None of the RUC or British army did a day in jail for torture and ill-treatment of hundreds of people arrested under emergency laws. None of the middle or high command in the security forces resigned in protest. There were some 150 cases of unjust killings and murders by security forces. Only a few soldiers were convicted of murder. The military establishment and the imperialist-minded campaigned for their early release and a declaration of their 'innocence'. We still await the uncovering of the involvement of

British intelligence and loyalist paramilitaries in the Dublin and Monaghan bombings of 17 May 1974 when 33 people were killed. Successive Irish and British governments stubbornly refuse to reveal the facts. They are terrified of the truth. The law over many years was bent and used as a weapon in counter-insurgency. People were brutalised and sent to prison on forced confessions or on concocted evidence or on the uncorroborated evidence of accomplices and convicted persons. The 'lion' reaches for the nearest victims: Carol Ann Kelly, a child returning home from the shop with a carton of milk, was killed by a plastic bullet fired by a soldier; Richard Moore, a ten-year old boy dashing out from school, was blinded by a rubber bullet fired from a British army post; Mrs Nora McCabe was killed by a plastic bullet fired at point blank range from an RUC landrover on a quiet street while on her way to buy a packet of cigarettes; Patrick McElhone, a farm labourer, was taken from his home and shot by the British army within sight of his aged father. These little people and many others were gravely injured or died at the hands of the state. The long arm of the state and the controlled media tried to bury them under the clay of official files. Of course the power of the state in its civil service and money is immense. This book removes some of the clay.

The rôle of the academic is changing, I hope. Today the historian must live with history as it is being made. We have seen historians expose the hypocrisy of the public statements and the private orders of the last world war and the wars in Korea and Vietnam. I think historians should close the gap and become investigators of current public affairs. They should expose and challenge the prejudice that the ruling class presents through the media and through their spokespersons. Similarly, what good are theologians if they can only speak for the past? And why did the philosophers in the universities sing dumb in post-war Northern Ireland while the whirlwind gathered? We had five years of internment and a decade of torture. Only a few notable academics spoke out. Do academics only comment on the dead?

The historian of today should expose the workings of modern government and reveal the enormous amount of truth that is concealed. This book gives examples of the violations of human rights in Northern Ireland, 1969–1997. Fortunately, the interest of national security, patronage and power did not suppress all the truth.

I

HUMAN RIGHTS

Peace and Reconciliation

THE BEAUTY AND DIGNITY OF CREATION
Welcome to Paradise, to a world wrapped in light, dashed with colours, veiled in shades and darkness. Welcome to beautiful Earth made by God. I have seen a blue haze like a filmy net hanging over the vast expanse of the bush in Australia under the shimmering desert light. A missionary friend has described to me the tropical jungles of Burma dank with oppressive heat and moisture. I have often seen pictures of the sun gleaming on the soaring white mountains of the Himalayas. We are happy in Ireland to walk among our familiar brown bogs and green fields. How lovely the pleasant waters of the River Lee! How delightful to wander along the meandering banks of the Callan in Armagh! To listen to silence or to drink in the sound of music is to be transported back to Paradise. This world is given to us to honour and love. How mysterious it is! Its stewardship is entrusted to humankind. Our responsibility is very great.

Welcome to Paradise and Peace. The peace of God which is greater than all understanding. God breathes within us linking us in our Garden of Eden to individuals of every description, linking all peoples in one great family. Humanity is the community of God. This is Paradise. Peace with God, peace in one's own heart, peace among all peoples.

When God created us in his image, he endowed us with divine dignity. He taught us how to use the earth and its fruits for our own good and the good of everyone. He himself is reflected in the work of human hands.

THE FALL
We regret that we took the forbidden fruit. Man refused to ack-

nowledge his Lord and Creator. He believed that he was his own master. Man destroyed the harmony between himself and others and all the creatures around him. 'When they were out in the fields, Cain turned on his brother and killed him. The Lord asked Cain, "Where is your brother Abel?" He answered, "I don't know. Am I supposed to take care of my brother?" Then the Lord said, "Why have you done this terrible thing? Your brother's blood is crying out to me for revenge."'

Are we brothers and sisters to others? We hear the daily death toll from Rwanda and Bosnia. We have listened to and experienced the tragedies in this tiny part of Ireland for twenty-five years. 'A mountain of suffering', Cardinal William Conway used to call it. Last week we buried a young woman in our parish, victim of a sectarian murder. She was badly beaten and her throat was cut in a sectarian attack on Castlereagh Road, Belfast. On Wednesday a Catholic man was murdered near Armagh, shot dead in his lorry while at his work. Last month an IRA bomb blew eight Protestants to bits in Teebane, County Tyrone. Last month the UDA shot dead five Catholics in a bookie shop on the Ormeau Road, Belfast.

JUSTICE AND PEACE IN THE OLD TESTAMENT
The Old Testament is full of evil behaviour of this kind, man using the gifts of creation to burn, ravage and kill. The People of God, our ancestors in faith, the Hebrews, carried out cruel acts of violence and wars against other nations and got itself entangled with their wars. The war God protected them from their enemies and made them victorious over other enemies.

But this image of a war God is not the only image in the Old Testament. Amid the tragedy is a God of Israel who is not only the God of a single nation but also the creator of the world who wishes all peoples to be saved. The Old Testament testifies to the life of justice and peace which Israel is asked to seek in union with God. The chosen people were called on by God to seek not only freedom, justice and security but also a peace founded on God's covenant. It was more than a social and political peace. It was also a religious peace. This peace expressed itself in justice to one's neighbour. Peace is the work of justice says Isaiah. 'Everywhere in the land righteousness and justice will be done. Because everyone will do what is right, there will be peace and security for ever'(Isaiah 32:16–17). The lament of Isaiah 48:18 makes clear the connection between justice, fidelity to God's law and peace; he cries out: 'O that you had hearkened to my commandments! Then your peace would have been like a river, and your righteousness like the waves of the sea.' Peace was strengthened by God's help and by man's adherence to God's laws. The Old Testament message is true for us today. Whenever we accept God in our life, justice and peace are possible. This is the fulfilment of the words of the psalm: 'Mercy and truth have met together, justice and peace have kissed each other' (Psalm 85:10). We pray this evening that we will recognise and acknowledge God's rule, that God's truth and justice will prevail in our thoughts, aspirations and actions.

THE GOSPEL OF PEACE
Peace in this world is always under threat. There is no utopia, no final state of peace in a new political order. We look forward to the parousia, a new heaven and a new earth, but we have learned that that is kingdom come when all creation will be made whole. The 'gospel of peace', the message proclaimed by Christ, announces the presence of God's rule. It brings about our reconciliation with God and people. However, the full realisation of God's rule remains to be brought about in heaven. The old world of sin has not simply disappeared. We still have to struggle against the forces of darkness, a struggle which began with Adam and Eve, with Cain and Abel, and which will last until the end of time. Pride and disobedience harden the hearts of us all. Even Christ's new creation, redeemed people, can yield to the temptations of power. War and enmity are still present, injustices thrive, sin still manifests itself. Hatred, oppression and violence lurk in the social, political and institutional spheres of our human existence. 'All creation groans with pain, like the pain of childbirth' (Rom. 8:22). There is evil in the world despite its redemption.

The final victory, however, is with Christ. The New Testament shows how people have experienced in Jesus 'the kindness and love of God our saviour' (Titus 3:4). Jesus himself is God's messenger of peace. His words and deeds bring God's liberating kingdom nearer. His words, especially as they are preserved for us in the Sermon on the

Mount, describe a new reality in which God's power is manifested and the longing of the people is fulfilled. In God's reign the poor are given the Kingdom, the mourners are comforted, the meek inherit the earth, those hungry for righteousness are satisfied, the merciful know mercy, the pure see God, the persecuted know the Kingdom, and peacemakers are called the children of God. Jesus is a healer who takes care of people in their concrete situations in life. He gives both a physical and spiritual salvation. He gives sight to Bartimaeus. He consoles and praises the Syro-Phoenician woman. He interviews the woman at Jacob's well by day and listens to Nicodemus by night. He forgives sin, 'Young man, your sins are forgiven'. He makes a friend of Mary Magdalen. Jesus teaches people to pass on to others the reconciliation which they have gained, 'go at once and make peace with your brother and then come and offer your gift to God' (Matt. 5:24). In the eyes of Jesus peace is not something that is easy to obtain. He talks about a peace the world can not give. This peace does not afford protection against those who oppose it. Jesus himself achieved the reconciliation between God and people on the cross. When we look at a crucifix we understand the power of evil. Violence and injustice in our world are so great that Jesus had to die on a cross to bring about peace and justice. He who lived a life of non-violence became a victim of violence. The cross and resurrection of our Saviour: these are our peace. In his death there is life. In his defeat there is victory. As disciples and as children of God, it is our task to seek for ways in which to make the forgiveness, justice and mercy, and love of God visible in a world where violence and enmity are too often the norm. When we listen to God's word, we hear again and always the call to repentance and to belief: to repentance because although we are redeemed we continue to need redemption; to belief, because although the reign of God is near, it is still seeking its fullness.

The Church and Peace
The Church of Jesus Christ faces a challenge to continue to testify to the peaceful words and deeds of Jesus and in a spirit of hope against hope to make them her own cause. She invites her members to become a community of reconciliation in practice. She invites all people to found the peace of the world on a relationship with God and in a

spirit of trust in his commandments.

Archbishop Oscar Romero, the martyred bishop of El Salvador, said: 'The way of Jesus leads to communion with all people. His enduring presence in the Church is the foundation of a profound brotherhood in the world just as God desires it. Love the Church as the Lord himself. Though she is burdened with the weakness and sinfulness of a long history, she is still the instrument of his Kingdom, his work of salvation for the world, the germ of a new creation.'

Moved by the example of Jesus' life and by his teaching, some Christians have from the earliest days of the Church committed themselves to a non-violent life-style. Some understood the gospel of Jesus to prohibit all killing. Some affirmed the use of prayer and other spiritual methods as means of responding to enmity and hostility. When the wall dividing Church and State fell in Roman times, Christians began to share the responsibility of wars. It is easy to see the weakness and sinfulness of the past. While making allowance for our difficulty to understand varied historical situations we would have to say that the Crusades to liberate the Holy Land were waged with great cruelty. Pope John Paul II has called on historians to prepare studies for the year 2000 and the new millennium, a recognition of errors committed by members of the Church and, in a certain sense, in its name. I am sure it will include a humble repentance for the excesses of the Crusades, the religious wars of the sixteenth century, the Inquisition, and reviews of Galileo and Copernicus, Luther and Hus. The Catholic Church will look at its own witness, culminating in the martyrdoms of the last hundred years and perhaps produce an ecumenical martyrology which would include martyrs from all the Christian Churches and communions. Nearer to our own times the colonial wars were barbaric in nature. Spain, Portugal, Great Britain, France, Germany, Holland, Belgium, Italy can hardly lift their heads with shame for the violence and death and suffering they brought in brutal fashion to America, Africa, India, Australia, New Zealand, the Middle East and the Far East. These countries still feel the pain of the wounds. Even in Ireland today we still bear the scars of the genocide policy of the nation-state established by the Tudors. A letter appeared in a recent issue of *The Tablet* – 'Why do Christians kill one another in Africa? is a question tormenting those attending the African Synod in Rome – in Europe have we become so hardened to the practice of Christians killing one another that we no longer bother to ask?' Yes, Christians still succumb to the temptations of power and violence and thus disregard the word of the Lord.

Looking back on the history of the Church, on the good side one can say that Christians have struggled hard from Augustine to Thomas Aquinas to debate the problems of war and peace. Pacifism has gained ground, especially in the recognition of personal conscientious objection. The theory of a just war was always something incomplete. Today it is heavily limited with the presumption against war, the immorality of nuclear warfare, and the immorality of conventional defensive strategy which violates the principle of proportionality, going beyond the limits of legitimate defence. There have always been movements and figures within the Christian denominations which have been exemplary in their fulfilment of Christ's testimony that we must love our enemies and practise peace. Such a spirit is embodied in St Francis and in the Franciscan prayer 'Lord make me an instrument of your peace'. Many Christians have proved themselves peace-makers in the midst of violent confrontation. The modern popes from Benedict XV to Pope John Paul II and other Christian leaders have grown louder in their calls for disarmament as the threat of annihilation of entire peoples and states by nuclear weapons has increased. They have deplored the incessant arms race, promoted world authority for the regulation of conflicts, directed attention towards promoting human rights and establishing humane conditions of life.

THE WORLD TODAY

It is difficult for us to understand the world we live in. Missiles and weaponry of all kinds abound, the cost of which would feed the world many times over. And yet one half of the earth, the northern hemisphere, prospers and the southern hemisphere is starved of rice, bread and medicines. The great economic powers of the world, USA, Europe and Japan and its neighbours may fight their trade wars out, or they may make a global agreement to share, but will they exclude the underdeveloped southern hemisphere? Is the power of Christians now so weak in the developed countries that it will not be possible for them to get these great powers to really accept that the globe is inhabited by a single family in which all have the same basic needs and all have a right to the goods of the earth, an interdependent world with a common nature and destiny?

Europe is still in a process of healing in the wake of the horrors of two world wars. Gorbachev and Pope John Paul, mighty giants of peace, have by their influence in Poland and Russia helped to end the east-west conflict. The United States and Russia have given new hope to the world, and to the planet, by their programme of progressive nuclear disarmament, begun by Kennedy and Kruschev and bearing fruit with Reagan and Gorbachev, with the present governments and we hope into the future. Surely there is tremendous moral pressure on the United States of America, Russia, France and Britain to destroy their nuclear weapons – in the absence of that surely it is hypocritical to comment on North Korea, India, Pakistan, Iran, Iraq and Israel?

There have been more than 130 wars in the Third World since 1945 which have cost the lives of 35 million people. Through television, the media and missionaries we have felt the human suffering in Nicaragua, El Salvador, Peru, Guatemala, Mexico, Ethiopia, Somalia, Liberia, Angola, Mozambique, the Sudan, South Africa, Bosnia and many other places in recent years. The Palestine-Israeli conflict seemed perennial. Their present peace evolution seems like a miracle. F. W. de Klerk has been magnanimous in his tribute to Nelson Mandela – 'You have come a long way', a far cry from Ian Smith's 'Not in a thousand years'.

Not all attempted solutions are praiseworthy. Sometimes we are deceived by the rhetoric of propaganda. The Roman historian Tacitus gives us the response of Calgracus, a British chief in the north of England to the conquest of the Roman legions under Agricola – *ubi solitudinem faciunt, pacem appellant* 'they make a wilderness and they call it peace'. His remark can be applied to wars today. We hear often that fifty thousand American troops died in Vietnam; we are seldom told that three million Vietnamese died. A million Algerians died in their war of independence. Robert Fisk has revealed the savagery of the Israeli invasion of Lebanon and the siege of Beirut in his book *Pity the Nation*. However just in principle the offensive against Sadam Hussein, the Gulf War in terms of civilian casualties resulted in perhaps the greatest single western atrocity since the devastation of the atomic bombs on Hiroshima and Nagasaki, which latter events were once described by Pope Paul VI as a 'butchery of untold magnitude'.

How do we face the tremendous discord in our world today? – ferocious new means of warfare threatening a savagery surpassing that of the past, deceit, subversion, terrorism, genocide, and forms of structural violence where resources and the control of resources are the property of one group who use them not for the good of all but for their own profit.

I think that since the last Great War the concept of 'Peace' has ideologically replaced the glorification of war. Slowly different governments have made public declarations of their past inhumanity to man. Reconciliation requires repentance as a first step. How can we repent for the enslavement of Africans, for the genocide of the Indians of North and South America and other indigenous peoples, for colonialism, for domination, oppression and aggression? Germany has done it for the immeasurable suffering it caused. Could the former allies not also ask forgiveness for the fire storms inflicted on Hamburg and the bombing of Dresden? Consider the magnificent words of John Baker, Anglican bishop of Salisbury. 'I consider it is perfectly right for Englishmen – as I and some of my friends have done – to go over to Ireland and say, "Look I am sorry". Not just we are sorry, but I am sorry for what we have done to bring about the problems you now face. And I believe that it would be an enormous step forward in the whole situation if our own political leaders, preferably the Prime Minister – I tried this on when Margaret Thatcher was in power – were actually to say something like that in a speech. Not to say we think that everything we're doing at the moment is wicked or anything like that, but to accept responsibility for having brought the situation or contributed to bringing the situation to where it is now. And that in itself is very important. You can't make other people forgive you, but you can at least say, "we need to be forgiven", and I think that is a very important Christian insight.'

Pope John Paul in his homily at Coventry Cathedral said, 'Peace is not just the absence of war. It involves mutual respect and confidence between peoples and nations. It involves collaboration and binding agreements. Like a cathedral, peace must be constructed patiently and with unshakeable faith'.

Because of the interdependence of the world we look to international organisations for solutions. They have mushroomed since the end of the last world war. Pope Paul VI called the United Nations the last hope for peace. However, it is clear that its bureaucracy and outdated Security Council greatly hamper its work. I think public opinion is more than disappointed in its failure to act in Rwanda. The same pope once said, 'If you wish peace, defend life'. He would be more than disappointed at the United Nations Preparatory Committee's choice of death rather than life in its contraceptive proposals for African countries for the International Conference on Population and Development to be held in Cairo.

The anxiety and impatience world disorder creates must be met personally with a spirit of strength. The temptation to shut ourselves off from the magnitude of the problem must be met with the toil of taking one small step at a time. The temptation to look only to our own welfare must be matched with a spirit of love which esteems the dignity, the rights and liberty of each individual and which protects our neighbours against degradation, bondage and injustice. Can we make the tender mercy of God present in a world of violence, oppression and injustice by our active forgiveness?

And as little individuals faced with such huge problems what can we do? A little story to end – 'It was a chilly, overcast day when the rider saw the little sparrow lying on its back in the middle of the road. Reining on his mount he looked down and inquired of the little creature, 'Why are you lying upside down like that?'

'I heard the heavens are going to fall today,' replied the bird.

The rider laughed. 'And I suppose your spindly legs can hold up the heavens?'

'One does what one can,' said the little sparrow.

NORTHERN IRELAND

In Northern Ireland there are some welcome signs of peace:

1. The major developments in Europe, namely the creation of a Single Market and the drive towards European political union, have profound implications for relations between Great Britain and Ireland. Britain is no longer interested in Ireland from its national security point of view. The forces of history and the forces of economics

21

are marching with great speed in Europe and they will take us along with them. The fear of Ireland's links with her European enemies once led Britain to colonise Ireland. Now the reverse is happening. Ireland's renewed links with Europe will draw us not only into friendship with Britain, witness the Anglo-Irish agreement, but into friendship with other European states. As Germany increasingly becomes the economic centre of Europe the Irish population in Germany will increase. The old German-Irish friendships of the early and late middle ages are reawakening. The Irish government should promote these Irish-German cultural links. They could bring German investment in Ireland and the north would certainly look towards a south that is economically sound.

2. Cultural groups in the north are engaged in a quiet revolution – They are searching deeply in their hearts – Who are we? What are we? Are our traditions necessarily opposed as in the past? Could we share our heritage and enrich one another?

3. Dialogue is the new bright word. It has burst upon the media with the news that Protestant ministers have engaged in talks with loyalist paramilitaries. We remember, however, that the Secretary of State, Mr Peter Brooke, the former Taoiseach Mr Charles Haughey, and recently Cardinal Cahal Daly, have hinted at a place at the negotiation table for republicans should the IRA call a ceasefire. Now is the time for this dialogue to gain momentum. Church leaders and political leaders can not move the dialogue unless the groundswell of frequent and varied talking on the ground brings them along. On this subject I would recommend that the south should form a Peace Corps, modelled on the good aspects of the American Peace Corps founded by President John F. Kennedy. Peace must not be confined to fine words and fine gestures. Our Christian testimony must be reaffirmed by deeds. This Peace Corps would work for justice and peace. Young professionally trained southern Irish men and women of all religions, and none, could give years to the investigation of complaints of injustice and discrimination in Northern Ireland. They would be the living alternative to the use of violence. By the dynamism of spiritual and ethical forces allied to professional skills they could reassure people that their problems will not be forgotten. The Peace Corps could win the trust of all in Northern Ireland, Catholic and Protestant, in working with the governments in Dublin, London, and Belfast, with Amnesty International and the United Nations, to restore a sense of trust and confidence among all the people of the north.

THE EUCHARIST

This evening we personally receive the peace of Christ in the celebration of the Eucharist. We thank God for peace and beseech him time and time again to grant us peace. We ask for the grace to be witnesses to peace before the world, to serve the Church in peace, to serve our community in peace, to serve our country in peace.

Sermon preached in St Francis Church, Cork, Sunday 8 March 1992, organised by PEACE (Prayer Enterprise and Christian Effort). Expanded for International Conference on Religion and Conflict, Armagh, 20–21 May 1994.

I am indebted to the Pastoral Letter of the German Bishops, Gerechtigkeit schafft Frieden, *18 April 1983, and the Pastoral Letter of the USA bishops,* The Challenge of Peace, God's Promise and Our Response, *3 May 1983, for many of the ideas in this paper.*

The Rich and the Poor

ADHMED KASSIM

Jesus did not redeem the world out of nothing;
he redeemed it out of a little boy's satchel,
That day in the desert
when he fed the five thousand with five barley loaves and two fish,
all that the youngster had.
The boy was reluctant to part with them.
His mother had prepared his lunch
at daybreak,
kissed his forehead
and bade him farewell.
Jesus did not throw a feast out of nothing,
he multiplied the boy's generosity.
The child emptied his bundle,
gave up his meal to be fed on words.
Jesus learned his first lesson.

23

On the fourth day of February
nineteen hundred and ninety-one,
Black Crows gathered in the heavens without fear,
the Allies from the Western World.
They quickly unburdened their gigantic sacks,
and destroyed a bridge in southern Iraq.

They killed the people fleeing from al-Nasiriyeh.
It was Jesus who recognised Adhmed Kassim,
the boy with the loaves,
lying on a stretcher,
still wearing the red cardigan his mother had knit for him
so skilfully without a seam,
his head crowned with shrapnel thorns,
holes in his feet, a wound in his side.
He was only ten years of age.
Jesus learned his second lesson.

That is a translation of a poem in Irish I published in *An tUltach*. If you think it isn't good I can say it suffered in translation!

Propaganda called the Gulf War a clean war, a surgical operation, but here was killing comparable to Hiroshima and Dresden, a re-enactment of 'Bomber' Harris' aerial murder raid on Lubeck on 28 March 1942. Abrams tanks of the 1st Mechanised Infantry Division equipped with bulldozer blades drove parallel to Iraqi trenches and buried soldiers alive. The Basra road carnage of fleeing helpless soldiers reminded one of the worst features of the First World War. The systematic destruction of the civil infrastructure of Iraq has led to the ill-health of millions of people and a high infant mortality. The allies sought to destroy *en masse* the Iraqi forces in Kuwait and south-eastern Iraq. These were mainly peasant conscripts and reservists. Their surrender would have been a matter of course but the allies chose to treat them as 'target rich'. Thousands of fuel-air explosives and slurry bombs and cluster bombs which spill out hundreds of grenades, and missiles from the Multiple Rocket Launch System (MRLS) poured down on the unfortunates. There is little sympathy in western Europe and in the United States of America for the victims. Governments of western Europe and the USA deliberately deny their peoples access to the culture of the Arabs. Pope John Paul stood almost isolated in his condemnation of the Gulf War. The disciples of the Lord fled as at Gethsemane.

I welcome my inheritance of western culture. I hope I am positive about accepting the benefits of modern technology. I do not, however, accept as utopia the ideology of secular liberalism, pluralism or a 'democracy' based on capitalism. The Brandt report, which exposes the north-south divide of the earth, is too much a reproach for that. History repeats itself. Empires rise and fall. Each great new power regards itself as 'civilisation' and frowns on the rest of the world as 'barbarism'. New Caesars need not lop off the enemy tribe's right hands. They can bury them alive in trenches. The Rockeye II, weighing about 500lbs, dispenses 247 grenade-sized bomblets which produce a hail of around half a million anti-personnel shrapnel fragments which can kill or severely wound anyone within an acre. All that is needed is a target-rich area of human beings.

I believe there is a utopia or a parousia – the redemption of Jesus Christ. That demands moving into the world of spirit. Redemption like creation is an ongoing thing. People in every age are heroic in their suffering, sacrifice and generosity. Jesus is eternally alive and he learns from every age of humanity. The boy with the loaves in the desert and Adhmed Kassim are telescoped.

ON THE WRONG SIDE OF THE TRACK ...
I do not find the Northern Ireland problem difficult to understand. It is in microcosm the problem of many countries and states in the world. The division of rich and poor is the basis of the division in Northern Ireland. Discrimination against Catholics was administrative policy of the Stormont government for fifty years. Its rule lacked charity and justice. In that sense the war in the north is a religious war. The facts of this injustice were admitted publicly by the British government in the Cameron Report on Disturbances in Northern Ireland of 1969. Justice in the work places is still being pursued by the Fair Employment Agency in Northern Ireland and by Irish people armed with the McBride Principles who lobby institutions of power in the USA. Sharing, power-sharing, is an answer to the Northern Ireland problem. The British government has further aggravated the dominance of one community and culture over the other by the one-sided structuring of the Royal Ulster Constabulary and the Ulster Defence Regiment which places security and power solely in the hands of unionists.

This serious mistake has led to corruption of law, harassment, state killings and collusion of government forces with loyalist paramilitaries.

The ghetto people of Northern Ireland, particularly those in Derry and West Belfast, are like other ghetto people. They regard themselves, in John Steinbeck's phrase, as on 'the wrong side of the track'. Problems like vandalism, illiteracy, drugs and violence in ghetto cities are basically the result of deprivation. There is a temptation on the part of government to regard these problems as a matter of 'law and order'. That embitters the situation. The 'haves' and 'have nots' divide seems to be perennial. It has led to major conflicts in today's world – South Africa, Nicaragua, El Salvador and the Philippines.

The rich eventually are forced to take notice of the situation. What do they say to the poor? They dictate to them from government offices, palaces, penthouse flats and mansions. The more they dictate to them, the more the poor resent their solutions. They presume the loyalty of the ghettos to the state but many ghetto people hate the state. Sometimes the poor reply with bombs and guns, as much as to say, 'Well, if I don't share, you are not going to enjoy your wealth in peace'. That is the *raison d'être* of anarchy.

Why, for example, should the Northern Ireland Office presume the loyalty of the people of Ballymurphy, a little housing estate of nationalists in Belfast where in the past twenty years over sixty people have been shot dead by security forces and loyalist gangs, where houses on numerous occasions have been systematically wrecked by police and soldiers, where nearly every able-bodied man has been interned or imprisoned? Who built that ugly ghetto in the first place?

LISTENING TO THE POOR

Liberation theology has something relevant to say to us here. It can be summed up in the phrase 'Listen to the Poor'. The rich have an attitude, 'Can anything good come out of Nazareth?' Can anything good come out of Ballymurphy? Can anything good come out of Bally-fermot? The poor want no plan handed down to them, neither from the USA government, nor from the Northern Ireland Office, nor from Leinster House, nor from the Irish Episcopal Conference, nor from the National Conference of Priests of Ireland, nor from the International Funds. What are the poor saying themselves? Come down and listen to them. They don't want people telling them, 'What you want is ...'

Northern Ireland mirrors the world-wide problem of the rich and the poor, the resource-hungry northern hemisphere devouring the southern hemisphere. If oil or any other aspect of economy is a problem then the powerful, in the name of democracy and the free world, will bury the weak with great earth-movers. The creed of secular liberalism, materialism and capitalism provides the philosophy to do so.

Secularism can be a pseudo moral voice that offers us more and more to eat and drink, comforts us with block-buster bestsellers with sex and violence on every page, assassinates the characters of other moral voices in competition and shields the sins of media bosses. It wrecks the unity of the family and aborts children from the womb. Its bland monotonous sameness provokes the revolt of the small nations and cultures anxious to preserve their national heritages. It threatens non-conformists with nuclear and chemical weapons and aspires to star wars. But what about the enemy within? Could it be that as the ghettos expand in this brave new world we will live to see the poor rise again in a new socialist revolution? Who says socialism is dead?

Where does the world of the sacred stand confronted by the pervasive dominance of this heady secularism? Does it respond by tirelessly proclaiming the old virtues – disciplined prayer, disciplined charity, disciplined chastity, conservative authority?

Or will the sacred try to survive in dialogue with the secular and content itself with small committed Christian communities, bright faith globules in the darkening pagan sea?

Priests in the field have no time to answer. Every day a desert boy hands them a satchel of bread and fish. Every day they find Adhmed Kassim lying wounded on a stretcher. Like Jesus they have learned their lesson.

A response to papers read at the 1991 AGM of the National Conference of Priests of Ireland. Published in Good News in a Divided Society *(1992).*

The Ghetto Poor and Human Rights

A Chathaoirligh, a dhaoine uaisle, is mór an phribhléid dúinne, lucht feachtais agus gaolta ar son na cóire bheith i láthair ag an bhFóram agus bheirimid buíochas daoibh as an fhaill seo a thabhairt dúinn labhairt.

Madam Chairperson and members of the Forum,

Thank you for the privilege of addressing the Forum as chairperson of Relatives for Justice and chairperson of the Campaign for the Right to Truth. The Campaign is an umbrella group of eight organisations. There are six speakers on this panel and there are some thirty members present at the Forum. You will meet many of them informally and hear their stories. We are happy that you are willing to listen to poor, humble and vulnerable people who have suffered at the hands of the state in the past twenty-five years. You will have heard, and doubtlessly will hear more testimonies from victims and their relatives who have suffered grievously at the hands of the paramilitaries. We sympathise with these victims and encourage you to do all you can for them. Today we are focusing narrowly on a section of people, victims and their relatives who feel they have been neglected and ignored. The ghetto poor have to a great extent been a voiceless people – although they can be eloquent – voiceless because they are without power. Government officials, religious people and academics were not always willing to listen to them and so their lack of human rights and civil rights and justice went unredressed. They found it difficult to get their story told. The people represented here, madam chairperson, have been the victims of the corruption of law. Such a problem is worldwide. We are focusing here on Northern Ireland and Britain but we have also a speaker here to challenge governments and politicians in the Republic of Ireland whose silence on the Dublin and Monaghan bombings is as deafening as the explosions themselves. The agents of the law in Northern Ireland and Britain, people in charge of the law, have violated the law to use it as a weapon to torture men in interrogation centres, to send some innocent people to jail for life, to kill and injure civilians with plastic bullets, to shoot citizens with army guns, to act in collusion over twenty-five years with the

28

murderous intent of the loyalist paramilitaries. A second hurt, added to the injuries, is that the law has provided no adequate remedy for proper investigation; no truth or justice for the Relatives for Justice. Hence the appreciation of our groups to have a voice here today.

The British government does not hold the high moral ground. Like the paramilitaries it should also acknowledge and repent for its crimes, the deaths and suffering of innocent people it has caused. Truth helps a peace process and has healing effects. Justice and charity flow from it. Our submission to the Forum outlines 16 classifications of the violations of human rights. The headings are:

1. *Murder and unjust killings by the security forces.* 148 members of paramilitary oganisations and 138 innocent civilians have been killed by the Royal Ulster Constabulary (RUC) and the British army; some of these can be classified as murder and some as unjust killings. Prosecutions and convictions of members of the security forces have been avoided in most cases.

2. *Collusion* of the British Intelligence system, members of the Ulster Defence Regiment (UDR) and the Royal Irish Rangers (RIR), members of the RUC, with loyalist paramilitaries leading to the murders of hundreds of Catholics.

3. Widespread and deadly use of *rubber and plastic bullets* resulting in severe injuries and the deaths of 17 people, of whom 8 were children and one was a woman.

4. *Internment* of *c.* 2,000 Catholic men and 32 women under special powers and the cruel ill-treatment of same.

5. *Inhuman and degrading treatment* of detainees in Palace Barracks, Holywood, and Girdwood Barracks, Belfast, 1971–2.

6. *Torture* of 14 hooded men by sensory deprivation in Ballykelly Barracks in 1971.

7. *Duress:* Arrested people in the 1970s were forced to sign statements admitting crimes the police wanted to connect them with.

8. *Harassment:* For 20 years nationalists were subjected to arbitrary house searches, house wrecking, beatings, verbal harassment, and census taking by security forces.

9. Ill-treatment of arrested persons in *RUC stations 1972–75.*

10. Ill-treatment of arrested person in the *interrogation centres* at Castle-

reagh and Gough Barracks 1976–77.

11. Alleged verbal statements of accused given out by the police were accepted on their word in the *Diplock Courts;* beating, thumping and kicking prisoners and interrogating them for long periods and putting them in positions of stress, were not accepted as cruel and degrading treatment and statements taken after these forms of ill-treatment were accepted in court. There followed great disparity in sentences and some of the sentences were inhuman. Despite the censures of the British domestic report, the Bennett Report, in 1979, ill-treatment continued centred on beatings designed not to leave marks, on psychological torture and threats, blackmail and the use of supergrasses.

12. Severe *punishments* were inflicted on prisoners who refused to do prison work and wear prison clothes in the 1976–81 period.

13. Degrading *stripping* naked of the women prisoners in Armagh Prison 1982–1986.

14. *18 innocent* Irish people were imprisoned for long years by police action and judicial procedures in Britain which were contrary to human rights.

15. Some Irish political prisoners in British prisons were treated with *cruelty.*

16. *The Prevention of Terrorism Act* brought great suffering to many thousands of Irish in Britain.

When those charged with upholding the law appear to violate it with impunity in this way, the foundations of respect for law and order disappear. The question is: will the new Northern Ireland with a radically restructured police force, with strict regulations re appointment of judges, magistrates and coroners, avoid political prejudice, guarantee the human and civil rights of all citizens, provide independent modes of investigation of police and legal abuse, and will citizens in positions of power show concern for justice regarding security and social justice? We hope so

My Introduction to Oral Submissions from Relatives for Justice and from the Campaign for the Right to Truth to the Forum for Peace and Reconciliation, Dublin Castle, 11 April 1995.

The British Media and Ireland, 1979

On 13 March 1977 British media workers formed the Campaign for Free Speech on Ireland and in 1979 published a pamphlet *The British Media and Ireland – Truth the First Casualty*. It listed some television programmes from 1970 to 1978 dealing with Northern Ireland that had been banned and carried articles by journalists and other commentators on the difficulties of reporting on Northern Ireland, censorship and distorted images of Ireland. The blurb on the back of the pamphlet has a quotation from a BBC television news sub-editor, 'I've always assumed that the official line is we put the army's version first and then any other'.

At the inaugural meeting of the campaign Jonathan Dimbleby, Thames television reporter, said, 'Those who have access, anywhere, at any time, to our media, should be pressing to ensure that in those media Northern Ireland is put in context, the events there are explained, the possible future analysed. Otherwise it will continue to deny the British public the kind of information it needs to form a judgement about the most important political issue that any government has had to face'.

I contributed the following piece to the pamphlet. It was written for the Theatre Writers' Union conference on censorship in London on 28 January 1979:

'The one means of redress left to people in the north of Ireland is publicity. There has never been in the past ten years proper machinery for the hearing of complaints regarding the violations of human rights – murder by security forces, torture and brutality in interrogation centres, imprisonment without trial, excessive punishments in prisons. It is quite clear that the sanction for these violations came from the British government itself. It therefore used the law and counter-terrorism as part of its war effort. In short, people with a grievance were asking the very people responsible for the violations of law against them to hear their complaints and grant justice.

'The British government therefore exercised great pressure at home and abroad to distort the truth, their simple case being that they were honest peacemakers caught in the middle of a savage war between Catholics and Protestants.

'On the unjust killing of civilians the army and RUC always got their story to the media – they were fired at first, the civilian was carrying a weapon, etc. The British media accepted the army spokesmen as did Radio Éireann often. The big lie was one of the most hurtful things to people who suffered and knew the truth. The British army version was what the people in charge of the British media wanted themselves; so they would not speak out the truth.

'Fr Denis Faul and I tried to break through on this many times: we had to resort to writing our own pamphlets – on the murders of Leo Norney, Peter Cleary, Majella O'Hare, Brian Stewart, for example ... the eleven men killed by the SAS in the past year. Which of the media has undertaken that? They are guilty by their silence and omission. These are the big sins of the British media.

'We are convinced that a D notice was served on the British papers at the time of internment and the torture of the hooded men in August 1971. *The Sunday Times* was given statements on the cases of the Hooded Men weeks before they printed it. John Whale then got the scoop of the year – and was honoured as journalist of the year – although this information was available weeks before it was printed.

'On the question of torture and brutality one could only break through occasionally in the British media (nothing to compare with the immense time and orchestration of media for the Peace People). Again one had to resort to one's own pamphlets – *The Hooded Men, British Army and Special Branch RUC Brutalities, The Castlereagh File, The Black and Blue Book.*

'Catholic papers like *The Tablet* and *The Catholic Herald* would print little or nothing. *The Tablet* refused information from me, even though I got a letter of recommendation. *The Belfast Telegraph* also refused copy on torture.

'The first time the BBC television approached Fr Denis Faul was six years after the 'troubles' had started – and then for a programme on abortion. He asked them where they were for the last six years.

'The same is true now on prison conditions. The British media still accept Mason's lie that the punishments in H Block are self-inflicted (as they accepted that torture was self-inflicted despite Strasbourg and the Amnesty Reports). So we resort to our own publications on the prisons – *Whitelaw's Tribunals, The Flames of Long Kesh, The Iniquity of Internment, H Block.*

'In short, only occasionally and at a late stage do the media take an interest in the serious problems of violations of human rights in the north of Ireland. On the rare occasion they do act it is of infinite value – for example, Keith Kyle's programme on Bernard O'Connor, ITV's *A Question of Torture,* and the recent *Nationwide* programme on H Block.

'Truth is a pillar of peace. The media have failed us utterly over ten years'.

The Royal Ulster Constabulary, 1992

After the Metropolitan Police the RUC is the largest police force in Great Britain and Northern Ireland. In 1970 the force had 3,500 officers. Its full establishment in 1992 is 13,450 officers, of whom 8,500 are regular members, 3,250 full-time reserve officers and 1,700 part-time reservists. Fewer than 8% of the RUC are Catholic, a lower proportion than at the start of the conflict in 1968. This is not acceptable.

There are probably between 200 and 300 RUC officers in Armagh city. I could not name one and I doubt if a dozen Catholics would know a single RUC officer in the Armagh district.

The RUC station is a forbidding place – a barracks. Millions of pounds have been spent in barricading police within protected compounds. Only utter necessity would persuade any Catholic to call there. Is physical force the only way to protect the RUC against the IRA? Could the millions of pounds have been spent in breaking down prejudice barriers rather than setting up ugly fortresses in 'Indian' territory?

The last thing a nationalist in difficulty in Armagh city wants to do is to seek the help of the RUC. Necessity – arising from prosecution or as an insurance requirement, forces some contact. It is common knowledge in the area that the police do not want to be called out to deal with a fatal road accident, a burglary, a stolen car, a hijacking or a domestic dispute. There are instances of their refusal to operate in these cases. The RUC assume that one should understand the danger they might face and therefore they do not always act.

There are no invitations from any of the Catholic schools in the Armagh area to the local RUC to address them, even on such vital matters for children as road safety. Career officers in the schools offer no encouragement to students to join the RUC, male or female.

What is wrong? Is it just that Catholics are afraid of being shot by the IRA? There is fear of intimidation but Sir Hugh Annesley and other RUC representatives suggest that this is the only factor.

The most important point is that Northern Ireland is made up of two strong cultural traditions, a British one and an Irish one. The RUC caters only for the British tradition. A man can not join the RUC and express his Irishness.

First of all, there is the weight of Protestant numbers drawn often from very loyalist backgrounds. There are elements of the Masonic and Orange orders in the RUC and these are anti-Catholic. Some Catholic police complain that they suffer from misunderstandings, mockery, taunts and bigotry. The trappings of the RUC are all British, union flag, name, crown, poppy-flaunting, music and games.

Above all, the RUC has traditionally been the defence force of the Northern Ireland statelet, a state which practised discrimination against Catholics for fifty years. It is regarded in this way by the Protestant leaders and their Churches. An Irishman joining a police force in the north ideally should be able to fully express his or her religion, nationalism and cultural tradition, proudly and without offence or constraint.

The gulf between the Protestant RUC force and the Catholic public has been widened by the counter-insurgency methods of the RUC and British army. In the 1970s, this involved one-sided intern-ment of Catholics and torture of detainees in Holywood, Girdwood, Ballykelly, Castlereagh and Gough barracks, and in police stations like Omagh, Strabane, Strand Road Derry, Armagh and Dungannon. The courts were corrupted by acceptance of forced confessions and the word of 'supergrasses'.

It is difficult for the RUC to win respect when cases of ill-treatment recur and there are doubtful court cases like those of the

'Beechmount Five' and the 'Casement Park Accused'. Worst of all is the Shoot-to-Kill policy, with the debacle of the Stalker Inquiry, and the collusion of RUC elements with loyalist gangs in the murder of Catholics and Sinn Féin members. There is great suspicion of British intelligence and elements of the RUC Special Branch and divisional mobile support units.

Furthermore, there has been a long history of complaints of verbal abuse and harassment of Catholics by members of the RUC. Nationalists unfortunately refuse to distinguish between these problems and the force as a whole. They feel that community policing can not exist while such problems continue.

This argument was advanced in 1973 by the Central Citizens' Defence Committee in Belfast, in *The Black Paper: Northern Ireland – The story of the police*. The argument is still valid. The book said: 'All the wishing in the world will not achieve the impossible. There is no way out of this torturous dilemma but the more difficult way that must be faced up to sooner or later. Law and order will not return to Northern Ireland on any basis but one. It will have to be seen to apply equally and fairly, to everyone in the land, whatever their position, even if they wear a uniform or hold a seat in parliament. Only when that is seen to be happening will the laws gain the respect from the community upon which its validity rests. This respect had been lost in Northern Ireland. It must be regained and strengthened. When those who make the law break the law in the name of the law there is no law.'

Catholics think that Sir Hugh Annesley and other senior RUC officers should attend meetings of Catholics and listen to what they have to say, not presume that they know why Catholics will not join the RUC.

In justice the sheer weight of the Irish Catholic nationalist tradition demands a change in the structures of the RUC. The recent census shows a 43% Catholic population, a growing one. In numbers the Catholic religion is the principal religion. Catholics comprise half of all young people in the north and a majority in most of the physical area of Northern Ireland.

It seems ridiculous that young RUC men from Larne, Coleraine, Comber, and Ballymena should police south Armagh and east Tyrone, west Belfast or Derry. In 1920 the number of Catholics and Protestants in the RIC in Belfast was almost equal. What a contrast to today's inequality!

Even from an economic point of view the combined forces of the RUC, Royal Irish Rangers, together with other security jobs and ancillary workers, entail very substantial employment, overwhelmingly for Protestants. This offends against social justice and the principle of power-sharing.

The Anglo-Irish Conference should spearhead a radical change in the police force in the north. There should be serious study of the possibility of regional divisions, or perhaps a second line police force that would separate the 'paramilitary' division from an unarmed civilian police force – the latter comprising all religions, culturally tolerant and carrying out the routine business of police work outside of the military conflict.

On 26 August 1969 an advisory committee was appointed by the then Minister of Home Affairs, R. W. Porter, 'to examine the recruitment, structure and composition of the Royal Ulster Constabulary and their respective functions and to recommend as necessary what changes are required to provide for the efficient enforcement of law and order in Northern Ireland'. Lord Hunt who was chairman of the committee underlined the essential problem in his report: 'Policing in a free society depends on a wide measure of public approval and consent. This has never been obtained in the long term by military or paramilitary means. We believe that any police force, military in appearance and equipment, is less acceptable to minority and moderate opinion than if it is clearly civilian in character, particularly now that better education and improved communication have spread awareness of the rights of civilians' (paragraph 81).

Over two decades later, this objective remains to be fulfilled.

Some of the ideas in this paper were originally outlined by me in a plan for the restructuring of the RUC at a sociological conference in St Patrick's College, Maynooth, in 1991. This text was submitted to Initiative '92 and the Opsahl Commission. It was subsequently published in Fortnight *magazine and as a separate broadsheet.*

The Repatriation of the Executed

INTRODUCTION
On 2 September 1942, Tom Williams, a member of the IRA, aged 19 years, was executed and buried at Crumlin Road Prison, Belfast. He had accepted responsibility for the death of Constable Patrick Murphy of the RUC. It is now over fifty years since his burial and the National Graves Association, following consultation with surviving relatives, have deemed it an appropriate time to request the exhumation of his remains and their reburial with full religious rites in consecrated ground where relatives would have dignified access.

There have been a number of precedents of similar nature:
1. The celebrated repatriation from Pentonville Prison of the remains of Sir Roger Casement in 1965.
2. The repatriation and reburial on 5 and 6 July 1967 of the remains of Reginald Dunne and Joseph O'Sullivan, executed at Wandsworth Prison on 10 August 1922.
3. The repatriation and reburial on 8 July 1969 of the remains of two IRA members, Peter Barnes and James McCormack, executed at Winson Green Prison, Birmingham, on 7 February 1940.
4. The repatriation from India and the reburial of the Connaught Rangers' mutineers on 2 November 1970.

In the High Court in Belfast on 5 May 1995 three judges ruled that the Secretary of State has power to exercise the prerogative of mercy and order that Tom Williams be exhumed and handed over to be reburied. The decision to release his body is now an administrative one. I write these words in the hope of persuading the Secretary of State to graciously accede to the request of relatives and a concerned committee who have sought to have Williams interred with dignity in a cemetery. Tom Williams was 18 years of age when he was involved with others in the fatal shooting of Constable Patrick Murphy.

I also hope that the IRA will be likewise persuaded to restore to their families the bodies of victims murdered by them in the last 25 years. They are buried in secret graves. One calls to mind, for example, Captain Robert Nairac of the British army abducted by the IRA on 14 May 1977 and presumed dead.

'SLEEPING WITH MY FATHERS'

In the Holy Bible there is a passage in the Book of Genesis, 47:27–31, which the Jerusalem Bible translation calls 'Jacob's last wishes'. We read that although Jacob had prospered in Egypt, he asked Joseph to promise not to bury him there but in Canaan. He says, 'When I sleep with my fathers (*i.e.* when I die), carry me out of Egypt and bury me in their tomb'. Joseph promised to do this and his father died in peace (49:29–33; 50). When the time comes for Joseph to die in Egypt, he says to his brothers there, 'I am about to die, but God will be sure to remember you kindly and take you back from this country to the land that he promised on oath to Abraham, Isaac and Jacob'(50:24). The text continues, 'And Joseph made Israel's sons swear an oath, "When God remembers you with kindness be sure to take my bones from here"' (Genesis 50:25–26; *cf.* Exodus 13:19).

The Jewish expression for dying was 'sleeping with my fathers' or 'being gathered to my fathers'; for this reason, burial among their own people was very important.

'THOSE WHO SLEEP'

Before rising from the tomb where he has freely 'gone to sleep', Jesus has expressed by signs his mastery over death, and over sleep, which is its image. He commanded the daughter of Jairus and his friend Lazarus to rise from their sleep, thus prefiguring his own resurrection to which the baptised will be mystically united. Jesus, St Paul says (I Cor. 15:20), rose 'as the first-fruits of those who sleep'.

We who 'sleep in the tombs' also hope to rise again. The hope of immortality and resurrection which comes to light in the Old Testament has found a solid foundation in the mystery of Christ. For not only has union with his death made us live with a new life, but it also has given us assurance that 'He who raised Christ Jesus from the dead will also give new life to your mortal bodies through his indwelling Spirit' (Romans 8:11).

COMMUNITY OF SAINTS

While putting an emphasis on the salvation of the individual, Catholicism also puts a great emphasis on the 'kingdom', the 'church', the 'community', the 'people of God'. This is carried on from the Old Testament. In the Old Testament the image of resurrection is used to express the collective hope of the people of Israel. God triumphs over death for the benefit of his people. Following this tradition, all the communal aspects of Salvation in Jesus Christ interest the Church. The baptised as a community have a vital union with Christ. St Paul says, 'We are all baptised in one Spirit to form one Body'. The baptised constituting the Church are, therefore, 'one Body of Christ' (1 Cor. 12:13). This unity is symbolised in the term 'communion of saints'. The church is the unity of the living on this earth with the faithful departed, those who sleep, who rest in peace. The Eucharistic bread is the bond of living cohesion. Therefore at Holy Mass there is a special commemoration of the living and the dead: both are united spiritually in Christ as the 'communion of saints'. Hence the use of the beautiful phrase for the Eucharist – Holy Communion, and the emphasis in Catholicism on praying for the purgation of the dead, praying with the dead, revering their memory at Easter, the feast of the resurrection of Christ, and in November. The dead are laid to rest in graveyards, in ground that is specially consecrated, like a congregation symbolically 'sleeping' around the building of the church; united to the people praying in the church who greet their memory as they pass their graves.

COMMUNITY GRAVEYARD
With this understanding one can see then that the executed belong to a community church in life and in death. Tom Williams and Captain Robert Nairac are brothers in the family of the faithful. That Williams is buried in isolation in a prison yard and Nairac in unconsecrated ground is a total contradiction of the community dimension of the faith they professed and a source of deep hurt to their surviving relations and to the people from which they came. They should be symbolically united with their brothers and sisters in a community graveyard where the 'church' sleeps in a great dormitory awaiting the arousal call of the Lord. The biblical idea of Christ as the bridegroom, who loves his Church as his bride and who will bring her resplendent to himself, expresses beautifully the idea of the corporate nature of the

Church, a single entity. These men should be buried among their own people, their 'bones resting with their fathers'.

A GLORIFIED BODY

Corruption in a tomb is a transitory state only, from which man will re-arise as one awakes from a sleep into which one has slipped. Ephesians says, 'Awake, sleeper! Rise from the dead, and Christ will shine upon you' (5:14). This fundamental conviction of resurrection of the body, the human person, whole and entire, dominates the whole Christian existence. It superimposes itself upon our thoughts in these cases of Tom Williams and Robert Nairac. We are mindful that all people are sinners. Tom Williams, aged 19 years, made a holy preparation for death in the company of Fr Patrick McAlister and he went to death holding his crucifix and praying. Cardinal Hume, former Abbot of Ampleforth where Robert Nairac was a student, made an appeal for the safe return of Captain Nairac when he disappeared. At least his body can be returned to 'rest in safety'. The religion of these two victims stretches beyond the grave. It would be fitting to respect the community nature of their religion, Catholicism, and the dignity of their bodies as individuals created by God and brought to a new creation by Jesus. Both men, like all Christians, lived in hope that their bodies would be transformed from present misery to a glorified state.

Abridged versions of this article appeared in Doctrine and Life *and the* Irish News.

II

INTERNMENT

Torture and Internment, August 1971

On 9 August 1971, 342 Catholic men were interned in Northern Ireland. Patrick McNally was among 23 of my parishioners in Armagh who were arrested. He and Brian Turley of Armagh were two of the twelve hooded men tortured in Ballykelly Barracks. I took this statement from Patrick on 18 March 1974:

ARREST

At 4.30am on the morning of 9 August 1971 the soldiers came to my house. I said, 'Is it internment?' One of them said, 'Yes'. They brought me to the grounds of Saint Luke's hospital in Armagh There was a lorry waiting there. I was the first into it, and shortly afterwards they brought in a few others, Corrigan and McGinley. Then we headed out to Gough Barracks, Armagh. Our photographs were taken there. Then three of us were taken in a helicopter, Dermot Kelly, Kerr of Navan Street, and myself.

BALLYKINLAR BRITISH ARMY BARRACKS

We landed in Ballykinlar Barracks and were put into a hut. Only a few of us at the start, about a dozen from all over. I was taken out and had a medical examination, very brief, just strip and on me again. He was a youngish doctor, pleasant enough. Then taken to a different hut. It was full. We were left alone for a long time. Then the army came in a few hours afterwards and started making us do the 'exercises', continued until that night, thumping you if you were not doing them right. All this time they were taking people out and questioning them; some would come back and some wouldn't. But I never was questioned the whole time I was there. Then processing us and moving us to different huts. On the 9th of August we were allowed an hour's sleep, but I couldn't sleep. I was only wearing a tee-shirt and trousers. I was freezing. On the tenth day of August we had the exercises all day again but the number of men was getting less all the time until there were only four of us in this particular hut, Brian Turley, Gerry McKerr, Seán McKenna and myself.

Gerry McKerr asked for a mattress for each of us and we were given this and a blanket. But they kept making us carry this mattress in turn and jump over the other three lying down. In between times you had to run outside between the two huts, ten times, getting faster all the time. At the end of this you were made go to the toilet which was a hole in the ground. You had to go through lines of soldiers and police standing round, watching this and laughing. They made swipes at you, odd thumps of the baton on the arm. Then when we came in again more 'exercises'. All were told to go in and sleep, but each time we dozed over they would waken us up again and make us run round again. That went on all night. Before we went into bed each time we had to say together, 'Good night, Sir' and 'Good night, Sergeant'. Once on the tenth I asked to go to the toilet but then I didn't go because there was no paper provided and they stood there watching you all the time.

BALLYKELLY BRITISH ARMY BARRACKS
On the following morning, 11 August, just about daylight, three or four soldiers and about three police to each man came bursting into our hut, and they had the hood and handcuffs. I was held by a soldier and I think it was the policeman who put on the hood. I knew I was in for some sort of treatment. All sorts of things were going through my mind. Then I was bundled into a vehicle, thrown into the back, kicked and trailed. Then into a helicopter, grabbing your hair under the hood when they walked you along. Not a word was spoken the whole time, but I would say, about an hour, or between half an hour and an hour in the helicopter. Then out of the helicopter again into another vehicle, all the time very roughly handled, odd kick, punched and trailed. Getting into the vehicle you were banged against it and then you scrambled in on your own. Brought in the vehicle for a short distance.

AGAINST THE WALL

Then we had a medical examination, stripped naked, still with the hood on, a short examination. No words spoken. Then into the boiler suit, about three sizes too big for me, open down the middle. Then taken out and stood against the wall, inside a building somewhere. At this time, in the beginning, I think we were lined together because you could feel people standing beside you. After a while I began to move and became restless. That was the first contact I had with anybody; my arms were falling down; they would raise them up and bang them against the wall. You were never allowed to keep your head down, just a few minutes and then it was pulled back. The noise was there at the start but at the start it didn't annoy me much. I was expecting it to be turned off. Only after a few hours that I began to think more about it. In the beginning it didn't seem loud but after a while seemed the only thing that mattered, nothing seemed to matter only the noise. After a while your hands and arms were numb. I imagined I was on a round wall, kept thinking it was a massive big pillar, kept thinking there was a roundness on the wall. After, I don't know how long, I think I fainted, was lifted up again. They got my arms and wound them round.

From I went in till the time I was taken away for the Removal Order I thought it was a few days. I was against the wall all that time except for the short interrogations. At the time the first interrogation came it just seemed an endless time against the wall. I know I had collapsed a few times. If you made any movement, if your hand crumbled, they would bang your hand against the wall, give you the odd dig in the ribs to remember you to stand right. One time I did fall I was left there for a good while but I am not sure if this was after the Removal Order or before it.

FIRST INTERROGATION

Brought out for the first interrogation, I was lying on the ground. They trailed me along the ground by the collar of the overall. I know I was trailed off something, like a short stage, a few feet high or more, two of them trailing me, kicked and punched, seemed a long distance. All darkness. Brought into a room. I was sat on the floor. On the first occasion the hood wasn't removed, but after that at the other interrogations the hood was rolled up but only up to my nose.

The first interrogation was very short. A voice just said, 'You wanted to see me'. I never answered. The voice said again, 'Have you anything to say?' I answered, 'No'. Same voice said, 'Take him away'. I was brought back again, but more roughly this time and pushed up against the wall. And so on.

SECOND INTERROGATION

Interrogation again in similar fashion. Seemed a good number of hours to me between this and the other one. Sitting on the floor again. After about half a minute sat up on a chair. Something similar. Heard only one voice. I was being held in the chair and the voice was coming from the front of me. All darkness under the hood.

DETENTION ORDER

Back again against the wall. Seemed another long time. I fell another few times. Next taken away in a jeep. I felt other people in the jeep. I knew Brian Turley was in it. He was shouting for air; he couldn't breathe. I was lying on top of him and somebody was lying on top of me. At one stage I saw underneath the hood – I could see black trousers and black boots of police. We were handcuffed in the jeep. My skin was caught in the handcuffs. An English voice said, 'Look at the bastard's hands'. I was thumped on the hand with a baton where the skin was caught. I had a scar there for a long time after it. Lot of kicks on the journey, lying in a heap on the floor, just kicking free-for-all. This was the most kickings I got.

Then into a helicopter and about half-an-hour in it. Then brought out. Taken on foot for a good distance. Held by the neck and arms. Run over tin and grass. Brought into a building, down steps, hood was taken off my head. There was somebody in front of me in a black uniform. That was the first time the hood was taken off me. The man in the black uniform was standing beside a table. He just held this paper up. I said, 'I can't see'. Everything was just a haze. I could only see the white paper and that was that. He didn't say anything. I couldn't see anybody else. Hadn't time to see them, all so quick. The hood was put on again. The piece of paper was put into the pocket of the overalls. Then the same journey back again.

I was wondering the whole way back what was going to happen. I had hoped at this stage that I might be going to jail. When I got back and was put against the wall again then I was really bad. Then started thinking all types of thoughts. After a few more hours of that I was thinking I would never come out of it.

MORE INTERROGATIONS

A few more interrogations, about twelve to fifteen hours in between. Something similar the whole time. After what seemed a few more days to me, I couldn't stand at all. Must have been collapsing and falling all the time. One time I felt somebody lifted my leg and a sharp needle was run along my foot. I was up against the wall again after that. By this time the noise, which was there all the time, was such that it is just impossible to explain; you couldn't have sensible thoughts. I had come out of the helicopter listening to see were we going to the same place and when I heard the noise it just knocked the heart out of you.

After one of the interrogations I was brought into this small room. No noise there. It was completely black. I took the hood off after a few minutes. The room seemed very small, about six feet by four feet. I was exhausted. I rolled the hood up, made a pillow. It was a concrete floor, freezing out. But I was totally exhausted and I slept. That was the first sleep I got. I had never been offered any sleep.

I got only half a cup of water, only once, and it seemed after days. My lips were all dried up. They tried to put bread in my mouth, couldn't take it, just choked me. That was the first and only water I got. They had given it to me sitting on the ground after I had fallen.

SAS

One time I took the hood off when I was standing against the wall. There was light in the place but I couldn't see well, just seemed to be a dim orange light from the roof. I saw two men both stripped to the waist.

One of them said in an English voice, 'Do you want to see anybody?' I answered, 'No'. Immediately they put the hood on again. I got a few thumpings. They were wearing what seemed to be the bottom of a track suit or a gym suit. Looked to be blue trousers. As the hood was being put on again I could see the white gym shoes. I have the idea that one had tight blondish hair. They were very fit and strong looking. This incident happened after I had come back from getting the Detention Order. The soldiers in Ballykinlar had told us there was civil war and that people and children were being shot. All this was coming back to me.

After I had fallen asleep in the small room, I was told by a Northern Ireland accent to put the hood on. Then they came in. Taken out this time walking. Taken down what seemed to be a corridor, blankets hanging down, roughish hairy material. You had to move in and out between them. Then brought in for interrogation again.

SMOOTH INTERROGATOR
This was the first interrogation with the hood off. Before Detention Order it was just rolled up a bit. Table there. Sat in a chair. Told not to look behind me. Hand was placed on each shoulder. The interrogator had black hair thinning a bit at the front, wearing a blue anorak, thinnish, round about thirty-five years old, spoke in educated type of accent, no Northern Ireland twang about it. He said, 'You are in the IRA'. I said 'No'. He talked about Republican parades. He said, 'Do you deny you are a Republican?' I said, 'No'. Then sort of casual questions. This particular interrogator never cut rough in the interrogations. Just straight forward simple questions.

ROUGH INTERROGATOR
Taken into another room. There was a mattress in this room. Later a blanket. After the door was closed I knew I was on my own and I could take the hood off. I took it off. I lay down on the mattress and went to sleep. The next thing I heard a banging on the door and a voice shouting, 'Put on your hood'. I was taken by the arms and into a room. Sat in the chair again. The hood was taken off and the fella immediately grabbed me by the lapels of the boiler suit. He lifted me up roaring and shouting, 'I don't want any nonsense out of you. I want the truth. You are going to tell me everything'. Then he sat down again. Then he started asking questions. 'We know you are in the IRA, what is your rank?' Just general questions but pretty rough all the time. Shouting and slapping the table, pushing you about and things

like that. I had about three separate interrogations with him. This man had a black heavy curly beard, black hair, combed straight forward, medium length, well-built, about just over thirty, maybe thirty-three. Always rough, losing his head, roaring and shouting.

Round about this time too I was sitting in the mattress room, might have been some time after I came out of the room where I got the first sleep. They came in and pulled the hood up to my nose and gave me some stew. I had to eat it with my fingers.

SOFT INTERROGATOR

The period between these interrogations was not very long. I was brought into a different interrogator, in his fifties, going grey-haired, very big, heavy, about six foot two or three. He acted real nice, put his arm around me. Sat down. He talked about politics – where did I get my views from? Did I read any books? Did you ever join the IRA? and so on. He wouldn't ask the same question twice. If you said 'No' to anything he would make you feel he believed you. He talked about Germany, Japan, the Free State, how well they were doing since the war. I was brought into him two or three times for interrogation. One time there was a plate of beans on the table. He said, 'You can eat them'. I didn't. I was very sick at this stage.

I had never been to the toilet since I was put against the wall. When I was in the mattress room I was very nervous and tense at this stage and asked out to the toilet, anything to get out of the room; even looking forward to the interrogation.

On the last interrogation, the big tall grey-haired man came in and shouted, 'Face the back wall'. He came in and spoke to me, 'Come on, get your hood on, you are coming with me'. I went into the room again. The hood was taken off. This was the last interrogation. The big grey-haired fella interrogated me. He said, 'Anything you want to eat at all, you can have'. I got a cup of tea, beans and sausages, bread. Then he put the hood on again. He himself took me to the washroom. I was filthy. He told me to get washed. Got sort of half washed. Then he told me I was for the Crumlin Road. I didn't really believe him at the time. I thought then this was a bluff. But I knew there was something on. Next he came in again. He had a sheet. He asked me to sign it. I told him I couldn't see. I got it and tried to read it. He got annoyed. I waited until I could see. Then I could make out 'boots and socks', so I signed it. He took me to this room and I was photographed in it. I had a sort of medical check before I went into the room, could feel hands going over me, the hood was still on. I was photographed along with this interrogator. I had no clothes on. Then photographed me on my own, back and front. Then brought back to the room.

CRUMLIN ROAD JAIL
Then next time brought out treated gently, sort of guiding you instead of pushing you into the vehicle, your foot was lifted up and set into it. From that into the helicopter. The guard kept touching me reassuringly, patting me. Still hooded. Landed. Put into another Land Rover. The hood was taken off in the Land Rover. I was sitting among six or seven police, just outside the Crumlin Road Jail, Belfast. I said to one of them, 'What day is it today?' He said, 'Mind your own business'. I was brought into the Crumlin through a hole in the wall. As soon as I got out of the Land Rover I could see the jail.

During the time I was away sometimes I would be stubborn with them. Other times you would have done anything. Other times I didn't really believe it was me. The whole time I was against the wall I don't think I stopped praying. I may have thought out loud but all the time I was praying. One time I thought a whole lot of children had been shot in Drumbreda but I don't know whether I was told that by one of the interrogators or not.

Letter to Jim Fields, Armagh, interned in Long Kesh Prison Camp, 2 November 1972

Dear Jim,
You have now been imprisoned without trial for 14 months. During that time you suffered heavy interrogation in a military barracks, Armagh RUC station, and Portadown RUC station. You endured the rigours of the condemned prison ship, *Maidstone*. You have been treated like an animal in a cage in Long Kesh prison camp, a place precisely

planned to break its prisoners by prolonged degradation. In Long Kesh you were beaten and injured by the British army on 25 October 1971, and on another occasion when being transferred from one compound to another.

This imprisonment, so terrible because of its injustice and its indefinite length, must weigh heavily on you, a man of nearly 50 years, considering too that you need medical care. As a peacemaker in the Armagh community you are appalled by the viciousness of the procedures employed to degrade men in Long Kesh. Not only the physical degradation causes you to suffer, but also the calumnies about internees of leading ministers of the British crown. Like the thousand or so Catholics who were arrested and detained, your basic liberty was taken from you. You had no just public trial and no proper means of defence – no warrant, no charge, no trial. Why are you being held without trial in Long Kesh prison camp? Was it because you were chairman of the National Graves Association? Would Mr Whitelaw, who reserves to himself the right to inspect each file, declare publicly or show you privately why you are being held away from your wife and family? Like yourself your wife is not in good health; deprived of her husband she has little to live on; she is on her own; she is one of 'Mr Whitelaw's widows'. Your son, Tony, on 3 October 1972 was sentenced to 4 years imprisonment after being found to have 6 rounds of ammunition. The people of Armagh have noted that in the same week a UVF man got the same sentence as your son for being in possession of 3 rifles and 1,163 rounds of ammunition, under suspicious circumstances. Why have you not been allowed to visit your son in Crumlin Road Jail? Why has your request been turned down so often? Why was no reason for the refusal given to you or to the welfare officer? Such permission has been granted to others.

I know that your heart contains no bitterness after having heard of the tortures of others imprisoned without trial. I understand your distress at the recent ill-treatment of the remand prisoners. What possible justification can there be for holding you and the other 211 prisoners detained without trial? Are you hostages? Are you being held for ransom by Mr Whitelaw? Are you prisoners of war? Have you, like privy councillors and ex-ministers of government, threatened to liquidate your neighbours? It appears to the community here in Armagh that you and others, Jim Fields, are the victims of English political expediency. Other Catholic men have spent 12 years of their lives imprisoned without trial. Does Mr Whitelaw with the help of Special Courts intend to do the same with you and your fellow prisoners? Does he really have any idea of what constitutes fair play, equality, and treatment of men in accordance with human Christian dignity? Is it true that Mr Whitelaw intends to keep you in the Long Kesh cages over a second Christmas? The Christmas message of peace, good will, and family unity means little to those implementing the immoral procedures of internment. The ordinary citizen wants a lasting peace, based on justice. The ordinary citizen wants all internees released immediately.

Extract from the broadsheet 'Whitelaw violates Article 6 of the European Convention on Human Rights'.

Visit to a Long Kesh Appeal Tribunal, 1972

The Detention of Terrorists Order (NI) introduced on 7 November 1972 provided that the British Secretary of State could appoint commissioners to adjudicate on persons arrested and determine whether they should be detained. A person who was the subject of a Detention Order could also appeal to an Appeal Tribunal. Special tribunals were set up in Long Kesh Prison to enquire into cases of those detained. They soon became known as 'Whitelaw's Tribunals'. I attended three, one on behalf of Patrick McNally, the same parishioner who had been tortured in Ballykelly Barracks and who had been brought to Long Kesh Internment Camp from Crumlin Road Prison, and the others on behalf of Éamon Hannaway and Brian J. Rafferty, also parishioners. These appeals were conducted by the doyen Armagh solicitor, Gerry Lennon. The appeals of Patrick McNally and Brian Rafferty failed. Éamon Hannaway's appeal was successful.

A DESCRIPTION OF THE COURT
Tuesday, 14 November 1972, at 1.45pm a prison officer arrives at the

door of Hut 82, Cage 9, and calls out the names of three internees. He tells them that they are to be taken to the 'court'. A grey prison van is waiting at the gates of the cage. When the three men and their escort of four prison officers are aboard, it begins its short journey to Cage 14 where the commission to enquire into their cases is being held. On arrival at their destination, the men are taken, one at a time, from the van and are shown into a prefabricated hut where, under the watch of two prison officers, they are asked to wait.

Cage 14 where the 'court' holds session is at first glance indistinguishable from the other cages in Long Kesh Internment Camp, four long Nissen huts with grey brick gable walls, corrugated tin roofs and sides. Directly in front of three of these huts are the tiny prefabricated buildings where the internees will wait, be thoroughly searched, and have all their belongings and the contents of their pockets, with the exception of a handkerchief, placed in a canvas sack. After waiting for perhaps a half-an-hour, the prison officers escort the internees into the main hut where the 'court' is sitting. The main Nissen hut is partitioned into three areas, the commissioner's chamber, the court-room, and a section made up of six small rooms severed by a narrow corridor, three rooms on each side. At the end of this corridor a small door opens up into the court-room.

The 'court' is a well-furnished room, the bare walls covered with sheets of brightly coloured insulating board and hung with scarlet and blue drapes. The floor is covered with a scarlet carpet. The main feature of the room is a large oval-shaped table of polished wood. The commissioner sits on a high-backed well-upholstered chair at the centre and to the right of this table. Above and slightly behind hangs a painting of the British coat of arms, complete with motto, *honi soit qui mal y pense*. The commissioner's chair is situated at the centre and to the right of the table. To the right of the commissioner sits a stenographer with a tape recorder and a microphone placed in front of him. Immediately in front of the oval table are a desk and chair at which sits the commissioner's clerk; on his desk are two microphones, one angled towards the crown prosecutor and the other towards the respondent. A few feet in front of him and facing the commissioner are two chairs, for the respondent and a prison officer. To the right of these two chairs is a desk behind which the crown prosecutor sits. There is a vacant desk and chair to the left and slightly behind the respondent's chair.

Three doors open into the court-room. One leads into the corridor already described. One is a few feet from this, but concealed by a screen of red velvet curtains, and through it come the Special Branch to take their seats and give evidence hidden from the 'court'. The third door in the opposite wall faces this. Through this door is the commissioner's chamber, from which he appears.

A drawing of the court

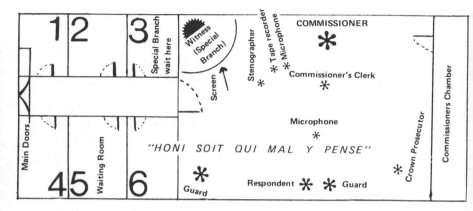

A TRIBUNAL HEARING

I wrote the following piece after appearing for the defence of Éamon Hannaway. It was published in *Whitelaw's Tribunals*.

The Tribunal and the Appeal Tribunal are held within the now great complex of the Long Kesh encampment. Yellow and black signs point to a special entrance towered over by a military post and guarding soldier. A shout from the soldier and a few accent misunderstandings before you realise that you have to wait. A soldier finally comes through a little door, checks your name and identity with his pad, and then disappears only to re-appear immediately to re-open the big gate and admit your car. Then you drive across a great waste-land surrounded by barbed wire and corrugated iron sheeting. To the right a worm-eaten cabbage patch catches your eye. It reminds you of your 'T. S. Eliot schooldays'. The next entrance is blocked by two Kosangas bottles. A soldier removes them and now you are through to a place where there is a little bit more life. It even cheers you to have your car searched and go into a wooden hut where there is heat and light! It is still even pleasant to dump the contents of your pockets and be amiably 'run over' by a smiling soldier. You go out clutching your permit which is now as valuable as a ration book. The two women witnesses have clambered into a van with two policewomen; the separation of the sexes of course for searching. You get into your own van. The solicitor is there and two other witnesses, the mate and father of the accused. And there are other lawyers who are putting their trust in their academic distinctions for their case, a formidable battery of learned lawyers.

The game we are playing is a different one. We know – the aunt, the girlfriend, father, mate, priest and solicitor – that our accused is an innocent man and we think that it will be a great compliment to the court to bring ourselves to it as human furnishings, because all the emphasis is on furnishing. One lawyer grunts in the van, 'This court has all the incidentals down to the last detail. In fact half the courts in the country have not had the expense and detail of court trappings as this one has. It lacks only the essence of a court'. 'But', I remark, 'how can judges and lawyers go through with this? Have they no professional shame?' 'My dear boy,' he says, 'they are Englishmen and you are a Hottentot'.

And true enough, when we disembark and go in, one is amazed at the beauty of the Nissen hut interior, beautifully painted, carpeted, separate rooms for lawyers and witnesses.

It is 10.30am. But it is an hour and more before any of us are called as witnesses. There has been much reminiscing about the beloved internee. His mate and girlfriend devour cigarettes. His aunt is womanly silent. I keep on building up their hopes, but not overdoing it. One poor internee was turned down at the first sitting of the appeal court the day before (and those who know him know how innocent and unfortunate he is). So today our lad stands a chance. Yesterday it was shown that the appeal isn't just a formality by not releasing the internee. Today just might be the day it isn't a formality by granting a release. But if our lad is released, even in this buffoon court, none of us are going to argue, because he will be going to his home that was lonely without him and his girlfriend will now plan her marriage. His mate will no longer go around like a lost dog. His father and aunt have prayed for fifteen months and have suffered. The father keeps mumbling of his release, 'I can't see it'. I try to reassure him.

Two policewomen and a policeman sit at the other end of the waiting-room. There is just that difference hanging in the air but it doesn't prevent an odd loud groan from the witnesses on the injustice of internment. There was a time in Northern Ireland when you wouldn't even have heard that groan. All are nervous about being called in. People have never been through this before. At last the bearded clerk comes in and takes out the first witness. And so the five of us are called in turn, his intimate friends, all rooting for him. As witnesses we go and come back as if we had been led to the slaughter.

My own turn comes. Into the corridor I go, at the top a small door marked 'Private'. It reminds me somewhat of the atmosphere below deck in a submarine.

The clerk is mumbling something, whether I have any objection to the James Bible. Two things flash through my mind – how strange in these ecumenical days, and should I quip 'James the Second?' On the exterior I reassure him. I am going to be nice and grovel if that means the release of an innocent man.

The door opens. I enter the court-room. It seems very bright and is slashed with royal blue and scarlet curtains. I am instantly greeted by a dozen murmurs. The accused is seated. He reminds me of Christ, patient and forbearing. A look of suffering.

The swearing. I have already made a statement for the solicitor. He just runs me through it in question form. I answer the questions a little more elaborately. I know the shorthand is at work and the tape recorder. A testimony to the good character and good behaviour of a friend. The defence solicitor is at my right at a desk. The prosecutor is seated opposite. The prosecutor questions me – going back to the day of internment, was I surprised he was taken? would I accept his word? I would. Any more questions? I take my first good look at the tribunal. They are all smiling. All three grey grave men. The Irish traditional saying to beware of the smile of an Englishman tempts my good will. But they are still smiling. Is the adage true? I feel as if I would like to hear the rest of the proceedings but I have to leave.

It is one o'clock. We await the verdict in the waiting-room. The solicitor comes in. 'Court adjourned until two o'clock. We can go to a canteen'. Another long hour of waiting but, if the tribunal has a working lunch, we console ourselves that the adjournment is a good sign. It all fits into the serious trappings of the show. The court has been an extraordinary affair. The prosecutor can not open up the prosecution case too much because then he would reveal the secrecy of some of the RUC Special Branch officers' testimony and this he cannot do. The defence lawyer is shadow-boxing too because he is not aware of all that he is supposed to defend, except that he knows his client is innocent and it is hard to prove that an innocent man is innocent. Our solicitor is very competent and so he shadow-boxes until the tribunal fixes on something that might at first seem a minor detail but it is something to go on and is soon torn asunder by legal ingenuity. All hypnotise themselves into a real court. There has been no precedent in this kind of court proceedings of appeal. The learned tribunal feels its way.

We are back at two o'clock. Twenty minutes later the respondent enters the waiting-room. 'I am released'. Smiles and tears.

Brian Rafferty's Hearing

My appearance at the tribunal hearing of Brian Rafferty culminated in an attack on my character from the 'prosecutor'. Reference was made to my campaign against the ill-treatment of detainees in RUC interrogation centres and RUC barracks. I then wrote to the Rt Hon. Merlyn Rees, Secretary of State, on 6 July 1974:

Dear Mr Rees,
On 13 June, 1974, I went to the Maze Prison, Long Kesh Camp, as a witness in the Tribunal Hearing of Mr B. J. Rafferty, Armagh. I have serious reservations regarding the morality and legality in international law of these tribunals. This you know from the pamphlet *Whitelaw's Tribunals* which was forwarded to you when you were an MP in opposition. Yet Armagh priests, Fr Malachy Coyle, Fr Peter Makem and myself, all of Armagh Parish, have participated to help wives and families.

The 13 June, 1974, was my third appearance as a witness in the Tribunal. I was put into an embarrassing position by the prosecutor and the commissioner. It is my opinion that the prosecutor set out to smear and discredit me with the allegation of association with the guilt

55

of men taking part in illegal activities. He presumed such guilt on the part of all Catholics for whom I have made representations and who were arrested in Armagh City. It appears to me that he could only have attacked me on the calumniatory information supplied by the police in Armagh to discredit me as a character witness.

The commissioner astonished me by his lack of objectivity, presuming the accuracy of what might well be fictitious informers. It appears to me that he tried to get me to support the immorality of what he was doing. I was astounded at his lack of objectivity. I did not realise that the prisoner had such a poor chance. His remark that the prisoner had refused to come to the tribunal initially and therefore was an IRA man was ridiculous.

Mr Lennon, the solicitor, said he would not expose me again to such a tribunal. I wish your department to furnish me with a transcript of my interrogation, which I wish to forward to the Lord Chancellor. I am also making a report to the International Commission of Jurists.

The reply came on 24 July 1974 from Mr Rees' private secretary, A. Huckle, Northern Ireland Office, Stormont Castle, Belfast.

Dear Father Murray,
The Secretary of State has asked me to reply to your letter of 6th July in which you referred to the review by a Commissioner of the case of Mr B. J. Rafferty, who is a detainee in H. M. Prison, Maze.

Although Commissioners are appointed by the Secretary of State they act quite independently and regulate their own procedure in accordance with the provisions of the Northern Ireland (Emergency Provisions) Act, 1973. You will appreciate, therefore, that the Secretary of State is unable to comment on your criticisms of the conduct of Mr Rafferty's review hearing in which you participated as a witness. Finally, you asked for a transcript of your cross-examination but I regret that it is not possible to provide this.

Poem – Long Kesh, 1974

Little flies, quivering and shaking with the wind gusts,
I look at the biological detail
of your wings.
Lightsome bloodless corpses,
glittering,
fluttering,
slightly caught on the silent strings
of the iron web,
mesh of grey, distorted vision.
Invisible men –
your escape is wider
wider than another day.

RAYMOND MURRAY, 1974

In memory of those who died in Long Kesh – Patrick Crawford, Francis Dodds, Éamonn Campbell, Patrick Teers, Hugh Gerard Coney.

III

TORTURE AND ILL-TREATMENT

Torture in Girdwood Park Barracks, 1971–72

Mgr Denis Faul and I recorded the torture of men in the RUC interrogation centres in the Palace Barracks, Holywood, and in Girdwood Park Barracks, 10 December 1971 – February 1972 in a pamphlet, published in 1972, entitled British Army and Special Branch RUC Brutalities. *Among the torture methods used in Girdwood Barracks, Belfast, was the use of electric shocks. Patrick Fitzsimmons, John Moore and William Johnston of Belfast related their experience to me in Armagh Prison. Patrick Fitzsimmons had been a celebrated Irish amateur boxer.*

PATRICK FITZSIMMONS

I was arrested on Thursday morning at 4.20am, 13 January 1972, in a house in Duncairn Gardens, Belfast. The soldiers came and arrested me and another fella. We were up the stairs. I had no shoes on. They started beating us. I was kicked down the stairs, beaten with batons. I was thrown into the back of a saracen. I was told to stop shouting or else I would get more beatings. I was handcuffed to the other fella. We were beat in the saracen. I gave them my name there.

We went to Girdwood Barracks. We were kicked into the entrance of it. I had been hit in the groin with a rifle butt when arrested. We were still handcuffed. I was made sit in the room. An SLR was put to my head and I was told I was being taken out and shot. I was made to sit in this hall till an army sergeant came in. He asked which one was Fitzsimmons. I replied. He said, 'You are just the little twerp I have been looking for the past two months.' Another fella returned and I was taken away. I was taken down a corridor, three soldiers on each side. They had wooden batons. They beat me as I went down the corridor. We went to the commanding officer. He gave me twenty seconds to give names of my brother and other fellas and where they were staying. When I told them I didn't know they beat me. They took me back up the corridor again. I was beat on the way up. I was put in the toilet. I was beaten with batons and rifles on the back of the neck and the privates. I was brought back down the corridor again, still being beaten by the batons. I was brought before the commanding officer again. I was asked had I thought where they were. I said I didn't know. I was beaten again. I was taken out and made stand against the wall. The sergeant replied, 'You are being taken out to be shot.' Another officer came along. He showed me a photograph. When I said I recognised the photograph they said I was reprieved. I was then taken out to the back and handed over to the 'duck squad', the fellas with black soot on their faces. I was beaten up outside and kicked. They put me in the saracen and kicked me in the saracen as it was taking off. There were four soldiers in the saracen with me. We made a lot of circles. I thought I was still in Girdwood.

I was brought round to the interrogation centre. Then stripped of all personal belongings. I was made sit in the cubicles. I was taken out and questioned by the Special Branch for periods, different lengths of time, sometimes half-an-hour, sometimes one and a half hours. The second last one I was brought into a room. The lights were off in the room. I was made sit in a chair. As I made to sit in the chair it was pulled below me. I fell to the floor and the lights went on again. There were three men there with stockings on their faces. The head man says, 'if you want to have it easy tell us everything you have done'. When I said I had nothing to tell, I was made stand against the wall, fingers distributed and legs outstretched. I was beaten and kicked in the stomach and privates for about half-an-hour. I was made lie on the floor. My pants and underpants were removed. One put his foot on my throat and the other held my legs. The other one lit matches. He blew them out and then put them to my privates. Then they made a few rude remarks about my wife and made me get up again. They made me stand against the wall again. That was a rest for about fifteen minutes.

Then they took me into another room. They told me not to look around but I saw a man with a green apron and green overalls with a mask like a doctor. He was a big heavy-set man. They made me sit on a chair facing the wall. They blinded my eyes with a cloth. They rubbed my arm with some stuff and I felt a jab in my arm. I felt my head dizzy. Then I thought they were taking my blood pressure for a band was wrapped round my arm. Then I felt an electric shock going through my arm. It got higher and higher and I felt it going through my legs and the rest of my body. I was holding on to the arm of the chair. Another person lifted my arm off the chair. The person who lifted my arm off the chair told me to sit ordinary without holding anything. The shocks went all through my body, down through my feet and all. Then I heard a voice, 'I think he has had enough'. The other replied, 'Electrocute the bastard'. The things round my eyes and arm were taken off.

I was told not to look around. I was taken into the same room I got the beatings. Made stand against the wall. Punched in the stomach and then the one punching replied, 'I have hurted my knuckles on the bastard'. Then they started to kick my stomach. They brought me over an electric fire as I was standing against the wall, fingers outstretched. One says, 'Are you too warm?' I never replied. He put it up to the full height. The sweat was running out of me. I was soaking. I said, 'That's it. You can take me out and shoot me. I don't care'. One who said he hurt his knuckles kept on punching me. He was about fifty, a big man, well-made, grey hair. Before this, after he had beaten me and taken the mask off, he said, 'You know I did a bit of boxing myself'. He punched me four times in the face. I says, 'I'm down but I would still do you if I was on my own'. I felt a punch on the back of my neck. They threw me out of the room.

A policeman outside linked me into a chair where you sit looking at the wee holes in the wall. When he saw the state I was in, he asked me to go to the toilet and get a drink of water. I came back and was set down on the chair for about two hours. Then a camp bed was brought in, must have been the early hours of Friday morning. I was told to make a camp bed and lie down on it. But a policeman stood over me all night whistling party tunes. He kicked me on the ribs and called me a bastard. I was awake all night. Didn't sleep, the lights were on, and he was standing over me.

Then I was made get up and sit on the chair and then brought out into another interrogation room. A man in his thirties with a beard was questioning me, more a talk. He said I was a Communist. He told me how many men he killed and he thought nothing of shooting me.

I made a statement after the electric shocks but can't remember whether I signed it, don't think I signed anything.

I was examined by five doctors altogether. I was examined by two doctors in Girdwood. One examined me and just went out. Another time after the beatings one examined me in Girdwood. He was worried about my kidney. He made me strip. I was examined by three doctors at Townhall (police station), by my own doctor, Dr Duffy, Duncairn Gardens, by a police doctor, and by the solicitor's doctor.

JOHN MOORE

In the early hours of Friday morning, about 4am, 21 January 1972, I was arrested. The soldiers came into the house. They said they wanted to search the place. I told them to go ahead. They searched the house and brought down five jackets belonging to me and said they were taking them away with them. They told me to get dressed. As soon as I went on the landing, they read a paper saying they were arresting me under the Special Powers Act. They kicked me downstairs into the car park. They said, for my own protection and the protection of those in the 'pig', they would have to blindfold me. They put a blindfold on and turned me round a few times. They brought me over and put me into the 'pig'. They drove around for about twenty minutes. I thought I was at the *Maidstone* (prison ship in Belfast harbour for detainees). I thought I smelt sea water. The 'pig' stopped and I was brought out and put up against the wall. They left me there for about ten or fifteen minutes. They came back about fifteen minutes later and brought me into a building. They set me down on a chair and took my shoes and socks off.

I was brought into a room, still blindfolded. I was facing a voice talking to me. He asked me what I did with the gun. I said I hadn't got the gun. I got kicked on the shin. He repeated it. Same answer. I was kicked on the other shin. Same question again. I was tapped on the head with a baton six or seven times, each time getting harder. I said I never used it. One of them said, 'Bring in the witness'. They took off the blindfold. They brought the witness in. He asked, 'Is this the man you saw from the building site?' 'How many children have you?' I said, 'Five'. He said, 'Did they know that you are getting eight and ten years for burning a bus, and there will be a long time for shooting at my troops'. I said I didn't do it. He said, 'Take him away; you know what to do with him'.

They brought me into another room. I was made sit down in the middle of the floor. They put on my shoes and socks. I was blindfolded again. I put them on. I was brought out again. Put into the 'pig'. I was given a couple of digs in the ribs getting into the 'pig'. They took me somewhere. I don't know where. Same thing, 'What did you do with the gun?' and all. I said the same thing. Back into the 'pig' again. A voice from the front of the saracen said, 'Take the blindfold off him'.

I was brought to Girdwood. As soon as I was put into Girdwood, I was brought into the back into a small hut, different cubicles, small, chairs. I was made sit there. I didn't know what time this was at. I sat in the chair, just looking at wall with holes in it. It was near breakfast time; they were coming in with breakfast for other men lying there. I sat there all day.

Just after supper time, a uniformed person comes in and took me to another chalet. I was interrogated there by 'plain clothes'. I took him to be a detective. He said he knew I fired a rifle that day and said I would have to tell him what I did with the rifle. I said I couldn't tell him anything, that I was in the house all day, the child was sick and the doctor was coming. Two more came in and asked questions. Then another two or three. There were six altogether, I think. They told me to stand up against the wall, fingertips, feet well back. After five minutes my fingers were getting numb, tired. Again, 'What did you do with the gun?' I said I didn't have it. Same again. The tallest stood directly behind me, tall, black blazer, football badge or something on it, wore glasses, greyish sort of hair. He was standing directly behind me chopping my sides with his two hands. There was a young one with a Scotch accent, a beard, gingerish hair, at my left side, one hitting me and then the other. Another one with two hands on my spine was pushing me towards the floor. One detective, about thirty, was sitting on a chair. He was asking where was the gun. I didn't have to go through all this here. I just gave the same answer, I didn't have it. He said, 'Give him a rest for a while'. About five minutes. Standing against the wall.

They all came round me again and told me to take off my pants. I had a blue jumper on. They took the jumper and shirt off. I was just in vest and underpants and socks. They started the same again, one at the back and front, punching and kicking all the time. One was still punching me from the back. I said I couldn't help them at all. They put this jumper on me, put it around my head and took me out of the room and marched me next door.

When I walked in there, there were surgeons there, and like an operating table. They had big green cloaks and masks, round hats. They sat me down on a chair beside the table. On the table was a small bottle of stuff, and two syringes with needles, something like dark blue in the small bottle. There were two syringes. I was sitting on a chair. Somebody came from behind and put on a blindfold. Then I heard somebody saying he was going to give me an injection on the arm. He gave me an injection on the right arm, then he tied something round it, then he did something to my fingers, fiddling about with them. Then he says, 'Are you going to tell us what you did with the gun?' Then I repeated the same answer, I never had a gun. Then I felt this feeling in my arm, electric shocks, but two given to start off with, not painful, just uncomfortable. Then every time they asked a question, it only kept increasing, got severer and severer. My mouth dried up. I couldn't even talk to them. They asked, 'What is the matter?' I pointed to my throat. I was going to say, 'I'm going to tell yous', but I couldn't talk. They turned it off altogether. I couldn't even feel my arm. They brought over a plastic cup of water and gave it to me to drink. I said, 'All right. I'll tell you what you want to know; I will tell you who fired the rifle'. They took the blindfold off then. One said, 'Don't forget this can be put on again'. I told them it was me who fired the rifle, that I was told to go to a certain spot. They let me put on me again.

WILLIAM JOHNSTON
I was arrested at my girlfriend's house in Ardoyne, Monday morning about 3am, 24 January 1972. and was taken to Tennent Street Police Station and then brought to Girdwood Barracks. I wasn't long in the police station and wasn't touched there.

I was 36 hours in Girdwood Park. They let me sleep there until the next day. I don't know what time, but an hour after going there I was let go to bed. They questioned me the next day, but later on that night (Monday). They started to interrogate me, insulting me, made me take my boots and trousers off. They stood me against the wall, fingers on the wall, feet as far back as I could. One of them chopping me on the sides from behind. The other was hitting me in the stomach. This went on for about an hour or so. Then they put a coat over my head and brought me into the next room. They took the coat off and put on a blindfold. I saw one beside me, tall, dressed in dark green uniform. I thought he was a doctor. But later I knew it was one of those who interrogated me by the sound of his voice. He was wearing a mask and hat like a doctor, dark green. There was a needle there with purple stuff in it. I thought they were going to give me a truth drug. I don't think they gave me the needle. I didn't feel one anyhow. They sat me on a chair. They put a thing on my arm, still blindfold. They gave me electric shocks. I couldn't stand the pain. Then I admitted charges. After they asked me for a lot more information, about my area. I said I didn't know anybody.

Then the CID came and took me down and said I would be out of Girdwood. On my own I did not intend to make a statement. I would have done anything to get out of Girdwood Park.

Castlereagh Interrogation Centre

Bernard O'Connor 1977
In 1975 complaints began to mount that plain clothes police were ill-treating people detained under emergency laws at Castlereagh RUC Interrogation Centre. The brutality increased towards the end of 1976. Some 1,700 people processed in the centre were charged in 1977. Amnesty International highlighted the ill-treatment in its report of June 1978. Fr Denis Faul and I had also brought the allegations of ill-treatment of arrested persons before the public in a book *The Castlereagh File* published in 1978. On 2 March 1977 Keith Kyle of the BBC presented a special *Tonight* programme on interrogation methods in

Northern Ireland. He interviewed two men who had been interrogated in Castlereagh, Bernard O'Connor and Michael Lavelle. In our book we published extensive extracts from Bernard O'Connor's statement to his lawyers and a medical and psychiatric report on him after his interrogation which indicated injury and stress confirming that he had been assaulted while in police custody. Following the European Court of Human Rights at Strasbourg's pronouncement on 18 January 1978 finding the United Kingdom guilty of violating Article 3 of the European Convention of Human Rights on two counts, Keith Kyle wrote an article in *The Listener,* 26 January 1978. He wrote, 'The Castlereagh situation involves, among others, Bernard O'Connor who was interviewed by me on the *Tonight* programme in March 1977 (*The Listener,* 10 March 1977). Mr O'Connor, an Enniskillen schoolmaster, made allegations on that programme in great detail that resembled closely the second category of cases in which the court found against Britain. This, and subsequent allegations by others, create the suggestion that the condemned "practice" – which in the usage of the European Human Rights Court means "an accumulation of identical or analogous breaches which are sufficiently numerous and interconnected to amount not merely to isolated incidents or exceptions but to a pattern or system (so that) it is inconceivable that the higher authorities of a state should be, or at least should be entitled to be, unaware of (its) existence" – is continuing today.'

Bernard O'Connor relates in his statement:

ARREST

On Thursday 20 January 1977, at approximately 5.30 in the morning, I was awakened to the banging of our front door. I jumped out of bed and ran to the window and saw outside a large number of army and RUC personnel. I thought there was something wrong and I wakened my wife. I ran down the stairs to the front door. When I opened the door, a soldier came in. He told me that he was searching the house under the Special Powers Act, or words to that effect. Two or three soldiers came through the door, then followed by a policeman with a large sheet of paper in his hand. He put his hand on my shoulder and asked me was I Bernard O'Connor and I said I was. He said, 'Well, you, Bernard O'Connor, are being arrested under Section

12 of the Special Powers Act (or words to that effect) for having knowledge of explosives and shooting offences in Enniskillen.' I asked him was he joking and he said 'No'. The other policeman said, perhaps I would like to put some clothes on, as I was just in my pyjamas. So I went upstairs. During this time a number of soldiers and some other police had come into the house. I went upstairs in front of the two policemen. They went to the bedroom. Two policemen stood there while I put on my clothes. One of the policemen then asked me did I want to have a wash and shave and I said 'Yes'. So I went into the bathroom and I cleaned myself up. Then they asked me was I ready to go and I said 'Yes'. By this time my children had been awakened and were looking over the banisters. I asked the police not to go near one of the rooms where some of the girls were sleeping, or if they did go near the room not to frighten them or disturb them or take them out of the room, but that they could search the room as thoroughly as they wished. They said they would do that. When I got to the bottom of the stairs I met my wife. I kissed her and said I wouldn't be too long away. The two police then took me away. My wife was annoyed at being left in the house on her own with the soldiers and two police officers (a policeman and a policewoman).

To Enniskillen police station

The two police put me into the back of a police car. One sat each side of me in the back seat. There was a third policeman in the car, with the engine going ready to drive me away. While in the car, one of the policemen, to my left, took out a pair of handcuffs and proceeded to handcuff my hands, one across the other. I told him there was no need for that. He said they were instructed to do that. Sitting as I was between two police in the back of a police car, I thought the use of handcuffs in the circumstances to be belittling. The handcuffs were extremely tight. At a later stage I found that the blood had stopped flowing to my hands. By the time I got to Belfast my hands were numb. The police car brought me from my home to Enniskillen RUC station. I wasn't taken out of the car there. The car was parked in the forecourt of the RUC station. One of them got out of the car and went into the station. We had to wait there a considerable length of time, about three-quarters of an hour I would say. Three or four other police cars came into the police forecourt as well. I gathered that there were other people like myself in those cars. I couldn't see who they were, or even make out [anyone] at all, because it was completely dark. The police in the car were extremely friendly to me and spoke about motor cars and driving and things of general interest like that. When the policeman who got out of the car came back, half-an-hour later, he said that things were nearly ready to go. I asked him where we were going and he said we were going to Belfast. He waited, talking again with the rest of the policemen about cars, as he seemed interested in that.

CASTLEREAGH INTERROGATION CENTRE
We set off from Enniskillen in convoy. I made [it] out to be about four cars in all. We were driven direct from Enniskillen to Castlereagh police station in Belfast. The police on the way did nothing, I could say, harmful to me; in fact they were very friendly to me.

When we arrived at Castlereagh police station, the car was driven up to a small side-door and I was taken out of the car and brought in through the side-gate. When inside the handcuffs were opened and taken off me by the same policeman who had put them on. I was then brought into an office inside of a hut-type building. A sergeant there asked me to take out all personal belongings that I had in my pockets. I had a pound note, a chain and a miraculous medal. The watch was taken off my arm, the ring was taken off my finger and shoe-laces were taken out of my shoes. These were put in a sealed envelope. The reason why I had not anything else in my pockets was that before I left home in Enniskillen I removed all other articles, my diary and personal letters and other items like that and I left them on the table back home. The policeman then filled in a personal form concerning my name, age, date of birth, address, family, number of children, names of children, etc. I was then taken by another policeman and stood up. He frisked me from head to toe to make sure that I had no other possessions.

After that I was taken to a cell, again another hut-type cell block. I was put into cell No. G8 which was quite a comfortable place really. In the cell I had an iron bed, red padded chair, two blankets, two white starched sheets. There was no daylight that one could see from inside the cell. There was a light in the cell, central heating and air ventilation. I was left in the cell for approximately twenty minutes.

MEDICAL EXAMINATION
I was then taken from the cell by a uniformed member of the RUC and I was brought back to the hut-type buildings that I was first in where my belongings were taken from me. A room in that hut was used for medical inspection and there I met a doctor. He was extremely friendly and helpful and asked me did I want a full examination. I told him 'No'. He asked me was there anything else I would like to complain about. I said that I had a strong cold in my chest. He asked me had I received treatment for such a cold before. I said that I had received mystecian capsules. He asked me had I ever got Penbritin. I said I had but that they were not much use in the past. He said he would try them again. He counted out twenty-four capsules to be taken two a time four times a day so that the total dose would last for three days and if I wanted to see him again then to ask the police and he would come again. He then filled in his own medical report from appearance that I was one hundred per cent. I signed the report and I was then taken back to my cell.

FINGER PRINTS
About twenty minutes later I was then taken from my cell, again by a uniformed member of the RUC. I was brought into another room in the original block. There I was told that I had to get my finger prints taken. I recognised two of the plain-clothed policemen there as being from ... The third I had never seen before. I know one of the men there to have been Detective ... from ... I only know the other plain-clothed man by sight. My finger prints were taken in duplicate, from both hands; went through each finger on two occasions. They did the palms of my hands. They did my hands with my fingers pressed together and my hand open. Having completed that, I was given a spirit substance to clear the ink off my hands. I was then brought to wash them. I was then brought back to the cell, G8. I was photographed in my cell by two men in plain clothes.

First interrogation

I wasn't very long back in my cell when it was opened again and I was brought again by a uniformed RUC man to be introduced to a plain clothed detective. He was a very tall man ... He had a beige folder under his arm. Behind him was another fairly tall man, very well-built detective wearing a brown suit. He was older than the 'taller' man. At no time did this man assault or ill-treat me but he was present while the 'taller man' did assault me.

They led me to a block of interview rooms. I was led into room one. In that room there was a table and three chairs. I was told by the taller of the two detectives to stand in front of the table. He looked at me and he said, 'So you are Bernard O'Connor. Man but you are an insignificant bastard'. He then put me standing on my toes, made me bend my knees and hold my two arms out in front of me. I was told to stay in that position. When my heels touched the ground, I was hit a slap on the face. At a later stage when I had to wipe the sweat from my forehead with my hand, I was also hit a slap on the face for not keeping my hands in the position I was told. Several times I wobbled to my heels and each time I was struck on the face. The 'tall man' generally used his right hand to slap the left side of my face. This man proceeded to confront me with various accusations about my life in the past. He was aware of my involvement in the Civil Rights and the People's Democracy, and in fact aware of many other events that took place in my own environment in Enniskillen which had nothing illegal about them. They both referred to my involvement in the Boy Scouts and to many other activities. The other man in the brown suit also wanted me to admit to taking part in several bombings and shootings in Enniskillen, and also to admit that I was involved in bringing injured people in Enniskillen to hospital in the south. Each time I denied these involvements I was again struck in the face by the 'tall man'. I went through this type of interrogation for approximately three and a half to four hours. My legs were trembling with the strain. The sweat was running freely down my face onto the ground. The 'tall man' said he was leaving the room for a drink of water. The older man in the brown suit told him to bring one for me. He came back with three white beakers full of water. The man in the brown suit handed one to me and told me there was no truth drug in it. I drank

half of the beaker of water. The man in the brown suit put my beaker
back on the window ledge and marked the letter 'B' on the side of it.

At the end of the interrogation I was taken back and put back into
my cell. A few minutes later a uniformed policeman came along and
gave me lunch which consisted of meat pie, beans and potatoes. I was
not in much form of eating. I tried to eat some of the potatoes and
things. I took two of the Penbritin tablets and a drink of water and lay
down on the bed awaiting the next interview.

SECOND INTERROGATION

About an hour later, I was taken from my cell and brought to interview room five. There I was confronted by two detectives who later
classed themselves as CID (Criminal Investigation Department) men.
All three told me their names. Two of them I remember as being a Mr
... and a Mr ... The third one I can't recollect but he had ... They
approached the subject in completely different vein to the previous
two. They were there, they told me, to help me to make sure that I
was treated properly and that I could admit to anything that I had done
wrong. They encouraged me to realise that if I had done anything
wrong that the best thing to do at that stage would be to tell it, to make
an open confession and that an open confession at that stage would
maybe even guarantee my release. They told me that in any event, that
if I had fringe involvement with terrorists' activities in Ennniskillen
that in the courts they would be extremely lenient on me, firstly because the offences were so long back and, secondly, that the involvement would have been so little anyway that I would get a very small
prison sentence. The prison sentence, of course, would be halved because the offences were committed before a certain date, and I would
also gain remission, which means that I would be away from my wife
and children for a period of two or three years.

They also told me, of course, that, if I didn't take this course and
that I was later on found to be involved in more serious offences, like
murder, that there would be nothing else for it but for me to do a
prison sentence for approximately thirty-five years; I would not see
the outside world in that period, and went on to explain that I should
understand what the outside world would be like in thirty-five years,
and how I would not be able to adapt myself to a community then.

They then went on quite a religious theme to point out that the Lord looks for his sinners to repent and that this was the time to repent and, if I was willing to confess that I was doing so at the hand of God, that that was the proper thing he wanted me to do and that, if I went to my grave with the offences that the file told them that I had allegedly committed, well then I would have nothing but damnation for the rest of eternity. Again, after four hours of this, it didn't seem to have any effect, so therefore they brought me back to my cell and there I was brought my tea.

Neither Mr ... nor Mr ..., nor the third man I have just described, physically assaulted me or ill-treated me at any time. My recollection of Mr ... is a man of ... My recollection of Mr ... is a man ... My tea was again something in the line of a fried egg, sausages and beans. I tried to eat as much of the egg as possible and as much of the food as possible because I felt that I needed strength. From the way that the previous two interviews had gone, I felt that they were going to put a terrible strain on me to admit to something that I had nothing to do with.

THIRD INTERROGATION

After tea I was then taken back again to room five. This time the gentlemen there, whom I didn't know, were very angry at the fact that I hadn't accepted the help that the previous people had tried to give me, that they were really doing their best for me, and I was flying in the face of help by not accepting what they were doing for me. One got to the stage that he would shout at me several times that he knew I was involved, he knew I was a murderer, he knew I was a terrorist, and he knew I was leading all the terrorists and young boys astray. He felt I was a top man in the Provisional IRA and if so from here on I was going to be cracked. He had about two and a half hours or more at this sort of thing. He was disgusted at the end of his interrogation and he again brought me back to my cell. He told me on my way back that I would rue what I had done. The man who conducted this interview was very similar in description to Mr ... He did not physically assault or ill-treat me at any time.

It was during this interview that I heard at least three other people receiving physical abuse as walls shook and I heard people shouting in the room adjoining the one I was in, in the one opposite the one I was in, and in a room some distance away. People were evidently being bashed against the walls and doors, and receiving other ill-treatment which caused them to cry out and roar. I was told by my interviewer not to pass any remarks as this sort of treatment was not for me. I wasn't ten minutes back in my room when a policeman again came and took me out again.

FOURTH INTERROGATION, ASSAULT
There I met a young gentleman and he brought me down to interview room number five again, after signing me out of the cell block. There we met another tallish, six foot, CID man. He was wearing ... Both these ... walked into the room and said, 'Bernard O'Connor, you have refused to help'. I said, 'I haven't been involved in anything'. 'Well', they said, their job was to prove that I had been. I said they were wrong and the younger of the two asked me what way did I want to get [it]. I asked him what did he mean, and with that he drew out and he hit me a box in the face. He landed me back in the corner against the wall. I was made again to stand up in the middle of the floor by the younger man and was told that was the way they meant. They then started to ask me again to go over the exact same things that the previous people had gone over throughout the day. I again denied all knowledge of them. Each time I kept getting hit in the head by both of them. One of the detectives, the fella in the ... tried to jump across the table and chairs screaming that he was going to kill me. The other one restrained him. They then decided to take me to room number two, which was a much bigger room.

Again there was a table, three chairs and a litter bin. The door was locked behind me from the inside. I was made to stand on my toes, bend my knees and hold out my hands in front of me, like the position the first interviewers had done, by the younger man. I was made stand in that position for about fifteen minutes. I was slapped on the face several times by the younger man, mainly to the cheeks and ears. My shoes were taken from me and kicked around the room by the older man. Several times the fella in the ..., i.e. the older man, hit me punches in the stomach. They both then took off their coats and their ties and rolled up their sleeves. I was told by the younger man that if

72

I wanted to talk I could sit down on the chair. While I refused to talk, they were going to proceed to make me talk. I was kicked around the room by both men, on the legs and buttocks. I was fired around the room from one to the other. I was punched severely in the stomach several times, mainly by the older man. I was made get down on the floor and do ten press-ups. If I let my body touch the floor, I was kicked by the younger man. I was made do ten press-ups. If my heels left the floor again, I was kicked by the younger man on the buttocks. I was again put back on my toes and made stand again with my hands out. This went on and on and on.

NAKED

Finally, they decided that it might be even better if I took off my clothes. So I was told to take my trousers off. They then told me to take my underpants off. They then told me to take the rest of my clothes off and I did so, leaving me naked. I was pumped up and down with my head between my knees several times after I was fully clothed again. I was pushed into a corner. The track-suit top which I was wearing was taken off me and put down over my head by the younger man with the arms tied around my neck. I cannot say who tied them around my neck. My nose was closed off with their fingers and my mouth was sealed off with another hand. I couldn't breathe. During this I heard the older man say, 'Choke the bastard'. I found even my very stomach trying to come up my throat, until finally I could re-member no more for a short stage. I felt I must have fainted for maybe just a minute, or maybe five or ten minutes. I have no idea, but I came round the same two people kicking me in the side. I was made run up and down at the time, jogging and running on the spot. Each time I ran past them they kicked me on the legs and buttocks. They couldn't get me to run fast enough. The younger fair-haired CID person started to shadow box in front of me. At no time did he hit me in the face with any of his punches until suddenly he would hit me very very hard in the stomach which would land me maybe five or six feet back against the wall with a very loud bang. He also punched me in the clavicle area several times. Again they flung me around the room. At another stage they made me put the clothes back on again. Because I was too slow putting on my clothes, they would kick me on the backs of my legs and buttocks for not being quick enough. The clothes incidentally were soaked, right out to the very jumper I was wearing, with sweat. They were terribly cold going on but, it is a strange feeling, it felt good to cool me down. This took place just before the pumping up and down which I referred to earlier.

Very shortly afterwards, I was made to take off my entire clothes again. In all I was stripped naked on two occasions. On at least three occasions I was kicked for being slow in taking off or putting on my clothes. I was hooded again by the younger man and again choked and tried to be smothered by them both but, except this time, I remember that I definitely didn't faint out.

FOUR MEN

There came, around two or three in the morning of 21 January 1977, two other people who had been doing a similar job on another person like myself in another one of the interview rooms, because I could hear the similar banging and shouting and thumping that was going on similar to my own. One of these clients was ... The other client was much smaller. This means there were then four men in the room apart from myself. The tall black-haired man took me and he spun me around above his head. He spun me round several times and then he threw me through the air. I landed on my back on the ground. When he was spinning me he held me straight up above his head and threatened to break my back on the table. I remember seeing a most beautiful shade of violet for at least half a minute. It would seem that length [of time] and was the most beautiful colour I had ever seen. I was then taken by the same dark-haired man and at another stage he hit me a massive box in the stomach which fired me straight across the room without my feet or anything touching the ground until I spattered against the wall.

IN THE NUDE AGAIN

I was back in the nude again at another stage. They took my underpants which had been severely soiled with sweat and excretion. They were then put above my head and hung down over my face. I was made run around the room while they mocked and jeered at me concerning my private parts, making references to the fact I had seven children, and then left [me] again standing on my toes with my hands out in a very awkward stance again. I never in my life ever sweated as much as I sweated during that period. At a later stage the two clients who had come in last went out and brought back two fish suppers and two drinks of water for the first two interrogators that started the punishment on me.

WASTE PAPER BIN

While they, the first two, sat eating, one of them, the older of them, took the waste paper bin and dumped it down over my head. The litter and paper and cigarette butts went all over the floor. I was made pick up each tiny piece of paper in my hand, one by one, and each cigarette butt had to be picked up in my mouth. If I wasn't doing it quick enough, again I was getting kicked by both of the first two interviewers. When they were finished their fish supper, one of them, the younger of the two, came over to me with a white plastic beaker of water and asked me did I want a drink. I was extremely thirsty and would have been very delighted to get a drink. I said 'Yes'. He handed the drink into my hand and with the other hand he smacked it out of my hand and sent it flying over the floor. I was then made get down on the floor on my hands and knees and lick the water off the floor. I was delighted even to get it like that.

THREAT OF ASSASSINATION

Finally at the end of, I would say, five hours or so of this sort of treatment, they threatened to put me into a car and drive me to the top of the Shankhill Road where they would have already informed the UVF, and let me free and that would solve all their problems. It was the first two interviewers said this. (The other two, i.e., the last two, left after bringing the fish suppers but came in from time to time.) They brought me outside to do this, but walking past the hut where the cells were, I was brought in and put into my cell. The parting word from the younger of the first two plain-clothed detectives was that, 1. he would get me himself, and 2. if he didn't get me, he would drive the car for the other person, i.e. the older detective, to shoot me. That was about four o'clock in the morning of 21 January 1977. All four interviewers last described had frequently used the word 'fuck' to me.

FIFTH INTERROGATION

I was awakened, and it is wrong to say I was awakened because I had no chance of sleeping that night due to my experience, I was called at seven o'clock in the morning of 21 January 1977 and told that my breakfast was there. My breakfast consisted of an egg on toast and some beans. I tried to eat as much of it as I could, because I knew from the experience I had the more food I could eat the stronger I would be.

I was then taken from my cell by another plain-clothed policeman and brought back to room two for interrogation at ten o'clock in the morning of 21 January 1977. I hardly knew what the time was. I kept asking the uniformed policemen who were taking me out of the cell what time it was, and they always told me. The two CID who were taking me now was 1. a smallish fellow, and 2. a taller fellow. These two clients were inclined again to go through the entire file again, to go through the same stuff all over again. But each time I would say 'No', the small fellow put his hand in front of my forehead. With his fist he kept punching me in the back of the head under the base of the skull until his knuckles got too sore to do it any longer. After the first five or six punches I didn't feel any more. I was numb to punching like that.

I was made continually stare through the window at daylight during this session and I could find my eyes getting very bleary. If I looked around to see the person who was talking to me, I got a box in the face for doing so, as I didn't obey them when I had to look out through the window. The thinner taller one of the two would keep roaring at the top of his voice. I thought my eardrum would burst open. This would last for fifteen or twenty minutes solid at one time. When the dark-haired one would be tired punching me in the back of the head, and after a slight rest, and again talking through the stuff in the file, he would then stand in front of me and slap my face from left to right with an open hand until his face got white with temper when he wasn't able to do it any longer. He got so tired hammering me that he left the room and said that he would be back in ten minutes after he got a break. He said he was fatigued and wasn't able to continue it any longer at that rate but, when he came back, if I wouldn't admit to any offences by then, he would take me to within an inch of my life.

When he came back he was more reasonable than he had been before he went out. For the rest of the interview, apart from an odd slap in the face and a lot of shouting and roaring at me right into my eardrum, the interview ended after about four hours. During this last interview the taller fair-haired fellow punched me several times in the stomach and poked me along the upper chest with extended rigid fingers. Both of these men told me that they were convinced of my guilt and they would personally, if I was released from there, meaning Castlereagh, assassinate me.

It was during the same interview that a third man came into the room and told me that a friend of mine from Castlederg had been shot dead by the UVF and that the same treatment would be suitable for me. One of the two interviewers asked me did I know anyone in Castlederg and I said I did not. I was then taken back to my cell and I was given lunch.

SIXTH INTERROGATION – EMOTION
After lunch I was again taken back to interview room four. Interview room four was a small room similar to the other ones with again three chairs. This time I was allowed to sit down. I was taken during this interview by a man called Inspector ... He told me this was his name, and another more friendly type of person who also told me his name. These men were out to prove that I had been involved in murders in Enniskillen. They spoke from a humane point of view of anybody being involved in a murder and the proper thing to do would be to confess. They tried to emotionally get me to admit that I had taken part in such murders. They said that they knew I wasn't involved in pulling the actual trigger but that I was far too intelligent for that; that I would be the godfather of the scene and that I would be sending young boys and killers out to do these jobs under my instructions and that they had at long last caught up with this godfather. They showed me photographs of the remains of bodies that were picked up, of people who had been killed in explosions and shootings in Enniskillen. They placed them on my knee and asked me to look at them for ages. I was asked to comment on them. I was asked to comment on the type of feeling I felt of people who would do that sort of thing. I was asked for my political views on the present situation in Northern

Ireland. My previous days in the Civil Rights Campaign were thoroughly discussed, my days in the People's Democracy; even a very petty offence of stealing steeples from a sawmill, a derelict sawmill in Enniskillen, when I was nine years of age, was brought up. They were very conversant with my private life in Enniskillen and had twisted everything round to the fact that I should admit now to murder, because it was only in all honesty and justice, looking at these photographs and that type of thing, that that would be the proper thing to do. Needless to say, as I was completely innocent of the whole affair, I would not admit to anything.

MENTALLY DISTURBING
The man who identified himself to me as Inspector ... was .... Neither of these two men physically assaulted or ill-treated me, though I did find their line of questioning mentally disturbing by reason of length of time and repetition. The two different new interrogators kept interrogating me until around two o'clock that morning, 22 January 1977, the following morning, which would have been Saturday morning. I would describe them as 1. ... he was the person who signed me out of the cell block to which I had been returned after the previous interview; up until this I had always been returned after each interview, 2. ... much older man. I would say that neither of these men physically assaulted me or ill-treated me. But, by reason of their line of questioning and repetition and unwillingness to accept my innocence, I found the interview mentally disturbing.

SEVENTH INTERROGATION – SEVENTEEN HOURS
I was put back in my cell then. Again I was in no fit state to sleep, although I felt the cell a relief and a comfort. I was taken from my cell again at ten o'clock on Saturday morning. I was put into room seven. I was kept in room seven from ten o'clock on Saturday morning until five o'clock on Sunday morning, 23 January 1977, which was approximately seventeen hours in the same room. The meals were brought to me there. I was not allowed back to my cell to get my meals. Even during my meals I was continually interrogated, although after lunch Mr ... , whom I have previously referred to, brought me to a toilet and wash-room to let me have a wash.

MADE-UP STATEMENTS

At one stage another CID man came in, and by the way in this period there would be changes of the CID men about every two or three hours, and they would come in pairs. At one stage one of them came in with a brief case, put it down on the table and said, 'Right, now I want the statements'. I refused to make the statements. He said if that's the way I wanted it then he would have to play it his way. He proceeded to open my file and opened it at the page concerning the murder of Constable ... He then proceeded to write down a statement concerning my alleged involvement in the murder of Constable ... He wrote down that I had committed or was involved in a conspiracy to the murder and that I was making the statement freely and not under duress and asked me did I want to sign the statement. I refused to sign the statement. He then turned over a page to the murder of ... and proceeded to write out a similar statement with my alleged involvement in it. He then asked me did I want to sign that statement. After some discussion he then took the two statements again and he handed them over to me and said to me, here write on those statements that I don't want to sign them. Again I told him I would have nothing to do with writing anything on those statements as I wasn't involved in them nor did I write them. The writing was on lined paper with the green crest on the top. He then said that he was going to keep those statements and use them in evidence against me in court as statements made voluntarily by me verbally but that I refused to sign them. I told him that if that is the way his conscience worked, well then that was up to him, but that he knew that I had nothing to do with them.

He then went to leave the room and came back and said that he hoped that I was aware of the fact that I would have to do a period like thirty-five years for not co-operating with the police in making the statements. He said in court, if I went in normally into court and made a statement freely and without persuasion, that the police in court would say this and I would get an ordinary life sentence, which would be about fourteen years, which meant that I would be released from prison, or I would get half remission because the offence was committed before a certain date. Not alone that but I would get one-third remission then on the remainder, which meant I would be released within five years. If, however, he was having to get up in court and say I would not co-operate in custody with the police in making these statements, the judge would rule that I would get a life sentence with a stipulated period of (as in the experience of [those convicted for the murders of] the Miami Showband) thirty-five years sentences. He then asked me to understand what the world was like and the changes that came over the past thirty-five years, and how over the next thirty-five years, if I was locked up in prison, when I would come out, I would be in no fit state to meet society. I wouldn't understand the changes that had taken place and I would, therefore, feel that I could not fit into society. I was asked to think of my wife and family. At one stage he said that the only time you'll get out of prison would be to attend your mother's funeral on a day's remission and, perhaps, maybe if I was good in custody, to get out to my son or daughter's wedding. Having finally, of course, convinced himself that I was not going to involve myself in these made-up statements, he left the room in expression of disgust.

This man was the same man who had me last thing at 2am that same morning 22 January 1977 and also at 10am that morning, i.e. 22 January 1977, that is, he was the much older man of the two who interviewed me until 2am on 22 January 1977. The younger man who was present at both interviews took notes.

AN EXTREMELY RELIGIOUS FELLOW

The next person I had was a Mr ... He was a tall CID man. Again he was a quite friendly sort of person. He even offered me cough sweets. He apologised from the point of view that he had a cold and he would just like to have a little talk with me. The talk lasted roughly about four hours. It went on the trend that he was an extremely religious fellow. He quoted several items of scripture from the Bible, all to try and convince me that I should in this point of time, under the eyes of God, admit to the guilt that he said that I was involved in. After his long and interesting at times discussion and lecture on religion, I seemed to disappoint him terrible when I said that 'No' I did nothing wrong, I was not involved in the acts of terrorism that they were trying to tell me and that I was sorry that he had got the wrong man in there. He then wanted to know as a result of that who did I think was the right man that should be in there. Again I told him that in no way did I know anything about terrorism in Enniskillen, nor did I want to know anything about terrorism in Enniskillen. I told him I never was involved in the IRA. I told him that I am not involved in the IRA and I never wanted to be involved in the IRA. He told me that was a lie, that he had complete evidence in that file to prove otherwise and, despite everything that he had said and that I had said, he was still one hundred per cent convinced that I was the man they were looking for. Again he left the room and this led up to some time in the region of about 11 o'clock at night. Now I had been in that room all day from 10 o'clock that morning up until then.

MY OWN DOCTOR

The only break that I had received out of that room was a twenty minute break, I'd say sometime in the region of around 5 o'clock and it was to be examined by my own doctor from Enniskillen, Dr ... , whose attendance I had requested the previous day, Friday 21 January 1977, from one of the uniformed sergeants. I was very thoroughly examined by Dr ... in the presence of another young doctor who was there under the direction of the RUC to act as a neutral observer to my medical examination. Dr ... medically examined me from the top of my head to the soles of my feet. He discovered numerous bruise marks and swellings on parts of my body. The other doctor that was there verbally agreed with what Dr ... noticed and then wrote them down on his report as well as Dr ... writing them down on the report he was making.

QUESTIONS ABOUT EVERYTHING

I was then taken back from that medical examination to my cell and then back to the interview room where I had been and there my interrogation continued. Around 11 o'clock that night, in the same room which I hadn't got out of, only for that twenty minute period or so, I was then confronted by two very tall well-built CID men. (One) threw his coat on the back of [the] chair, took out two large packets of Stirling cigarettes from [his] overcoat pocket and threw them on the table. He also threw a packet of Opal fruit sweets onto the table as well. He lifted the ash tray from the window ledge, threw it upside down to throw ashes out of it and then put it on the table. He threw the chair from the corner over to the table. He then sat down on a chair and put his feet upon a table. The man ...

Both the men smoked a lot. They offered me sweets which I was very glad to take. It appeared to me that these men were out to ask me as many questions as they possibly could about everything and anything. I was asked questions about religion, priests, nuns, pope, schools, civil rights, P.D., all forms of politics, united Ireland, political parties in the south, England, sex, personal sex life, practically everything one would want to ask questions about. The questions were mainly asked in a very slanted sort of manner. For instance they would ask did I believe that priests had intercourse with young girls; did I believe that priests had intercourse with nuns; did I believe that the nuns were in orphanages to cater for their own children; did I believe that the Pope was a bastard; did I believe that the Pope was the cause of starvation in parts of the world for not selling his wealth and his property. This type of question went on and on and on, roughly to about 4 and 4.30 in the morning of 23 January 1977. At times I was answering 'yes' and 'no' to things I honestly didn't believe in and I knew were completely untrue. I know for a fact that when they asked me did I believe the Pope was a bastard, I answered 'yes'. I know for a fact that I gave a completely unfounded answer in agreeing with them when they said St Christopher was being stroked off as a saint by the Pope. I may have let down my religion during this period through sheer fatigue, in not being fit to put my mind or to employ my mind into giving a reasonable and proper answer.

QUESTIONS FROM THE FILE
During this period I felt that I could relax my mind that bit to allow that sort of thing to happen but, when it came to approximately 4.30 in the morning, the questions started to come direct from the file and to implicate me in terrorist activities that had taken place in Enniskillen between the years 1972 and 1974. It was at this stage that my mind had to become suddenly alert again and to be very careful of the things I was going to say, because a yes or no in the wrong position at this stage would have incriminated me into something that I have never been involved in. At approximately 5 o'clock on 23 January 1977 I was brought back by these gentlemen to my cell. I had not seen these

two men before, nor did I see them again.

On Sunday morning I was called again about 7 o'clock for my breakfast. I ate the entire breakfast to try and again build myself up. I asked the police officer in charge of the cell block to give me a drink of water. He quite willingly gave me as much water to drink as I wanted. He was very helpful. At no stage did these uniform policemen at any time interfere with or ill-treat me, but I could only meet these men when I was put back into my cell.

During interrogation in no way could I have had any contact with any of these uniformed policemen. It was only when they put me back into my cell that I would be able to ask them for a drink of water or my tablets or, as one did later on, get me a towel and soap to take a cold shower. On Sunday morning I had no interrogation whatsoever. I was left in my cell alone without anybody to talk to until about 3 o'clock in the afternoon, Sunday afternoon.

EIGHTH INTERROGATION – BACK TO THE FILE
I was again taken out for further interrogation. This time by a Detective Constable ... who I would describe as ... Both these men told me their names. Also Detective Constable ... came into his interview on a few occasions. Again this interview was similarly based on previous ones where they went back to my file and asked me more questions similar to what I had been asked before and right through the whole rigmarole.

Among others who interviewed me on that Sunday, 23 January 1977, both before and after tea, was Detective Sergeant ... who told me his name. He kept expressing disgust at me being involved in the alleged offences and would not hear of my innocence. This was the first and only time I was interviewed by this man. I was also interviewed on this day by the small detective who was one of the latter two detectives who came into room two during the interrogation between 10pm and 4am on my first night in custody 20 January 1977. Incidentally every CID person who interviewed me had to write a report about the interview. My file was thick when it started, but it was now getting to be twice as thick with the extra reports they were putting in. That interview was again based similarly on the ones before, the same questions, the same idea, and again the same result. I was not willing to, in any way, accept blame for anything I had not done.

NINTH INTERROGATION
On Sunday after tea a similar thing happened, similarly taken for interrogation for a similar period of four hours and again it was the exact same thing happened. I was interviewed until approximately 3 o'clock on Monday morning 24 January 1977 and finally put back in my cell. But at no stage during these interviews on Sunday had there been trace or any sign of violence being used on me.

TENTH INTERROGATION
On Monday morning 24 January 1977 I had a shorter than usual interrogation from the two people who had interviewed me on Friday morning 21 January 1977 from 10 o'clock. They were again using the similar approach. Some of their ideas they had used before, except that this time they didn't attempt to use any violence on me but went through the same type of questioning again.

THE MEN OF VIOLENCE THREATEN ASSASSINATION
The next two that I had were the two main CID men who had used the most serious abuse against me on the first night that I was held in custody on that Thursday night early Friday morning, i.e., the first two of four men who saw me after 10pm of 20 January 1977. At this time they did not attempt to abuse me. They were there to give me good advice, and the advice was that I should take a short stretch in jail now or, if I was going to be now released, which they doubted very much, and said that in fact they were sure I wasn't but, if by any chance I was, that the UVF would only be too delighted to murder me. That was very strange. This reminds me of the first interview I had with them, when they were kicking me around the place, that they said that they personally would make sure that I would be assassinated, and they said that they personally would be the boys who would assassinate me themselves.

This was contrary to the two people I had on Friday morning first from 10 o'clock. Their threat of assassination was that one of them, yes, would personally do it, that is if the UVF didn't do it first. He would be very surprised if I wasn't assassinated by the UVF. In the event of them not being able to do it in two or three weeks that he would guarantee that it would be done by themselves within six months. The two interviewers that kept me from 11 o'clock on Saturday night until 5 o'clock on Sunday morning at numerous times said that the UVF would assassinate me because they had no doubt that I was the godfather. However, they felt that in no way were the UVF going to get me because they had cracked the Miami Showband murderers and they would have no bother cracking me too.

ELEVENTH INTERROGATION – A LIGHT-HEARTED INTERVIEW
I was put back in my cell for my lunch and after lunch at about roughly 3 o'clock I was taken from my cell again. This time I was interviewed by two CID men whom I know. One was Detective ... from ... and the other was a Detective ... from ... Both these men took the attitude that either I was as guilty and as black in guilt as the floor or as white in innocence as the ceiling. It was a light-hearted interview really because I believe that for the first time I met people I knew and who knew me. I wasn't afraid to talk freely to these men. There were no strong accusations made against me and I sincerely believe that they believed that I was innocent.

TWELFTH INTERROGATION
I was put back for tea and after tea I then met another member of the CID, this time a new face for the first time, [a] small man. He again decided to go back down through the file asking me the same questions as I had been asked by numerous other CID men before. Again I told him I was innocent. He said I was just telling him the same story as I told the rest, that it was about time now that I told the truth. He was getting quite nasty about the whole thing. He asked me did I think that a good hammering at this stage might help me to tell the truth.

RELEASE
This interview was interrupted by Chief Inspector ... from ... whom I was delighted to see. He asked the other CID man to leave the room. Another gentleman came into the room whom I now know to be

Chief Superintendent ... of CID. Mr ... had been one of the men who had come into the room at one of the previous interviews of which I have told you and produced the brief case and wrote out the two made-up statements about the two murders that I refused to sign. Mr ... told me that I was being released and that I had the option of going home with ... or having my wife drive to Belfast to collect me as she had wished. I said that my wife was in no fit state to drive to Belfast and that I would be only too pleased to drive back to Enniskillen with ...

BEFORE A DOCTOR

I was then brought back to my cell which incidentally now was G9 because the lock on G8 had failed two days previous. There I took the dirty sheets off the bed and put them into a pillow case. I was given a plastic bag to put my dirty clothes and belongings into. I was then brought before a doctor for a final medical examination. The doctor asked me did I want a full medical examination and I said 'No'. He filled in the recognised medical form and stated I had received no injuries since Dr ...'s examination, nor was I willing to complain nor had I received nor complained about any injuries received from the previous medical examination by my own doctor. I signed the form stating to that effect, that is, that I had received no injuries since the time I had been examined by Dr ...

COMPLAINT FORM

I was then taken to the Police Office and there the police sergeant gave me back my belongings that were taken from me the first day I arrived – my watch, my medal and chain, my ring, my pound note and my pair of laces. Also given back to me was a newspaper, two books, a packet of cigarettes, and some bars of chocolate which had been sent into me and which were not allowed to be given to me. I was then given a form to sign by the police sergeant which was stating – had I received any ill-treatment while I was in custody. I signed that part of the form which said that I had received ill-treatment. At the bottom of the form was a section which said 'other information'. I wrote that I had received injuries in accordance with the medical report already submitted by Dr ... I was given back all my belongings.

TO ENNISKILLEN

Chief Inspector ... drove me to Enniskillen. On the way he spoke about numerous political things that had happened in the past, like the Civil Rights Campaign, the People's Democracy affairs, the *Concern* newspaper which used to name him specifically and how he used to enjoy reading about himself, the present political state of Northern Ireland, and in no way did he at any time try to involve himself in any fringe interrogation about any offences back in town that I had been interrogated on during my stay there at Castlereagh. We arrived home at approximately 10.45pm to the delight of everybody.

STATEMENT MADE BY ME

This statement has been made by me Bernard O'Connor of ... Enniskillen, County Fermanagh, on the 28th day of January 1977, at the offices of my solicitors, Messrs ... & ...

I am 36 years of age this summer. I was born on the 1st June 1942. I have a wife and her name is Mary Patricia O'Connor, formerly Crosby. I have seven children, namely Philip, Nuala, Moira, Sinéad, Brian, Áine, Nollaig. I was married on the 28th day of December 1965 at Holy Rosary Church, Belfast. I am at present employed as a school teacher in ... , Enniskillen. I commenced employment there on the 1st September 1966. I have a post of responsibility for music in the school for the past three years. I am a scout master with St Michael's unit of the Catholic Boy Scouts of Ireland. I was a founder member of that organisation in Enniskillen in 1961 and I have been a scout master up until 1969. I am now the unit leader of that unit in Enniskillen.

At nine years of age in the year 1951 I was convicted of being involved in the theft of a small quantity of steeples from Acheson's mill in the Brook. I was involved also and convicted of obstructing the police in the course of their duty at a sit-down in the Civil Rights parade in Enniskillen in 1972. Other than that I have no other criminal convictions whatever of any kind nor have I had any other involvement with the RUC.

Supplement: Statement by Bernard O'Connor, 16 June 1977, on RUC interview based on the Catholic religion.

This interview lasted from 11pm on Saturday 22 January to 5am on

Sunday 23 January. Practically two-thirds of this interview was based on the Catholic religion. In previous interviews many of the interrogators would say abusive things about my Catholic religion, but during this particular interview there was a prolonged attack on the Catholic Church. The fact that I teach in a Catholic school and also give religious instruction to the pupils, and the fact that I am Diocesan Commissioner for training scout leaders in the diocese of Clogher for the Catholic Boy Scouts of Ireland made the two interrogators very bitter towards me.

The questions were asked in quick succession, giving little time to think of an answer. The following are an example of the kind of questions that they asked:

Do you believe that the majority of priests have sex lives?

Do you know that nuns and priests have sex together?

Do you know that nuns run orphanages to cater for their own babies?

Do you believe that when we (the interrogators) pulled into a lay-by two nights ago there was a priest in a car having sex with a teenage girl?

Would that priest be able to forgive sin in confession?

If you were lying on the path, would that priest be able to anoint you?

Do you believe that priests should marry?

Do you use contraceptives?

Do you think the Catholic Church has the right to forbid the use of contraceptives?

The Pope forbids the use of contraceptives so that there will be more Catholics in the world than any other religion.

Would you agree that over half of the Catholic parents in the country use the pill?

Wouldn't the Pope be able to solve the hunger problem in the world if he sold the Vatican and all the valuable properties that the Church owns?

Do you believe in the infallibility of the Pope?

What do you think of the Pope kicking out saints? Do you believe in St Christopher?

Why do I pray to the Virgin Mary?

Why pray to the saints, why not pray directly to the boss?

This kind of questioning went on for hours. When I tried to defend the teachings of the Church, one of the interrogators would stop me by saying the following, 'Such a stupid answer for a fucking intelligent school teacher'.

They went on to give me the details of their own sex lives and the freedom they enjoy with the pill, etc. Everything they said about the Catholic Church, the Pope and the teachings of the Church was most insulting. They used the most foul language throughout the interview.

BERNARD O'CONNOR, ENNISKILLEN, 18 JUNE 1977

Ill-Treatment of Women in Castlereagh

GERALDINE CRANE, 1977
Women were also ill-treated in Castlereagh Interrogation Centre. On 7 November 1977, eight women from the Short Strand area of Belfast were arrested by the RUC under emergency legislation and held in Castlereagh for seventy-two hours. Mgr Denis Faul and I published in *The Castlereagh File* statements from the Association for Legal Justice on the interrogation of these women.

The Short Strand is a Catholic enclave in east Belfast. In the 1970s and 1970s it was reduced from a population of 8,000 to 2,600, a result of the war in the north and unenlightened redevelopment. It is a district noted for its community spirit and kindly hospitality. Some fifty residents have been killed there in the recent troubles. In December 1997 there were 56 men and women from this little district in prison for political offences.

The first part of the following statement was taken by Elizabeth F. Murray and the second part by me.

STATEMENT OF MRS GERALDINE CRANE. AGED 21 YEARS. MARRIED WITH A CHILD OF TWO AND A HALF YEARS.
On Monday 7 November 1977 at 6.30am I was rapped up. When I got to the door there were four RUC men accompanied by the army and

two women officers in plain clothes. They said there going to search. I asked if they had search warrants. They said 'Yes'. Two RUC men went upstairs. One went into the scullery and the other one stayed in the kitchen along with the two women officers. I stayed downstairs. They all came down again. They didn't search much when they came down again, only the electric box.

I said I had the baby upstairs. He told me I'd have to leave him with somebody. I didn't want to leave him and I went up to get him. A woman officer came up as well. The baby was in his pyjamas. I got the bottoms off and struggled to get his underpants and trousers, etc. They then said, 'We'll have to go on'. So we had to go with his pyjamas top on. They lifted some of his clothing with him and hustled us outside.

I was put in a jeep with the child. I was taken to Castlereagh. There I was taken to a kitchen in it and left with two women police in plain clothes. A uniformed policewoman came in. She told them to go on, she would stay. A plain clothes man came in, put his hands out and said, 'Give me the baby'. He said he'd contacted the authorities and they would take the baby to a home. I started crying, saying I wasn't giving him to any policeman or any welfare. They said, 'He's not staying here'. So this RUC man came in. He asked where my husband was and said they'd get in touch with him. I shouted, 'You know where my husband is'. He laughed and said, 'Why, where is he?' I was still crying. I told him he was in jail. He then asked if I was going to hand Ciarán over. I said, 'No. You can send for his granny'. So they went out to get her and they brought her in to me in Castlereagh. I gave her the baby.

I was taken to a cell. I had to leave my coat and shoes outside the cell door. A man came in to take my finger prints. I was brought down to a room to have them taken. Back to the cell. I couldn't breathe in this cell because the fan was blowing out hot air and it was making a terrible noise as well. I kept rapping the door and asking for water and, as well, I had diarrhoea, so I needed to get to the toilet. I called, 'Miss, get me the doctor, get me Dr ...' The police told me afterwards he was too busy. Then I was photographed twice. I was then taken to the interrogation room.

FIRST INTERROGATION

There were two male interviewers and a policewoman. They said I would know what I was in there for. I said I didn't. He said did I know what Section 10 was. I said 'No'. He said, 'you know under this you are suspected of being a terrorist and being a member of Cumann na mBan'. I said that I was never a member of any organisation. They all started laughing. So they said, what did I know about the fire-bombs. I said that I didn't know anything. They banged the table. I was scared and I couldn't stop shaking. They told me they heard I was sick. I told them I never had good health. They said, how could I expect good health with the people I had bombed and killed. I said that I never hurt anyone in my life. I kept on denying it. I was taken back to the cell. A lunch was brought in. I never ate it. I was left there about an hour.

SECOND INTERROGATION

This time I had two different interrogators and a different police-woman: I planted the fire-bombs (they didn't say where), I ran around with republicans, I was at republican funerals in uniform. I said that the only funeral I was at was that of two friends and I wasn't in uni-form and the only uniform I wore was my school uniform. They said they had lots of photos of me and one was going to bring them down. They kept on insisting they had photos. I knew they had none. Then they said that my husband was awful good, that he even told them he was in the IRA and that I should be like him and tell them everything and get it all off my chest; I would feel better for it. I said that I had nothing to tell; I didn't know any IRA men, about Cumann na mBan, about fire-bombs. Back to the cell again.

THIRD INTERROGATION

This time again two different interviewers. One an older man, fat and long hair combed back. I've seen him at Mountpottinger. The other was a ... There was a policewoman in plain clothes. She had permed hair. She started off asking was I going to co-operate. I said that I told them all I could, I'd told the truth, I wasn't in anything. I said, 'I know nothing of fire-bombs'. He asked, 'Can you fucking read, do you know what that says?' It was stamped in red. It said, 'Geraldine Crane, Intelligence Brief'. I said, 'Yes'. 'Well, what the fuck do you think that means?' I said, 'I don't know'. 'Do you think we get paid for nothing?' I said, 'No, mister'. He said, 'We've got men watching you every minute of the day. We're not only talking about recent fire-bombs but things that go back years.' I told him that I'd nothing to fear because I was in nothing.

The ginger-haired one, when he interrupted, kept referring to Ciarán as a cub. The policewoman then said, 'Do you know the song "Nobody's child"? Well, that's what he will be singing one day'. She kept on referring to Ciarán, saying I wasn't crying, so I wasn't worried about him.

The older man said, 'You sicken me, sitting there shaking. Stand up against the wall'. Where I was standing I was close to, in fact right beside, the policewoman seated on the edge of the table. He stood beside me. The other one at my side. The ginger-haired one stood facing me. The one beside me struck the wall and shouted, 'Aren't you fucking in it?' I said, 'No'. She said, 'He said to stand up, not lean against it' and she pushed me. I had my hands in pockets and she said, 'Keep them by your side'. I put my hands down. He kept banging and shouting, just missing me every time. When I moved she would shove me back. He shouted at me then for staring at the brick wall rather than at your man's face. I said that it was ignorant to stare. He banged the wall. He said, 'Well, I'm staring at him and talking to you and he doesn't think I'm ignorant'. Your man laughed and said, 'You're my friend and I don't mind you staring, and I'll be your friend, Geraldine, if you tell us all.' Back to the cell.

WITNESSED: ELIZABETH F. MURRAY

This statement was interrupted by the arrival of the RUC who wished to interview her re her complaint made at Castlereagh. I took the rest of the statement at a later date.

The second day of my stay in Castlereagh started about 5am, when the policewoman turns the light up. You are left there until about 7.30 am, until the breakfast comes in. I couldn't eat mine. You have your breakfast in your cell, about seven minutes. I asked to get washed and they let me. I was very sick but could not vomit, so I asked for the doctor. They said I could see him when he came. I was still shaking a lot. About 9.30am they opened the door. Two young men were there. I thought it was for interviews but they asked my name and I told them. They asked me was I Raymond Crane's sister. When I said, 'No, his wife', they started to laugh. They told me to stand straight and walk up and down, turn around. Then they said, 'All right, bastard'. The one who did the talking had a beard. I was very nervous after that and I was glad when the doctor came. I asked the doctor for a medical. I told him that I couldn't stop shaking and that the Branch men were shouting at me for it. So he called the policewoman to come while he examined me. I was at least eight stone weight when I was arrested, but was only seven stone four pounds when weighed. I told him I was about eight stone before I was arrested. He said it wasn't possible and was quite angry. He said there was nothing wrong with me except nerves. He put me on three valiums a day. I went back to the cell. Not long afterwards a man brought me down to the interview rooms, as they called them.

FOURTH INTERROGATION
There was another man there and a woman. It was the same girl [as] was there on Monday night. She said had I thought it over, what they said last night, and was I going to tell the truth. She started shouting again, 'You are lying. You planted the fire-bombs. You are in Cumann na mBan, are you?' I wasn't and I never planted any fire-bombs, but they kept on about them. They then started about my husband again and said he was in the IRA and I was in it too. They then started about Ciarán, my son. They asked had I a pram. I told them he was out of his pram a month now and he walked. They said he was out of the pram because I was tired putting guns and bombs in it. I said there was nothing in his pram, that he had a buggy when he was young. They laughed at that. They said I put guns and bombs in the buggy. Then they said I didn't care about my son, I was going to jail for fifteen years. One of the men said he had a son the same age as Ciarán and he wouldn't like to think he would be left in a home because of his mother. I said, 'Ciarán's not going to the home'. They said, 'Why?' I said I had done nothing and was quite capable of looking after him. They said, 'You don't know what you are saying. You planted the fire-bombs and have to do time for it'. They said my mother had reared her family and had a bad heart and wouldn't be able for a baby at that

age, and Raymond's mother had a young family and couldn't take care of another. So I would be as well to tell them and they would make sure I would get a suspended sentence and would only be away for six months and six months was better than fifteen years. They said I could get twenty with the things I had done. I said I never did anything, I couldn't go to jail for nothing. They said I was hurting nobody but myself, I would be as well to tell them everything. I told them I done nothing, I was being held for nothing. So they were quite angry and started shouting at me, calling me a liar. They then said the woman there was a welfare worker and in the police as well and she could put Ciarán in the home or, if I signed a form she had, that she would get him foster parents. I said I never done anything. But they kept on about Ciarán and about jail. I just sat and cried so they would bring me up. I asked if I had been left in clean clothes. So he asked a man. He said 'yes', they were up at my cell.

I saw my sister on the passage. She asked me was I all right. I said 'Yes'. The man pushed me and told me to shut up and walk on. The woman police constable on duty in the passage gave me my clothes and said I could take a shower later because there was someone in the shower.

The interview finished about one. I had a shower and my dinner, although I could eat very little of it. The policewoman opened the door and said there was another doctor in and would I like to see him. I said 'Yes'. I went into the doctor and he said my mammy had sent him in along with the solicitor. He told me to stop shaking and crying. He took down notes of what had happened to me and said I was all right. I asked him about my little boy. He said he was all right. I told him to tell my sister I was all right when he saw her. I was brought out and put in the cell. I stayed for another half-hour or more, then brought down to the interview room where there was two men.

FIFTH INTERROGATION
They started off again about fire-bombs and Cumann na mBan. They finished that interview about five. I had my supper about 5.45.

SIXTH INTERROGATION
I was brought out again about seven to the interview again. It was an-

other two men. So they started again about fire-bombs and Cumann na mBan. I told them what I told the other ones. One brought his chair round and sat facing me. He started to push my chair with his foot. I was holding on to the chair and he asked me what was the matter with me. I said I was going to fall off the chair and would hit my head. He said, 'Don't worry, haven't you clean knickers on' and pulled my skirt away up and started laughing. Then he asked what was I was doing, out shooting at the Brits. I said I wasn't. They said I was telling lies because I was arrested with my husband and my sister, the one in Castlereagh. I said I wasn't lifted with my husband or sister and I was not shooting. They said they had it in black and white, was I calling them liars. I told them my husband was in jail from July and they must be telling lies. They kept on.

I was brought to my cell about 11 o'clock or shortly after that. The policewoman turned the light down. I kept on waking up. They put the light on about 5.30.

SEVENTH INTERROGATION

I was brought out about 9.30 to the interview room. They said they would keep me for seven days, it was nothing to them. I could hear someone getting shouted at and the table getting banged. He said I would get the same if I didn't hurry up and tell them all I knew. They then said about the electric shock treatment. They said I would get that if I didn't hurry up. They brought me to the cell about one o'clock.

EIGHTH INTERROGATION

I was brought down again about two. Again about fire-bombs. The two went out and came back with a piece of paper and said my friends told them I done the shops. I told them I planted no fire-bombs. They said, if I was threatened to do it, I would get off with my health and the child but I better tell them. The door opened and there was about three men there. One told me to walk up and down. Then he said, 'That's her' and closed the door. The man said, 'Do you know who that was?' I said 'No'. He said it was the police officer who had identified me. They kept on changing about. Then two came in and sat down and said they were charging me anyway. I said I never planted any fire-bombs and I want to see my solicitor. They said I was identified, my friends had said, and the judge would believe the police before he would believe me. They then said they would let me out if I told any man's name in the IRA. I said I didn't know anybody. They said they would let me out if I kept my eyes opened and watched the movements of them. They said to let them know and they would pay me well. They said they would put the money in my son's name and nobody would know. They said they would give me a phone number to ring if I saw anything.

I was brought up to my cell. It was 5.10. The man who brought me up said he would be back to give me the phone number. I had my supper and was just lying there waiting for him to come back but he never. It was the longest night I ever spent. I thought they were just going to charge me or keep me for seven days. Then the policewoman opened the door and said I had to see the doctor because I was being released. I asked the time. She said 5.15 Thursday. About 6.15 she opened the door. I signed the release form. I was brought out to a jeep with two girls already there. We waited for the other two and were brought down the Woodstock. The policeman started to laugh and said, 'Duck your head'. We were let out at the bottom of it. The Woodstock is a Protestant area. We ran over to our side of the road. It was a terrible experience.

SIGNED: GERALDINE CRANE
Witness: Fr Raymond Murray

Grand Central Army Post: Patricia Moore, 1977

Prior to the November 1977 sweep on the Short Strand, Belfast, other women had alleged ill-treatment while in custody in Castlereagh Interrogation Centre. Mgr Denis Faul and I included the case of Patricia Moore, Dunmurry, Belfast, aged 18 years, among a number of statements published in *The Castlereagh File*. It alleges ill-treatment at a military post. This statement was taken by Margaret Gatt of the Association for Legal Justice and was signed by Margaret Moore, Patricia's mother:

On Wednesday 30 July 1977, I was coming up Castle Street, Belfast, between 3pm and 4pm. I was stopped by a military policewoman. She asked me to open my bag. I had a tape recorder in my bag which was switched on by mistake. She also found a letter in my bag which I had found in a telephone box a few minutes beforehand.

I was then arrested and taken to Grand Central army post. I was put into a cubicle and then taken out and searched in the toilets. After about two hours I was taken in again and asked if I had anything in my pockets. I emptied my pockets and there was a dead match and a piece of tissue in them. I also had a bracelet on my arm which the policewoman dragged off me. She was shouting and yelling at me and saying I was 'a suspicious bitch'. I did not say a word while this was going on.

I was taken to a room which I took to be a medical room. A young soldier was in the room when I went in. I think he said he represented the medical officer. He asked me about previous illnesses and did I have any scars. Also did I want to be medically examined. I said I had no need to be examined. He asked me to sign a form which I did. He went out but the military policewoman was still there. He came in again and the two of them giggled and laughed about strip searching me. He went out again.

Then a black soldier came in. The military policewoman said, 'I want her strip searched'. He just walked out. The young soldier came in again and the military policewoman said, 'She's going to be strip searched and you have to leave'. He said something about 'his luck'. He then left and the black soldier came in again. I was standing facing the wall. The military policewoman came over to me and said, 'Right, you're going to be strip searched'. With that the black soldier left again. The military policewoman said, 'Get your clothes off'. I said, 'No'. She said, 'Take them off or I'll get three or four women to take them off for you'. I said, 'Go and get them'. She went out for about one minute and came in again with the black soldier. He said, 'You'd be better to make it easy for yourself'. I said, 'For what reason should I take off my clothes?' The military policewoman said, 'Because you are a suspicious bitch'. I said, 'I've been searched twice before'. She came towards me and grabbed my coat and tried to pull it off me. I resisted and she pushed me and I banged my head off the wall. She lifted her fist and I thought she was going to hit me. I slapped her face and she then hit me on the ear. With this the black soldier came in. She told him that I had hit her and that I wouldn't take off my clothes.

She left and came back with two other women soldiers. One was a sergeant major. She said to me about 'making it easier for myself'. I said again that I would not take off my clothes. She asked me again. This time I said I would, if some of them left. I took off my clothes, every stitch. I put my shirt and anorak on very quickly but the military policewoman said, 'Who gave you permission to get dressed yet?' With that she grabbed my anorak and a struggle developed. The black soldier must have heard it and came in again. I struggled and kicked like mad but eventually they managed to get me onto the table. They put plastic-like handcuffs on my wrists and on my ankles.

The black soldier was holding my arms and he asked one of the women to hold them so he could search me. He said he could not get at me, so he took the handcuffs off my ankles and he put his finger inside me. I was crying with the pain. They turned me over and he did it again. During this time they were shouting and yelling at me.

When I was getting dressed, this military policewoman kept hitting me on the back with her fist. They questioned me again and said they were going to charge me with assault. I thought I was going to be released then, but instead they took me to Castlereagh where I was kept for twenty-four hours. I was released on Thursday 31 August 1977 at about 8pm.

IV

THE PRISONS

H Blocks: Ill-Treatment of Prisoners and Human Rights, 1978

In 1973 Amnesty International reported 70 countries using torture and inhuman and degrading treatment against prisoners and political opponents. In 1977 they named 116, an alarming increase. In December 1975, a resolution sponsored by Amnesty International was passed by the United Nations condemning torture and inhuman and degrading treatment of persons. All the countries affiliated to the United Nations signed it. The conclusion is that either many of these governments are hypocrites or they are unwilling to classify their own treatment of prisoners and political opponents as brutal and inhuman.

The Irish government showed an interest in torture by the agents of the British government in Northern Ireland. They brought them to Strasbourg and won the case. But they did not show the least enthusiasm investigating the serious allegations made against the Irish government by the Barra Ó Briain Report and implement the worthwhile recommendations, namely access of family solicitors and the use of a custodial guardian for prisoners under interrogation. Only after a hearing in the Supreme Court and a Presidential crisis was Seven-Day Detention in the Republic reluctantly suspended.

The British government was very interested in the allegations of brutality against the Gardaí Síochána and their newspapers and other media gave a very inflated picture of these allegations and of the Amnesty Report of June 1977 (on the Irish Republic). Their crusading liberal spirit, however, disappeared when they themselves were confronted with the finding of the European Commission for Human Rights, January 1976, and the verdict of the European Court, January 1977, and the clinching of the subject by the Amnesty Report, June

1978. They showed no desire to rectify the serious damage and injustice. They were no different from the Russians who have come to Northern Ireland often looking for details of the British torture of the Irish people, but who deeply resent the public searchlight on their labour camps, mental hospitals and treatment of dissidents. So it is with governments. They are all interested in the torture of other governments but not in their own.

It is difficult to get governments to put an end to ill-treatment within their own countries. It is equally difficult to gain the interest of the opposition because they hope to win the next election and they will not risk losing votes by attacking the sacred institutions of the state, the police, the army, the judiciary, the civil service. There is need for real Christian witnesses at the present time, people with professional training, doctors, lawyers, journalists, priests, teachers to answer the demands of the Christian conscience and to stand up for the human rights of the oppressed and dispossessed every day and every week of every year. It is a lonely and unpopular witness that will meet with sneers and smears and misrepresentation from the leaders of state and society. But it is a genuine charity for the end of the century to fight the problem of the individual against the state with its control of power, publicity and patronage. From those who fight this battle will come the prophets, heroes, and saints of our age.

The H Block problem is a classic example of how the state can intimidate genuine Christian people into waffling about basic moral principles. H Block is an obscenity no matter what the prisoners may have been convicted of, justly or unjustly, no matter what protest action they have taken, no matter for what motive or purpose they may have taken it. The state has no right to do wrong. It has no right to ill-treat prisoners. It has no right to break its own laws. It has no right to break the international covenants on human rights. It has no right to break the moral law.

Leave the questions of political status aside. The factual position is this. The prisoners refused to wear prison clothes and work. These are trivial matters. In the Republic of Ireland prisoners wear their own clothes and prison work is voluntary. The British government removed all remission from the prisoners on protest. Wasn't that punishment severe enough? Is not the punishment of prison deprivation of liberty? But the British government also in the month of September 1976 imposed an inhuman degree of punishment on the men for this refusal – 24 hour lock-up, no physical exercise, no mental stimulation, harassment by internal body searches, casual beatings. All these taken together over a period of time constitute cruel, inhuman and degrading treatment contrary to Article 3 of the European Convention on Human Rights. The British government has inflicted all this for thirty months.

It is completely untrue to say that these punishments are self-inflicted. They are inflicted by the British government on persons who have broken trivial regulations, not wearing prison clothes and not working. The fact that in April 1978 the prisoners escalated their protest with a no-wash, no slop-out campaign is not really relevant to the real issue. The prisoners were merely using one of the few forms of protest left to them against an administration which had deprived them of many of the ordinary necessities of life.

I salute courage and sacrifice wherever I find it. Whatever the past deeds of the men in H-Block may or may not have been and whatever the justice or injustice of the sentences, one has to admire their courage, fortitude and endurance against impossible odds. The Athenian prisoners in the stone quarries of Syracuse could not endure their deprivations for two months. The American and British prisoners collapsed in Korea. The men in H Block, the majority of them 17–21 years, have already created a place for themselves in the records of human endurance. The words of Terence MacSwiney ring true – it is not they who inflict the most but those who endure the most who have the victory.

Extract from a lecture given in St Patrick's College, Maynooth, under the auspices of Cumann na Sagart, 6 December 1978. Published in H Blocks: British Jail for Irish Prisoners, *1979.*

Christ and the Prisoner

When men tried on a few occasions to carry Jesus off and make him king, he ran away and hid himself. He didn't want power. His kingdom was not of this world. He was a king, he said himself, in the sense that he bore witness to the truth. We admire in others, perhaps subconsciously, the good qualities we have ourselves. The picture Jesus gives of John the Baptist when he praises him may be a picture of Jesus himself, 'When you went out to John in the desert, what did you expect to see? A blade of grass bending in the wind? What did you go out to see? A man dressed up in fancy clothes? People who dress like that live in palaces! ... From the time John preached his message until this very day the kingdom of heaven has suffered violent attacks and violent men try to seize it' (Matthew 2:7–8, 12).

Jesus did not wear fine clothes. He did not live in a palace. He did not try to charm the world or show off. He was a friend of the oppressed and chose to live more in obscurity than in the limelight. He rebuked those who called for fire and brimstone. He took a safer line; he called for a change of heart. No crown, no seal of office, no signet ring, no purple band, no red cloak. These would come later in the castle-yard of Pilate. No presentations except the perfume in the house of Simon the Leper. Jesus appreciated Nathaniel because there was nothing false in him. There was nothing false in Jesus, friend, brother, reconciler. There was room for Simon the Zealot and Matthew the tax collector among the twelve apostles. He healed the government official's son and the Roman officer's servant. He touched lepers and ate with sinners. He taught that God 'makes the sun to shine on bad and good people alike, and gives rain to those who do right and those who do wrong'. This message is clear – kindness to all, not only to respectable people but to the outlaws and outcasts as well. The goodness of Jesus was closely connected with his obscurity. For thirty years he was the carpenter's son from Nazareth who shocked his village people in the three-year period of his public life. And always his interest is in redeeming and mercy. Not lording it over people. The greatest is the one who serves! No hatred, no hostility. He recognised the dignity of Bartimaeus and the Phoenician woman. He had room for all in his heart from the children to the thief on the cross. For our sake he opened his arms on the cross. His embrace is for all.

This attitude of Jesus is a scandal to humankind. The guests at the dinner party recoiled when the street woman touched him and kissed his feet. 'Does he not know what kind of a woman is touching him?' 'This day you will be with me in paradise' was his dying promise to his fellow prisoner.

Life is short. It has pain, sickness, tragedy, quarrels. War and killing seem pathetic. The unborn are killed. For some there is no happiness in life at all. Who understand more than the compassionate Christ who never condemns? 'Has no one condemned you?', he said to the woman taken in adultery. 'No one, Lord'. 'Neither will I.'

Nameless, obscure, hidden. Christ the teaching beggar. Even his death was as ordinary as the thousands of others who were crucified in his time. Only the film producers make it grandiose. Jesus in pain cried out in a loud voice; he was parched with thirst; he felt the abandonment of his friends.

Prisoners are not dressed in fancy clothes. In H Block, Long Kesh, in the north of Ireland nearly 400 are naked. They live obscure lives. Their names are replaced by numbers. They are dossiers. 'Show me his file!' They are outlawed. They are oppressed. They are vulnerable. The world goes about its business. Important men who travel long distances to discuss finance are not worried about them. Cars scud along the M1 motorway alongside the massive prison camp of Long Kesh. The occupants hardly turn their heads. Courting couples saunter in the Mall in Armagh. They don't even know that 34 girls on protest in the prison opposite them are locked in for most of the day. The world is too busy, too occupied. It is in a hurry. 'I was in jail and you did not come to visit me'.

Where are the Good Samaritans? Jesus told us the story of the Good Samaritan, not to make us think, not to weigh up reasons for doing this or that, not to calculate ambition or popularity – not even to be charitable for the love of God. All that Jesus said in the story is that the Samaritan looked and he saw a man, a human being. He did not even think. He saw, he looked, he stopped. The Good Samaritan never heard the story of the Good Samaritan! All Jesus is saying is that our very human existence should move us to compassion. Jesus was compassionate, not because he was God, because he was human.

In the H Blocks, Long Kesh, 370 prisoners are denied the basic status of life for going on a minor strike as a protest for political status. For refusing to wear prison clothes and work, excessive punishments have been imposed which, taken together and over a period of several months, amount to inhuman treatment. The punishments are: complete removal of remission; twenty-four hour lock-up; deprivation of mental stimulation of any sort, reading material, newspapers, books, television, radio, games, hobbies or writing materials. These are combined with intimate body-searching. Here is an extract from a letter written on toilet paper and smuggled out of H Blocks:

'Seeing it is a special occasion I have decided to write. The last time I wrote you on this date I was one year "on the blanket". I wrote then, I thought it was an achievement. But I don't know about this for it is hard to gauge even now how much longer I will be on it. What would I say after four or five years lying naked in a cell and times change so much? One would think being in our position we have lost out in experience in life, that is normal life. I can assure you that these last two years have changed my outlook in many things and have helped me to learn and realise many other things. Everyone of us has his regrets that he didn't do this or that, and we all have our desires and yearnings for this or that, which change every week. None of you outside could gauge fully the amount a visit or letter would mean to us or some small thing that indicates we are not forgotten. It is being deprived of the small luxuries of life that has helped us to face up to the harsher realities plus all the suffering and anxiety. We don't say any more that it is a hard station, as most of us believed long ago our station had reached its limits, only to learn this isn't the case. Well, I suppose there are those who say, "They made their beds so they can lie on them". I used to accept this, especially in regard to myself, but now I realise that this is another person's opinion. My own now is that our beds were well made long before we lay in them.

'Well, these are the thoughts in my head tonight. No harm in re-examining our commitment to things in life, in trying times like this asking what would be the best thing to do. You know you are strong and there is no chance of reneging on it'.

There is a crisis of human existence. The H Blocks are like the empty desert Jesus went into. The desert of the mind, the dry parched desert places of the mystery of man, the limits of human endurance. Amid the rocks and stones of deprivations, sufferings and anxiety a new man emerges. Out of Christ's H Block came his compassion. He recognised the dignity in the human person – the woman who suffered from bleeding, the deaf-mute, the boy with an evil spirit, the men killed by the tower at Siloe, the widow and her offering. For him no one was insignificant. He welcomed the lovable and the unlovable. He accepted the Samaritan woman at the well. He listened to Nicodemus. He told us not to show off, to invite to our dinner the poor, the maimed, the blind, the lame. Not to be anxious for our body. Who says the prisoners in H Block are bitter? Will they be bitter? No. They have learned compassion in the school of suffering.

Christ did not wear fancy clothes. He was a beggar who had nowhere to lay his head. He is still the beggar who keeps coming back to the door when we hurt him. His bloodied body still lies in death from Brazil to Iran. His little belly is still swollen with hunger in Kampuchea. He keeps coming back, for the love of people who are suffering, for people who die in tragedies, for their families and those who mourn for them. He is a human being standing defenceless before us full of goodness and understanding. He would not be ashamed to go into the H Blocks, or give clothes to the naked, or bury the dead. The risen Christ dwells in every man. This is the new creation. 'I was hungry and you fed me, thirsty and you gave me a drink; I was a stranger and you received me in you homes, naked and you clothed me; I was sick and you took care of me, in prison and you visited me.'

Christ wants us to be beggars too, to be moved with compassion for the helpless, the hunger and poverty of oppressed peoples. Not by words only. By action. We are to pour in the oil and wine and put the wounded on our own beasts. Not just because we are Christians but because we are human beings.

Homily delivered by me on a tour of Northern Italy. Published in The Furrow, *March 1980.*

Remembering the Hunger-Strikers, 1990

In Ireland the names of the hunger-strikers are hardly mentioned. Now when an occasional political prisoner in Ireland or the European mainland threatens to go on hunger strike to highlight an injustice, he or she is met with severe opposition from organisations and friends. Why is that? Is it because Irish people no longer revere the men who died so bravely ? No. It is because the whole episode hurt everybody too deeply. Everybody suffered. Everybody longed and prayed for an early and just solution of the prison problem. It was a simple enough problem; basic demands for prison conditions that would respect dignity and admit the fact that there was an extraordinary situation in the north of Ireland which had led to many people being imprisoned who otherwise would not. Everybody could see that a compromise solution was possible and easy; in fact now that the men are dead such a solution was found and the conditions they sought now exist in the Maze prison. Why then had they to die? Because the British Prime Minister Margaret Thatcher would not allow the plan worked out between the Irish Commission for Justice and Peace and the Northern Ireland Secretary of State, Mr Humphrey Atkins, to be implemented. That is why it is so sad. The men need not have died. Their families need not have suffered. The country need not have been torn apart. So one understands why, when Irish people think of these men, it hurts them so deeply that they do not want to talk about them. It is a kind of on-going grief.

The present war in Ireland has been waged for twenty years. It makes Irish people very sensitive to troubles elsewhere and makes them very wary of the policies and motives of powerful states. There is so much trouble in the world. It is all brought home to us because the world is a smaller place. The plight of starving children in Ethiopia, the civil war in Afghanistan, the agony of Lebanon, the oppression of the Palestinians, perennial problems of racial and religious conflicts, perennial power struggles between great powers, economic wars, political wars, tribal wars.

What lesson are to we to learn from the deaths of Bobby Sands, Kieran Doherty, Joe McDonnell, Raymond McCreesh, Martin Hurson, Thomas McElwee, Patsy O'Hara, Francis Hughes, Kevin Lynch, Michael Devine?

The world cries out for justice. Small nations, nations that are economically weak, the poor and the oppressed can not accept a situation where the Great Powers and lesser Great Powers and the Churches of the west condemn them for taking up weapons as a last resort to defend their basic rights and their human dignity. At the same time powerful nations loudly boast their own nationalism, control the raw materials and trade of the world, hand out 'gifts' and 'aid' with their own political strings attached and invoke 'God' 'democracy' and 'free world' at every turn. The powerful nations do not hesitate to use violent military might, either invasion or repulsion of every little revolution of the poor and oppressed. The same powers are weighed down with weaponry of the most deadly kind.

In time the deaths of the hunger strikers, their thirst for justice, will demand a chapter in the history of Ireland. Then the hurt will be over, the wound healed. The salve of time heals everything. It would be lovely to think that their deaths would also demand a footnote in the wider history of our world, that they would be taken as examples of courage, that it would be understood that they died for justice, and that one could learn not to leave the oppressed and the weak in the lurch but come to their aid with faith, justice and love.

The hunger strikers suffered. There are others like them in the world today. They will have hope if we are ready to carry the Cross with them, to share life and death with them.

> They need the *deeds* of our love.
> They must experience that *we are Christ*.
> ... For Christ has no other heart
> to have mercy on mankind
> except yours
> except mine.

This short talk was prepared for the annual Mass for the Irish Hunger Strikers in Holy Redeemer College, Washington DC, 1990.

Stripping Girls Naked in Armagh Prison, 1985

Dear Sir,

Since strip searching was introduced into Armagh Prison on 9 November 1982, Cardinal Ó Fiaich, Mr Peter Barry, congressmen and senators of the House of Representatives, USA, the Irish Missionary Union, the National Council for Civil Liberties, London, Amnesty International, Action des Chrétiens pour l'Abolition de la Torture, and many more national and international organisations and individuals have voiced their concern. Labour MPs in particular, such as Kevin McNamara, Joan Lestor, Tony Benn, Clare Short, Joan Maynard, Sarah Roloff, Jeremy Corbyn, Peter Archer and Clive Soley, have by visits to the prison, by letters or public statements, shown their distaste for this new procedure. Mr Kevin McNamara in particular has campaigned to have it ended by raising it in Parliament and by his pointed written questions at Westminster. The nationalist community in Northern Ireland will share his disappointment that the Minister for Prisons, Mr Nicholas Scott, finds the strip searching acceptable. As chaplain to the prison I would like to take Mr Scott up on some issues and explain to him some of the feelings of the nationalist Catholic community.

1. The stripping was introduced on 9 November 1982 shortly after a delegation from the Help the Prisoners organisation, consisting of Cardinal Ó Fiaich, Councillor Jim Canning, Fr Denis Faul and myself met Lord Gowrie, then Minister for Prisons, and some civil servants. We pointed out then how a restoration of lost remission, releases of young prisoners sentenced at the Secretary of State's pleasure, ill prisoners, those who had completed long sentences, improvements in legal proceedings, education and meaningful work in prisons, Irish magazines and journals, ending of degrading searching, would help to create a climate towards peace. Their answer was the stripping of the women, a new procedure, an end to dialogue. We took it as the customary slap in the face to our community from our colonial masters. The subject more than two years later fits into the 'Alienation' context.

2. Since there is no internal searching of the women, as the Northern Ireland Office has often pointed out, what is the logic of stripping them completely naked, even during their periods, and visually examining the genitals and anus? Can you blame people for logically concluding that the purpose is to degrade and cruelly punish them? Punishment was uppermost during the 'Blanket Protest' period; the authorities thought nothing of the mental suffering of the Armagh women prisoners at that time and only ameliorated the situation when public protest grew.

3. It is unfair for the Northern Ireland authorities to say that the prisoners do not object. They have objected in the past and were punished severely. Furthermore prisoners on parole or taking inter-jail visits may not want to jeopardise their position; this is a form of emotional blackmail.

4. The Northern Ireland authorities constantly point out that their procedure compares favourably with England and Wales. I am not convinced by arguments that compare degrading practices in England, Republic of Ireland, or any country. However the comparison does not stand up. Dr Susan Kramer has pointed out in the *British Medical Journal* from parliamentary questions, for example, that between 11 November 1982 and 1 March 1983 a total of 722 strip searches were carried out in Armagh on an average population of 40 women, most of whom were long term prisoners and never left the prison; during the same period 1,430 strip searches took place during routine cell and special searches in women's prisons in England and Wales where the average population was 1,400.

The serious decline in the standards of behaviour on the part of the Northern Ireland Office prison management took place on 9 November 1982 and has continued. This type of degrading inhuman treatment had not been used during the previous fifteen years of my chaplaincy, nor in the seventeen years of my predecessor, not in the worst times of the 1970s when the situation was very bad and there were some hundred political prisoners in Armagh Prison.

Why now, when the number of killings has decreased significantly, are we still faced with such grievances as plastic bullets, stripping of women, 'Shoot-to-Kill', corruption in the 'Supergrass Courts', the PTA? Is it not a matter of the authorities putting in the boot?

A letter from Fr Raymond Murray, Chaplain Armagh Prison, to Nicholas Scott, Minister for Prisons, 11 January 1985. This letter was issued as a leaflet by the Armagh Social Action Group.

A Visit wth Cardinal Tomás Ó Fiaich to English Prisons, January 1990

When Pope John XXIII visited San Angelo Prison in Rome, his simple action, screened universally on television, brought tears to many an eye. One could feel the gentle compassion emanate from him as he raised his arms in greeting to meet the outstretched arms of the prisoners, so wretched looking in their pyjama-like garb. He showed his solidarity, not only by his love and prayer, but by confessing that his own brother had done a term in jail for poaching. Like Jesus washing the disciples' feet, Pope John had given an example.

I often thought Cardinal Ó Fiaich in his attitude to prisoners was a true disciple of Our Lord and another Pope John. He reached out in love and compassion to them. I was chaplain in Armagh Prison for nineteen years. He took an interest in the prisoners there and did his best to intercede for them in times of stress and sickness, adopting some particular cases and pursuing the issue even though he met with criticism and opposition. Every November we had a Mass in the prison for the dead relatives of the prisoners. The women prepared the liturgy very well and it was always a moving occasion. After the Eucharistic celebration we would chat and put on an informal concert. The cardinal would oblige with the 'The Boys from the County Armagh', 'Henry Joy' and 'Tráthnóna Beag Aréir'. One looks back on those times with a nostalgic mixture of joy and sadness.

In January 1990 the cardinal invited me to visit some prisons in the north and midlands of England in his company. I was delighted to accept. I contacted Sister Sarah Clarke in London and she quickly provided me with a list of English prisons, complete with addresses and phone numbers, and where Irish prisoners like the Birmingham Six and the Winchester Four were located. As so often happened with the cardinal, we had a tight schedule. On Saturday 27 January we set out from Armagh to Belfast in the cardinal's car, John Ward driving. The cardinal was the special guest at a dinner reunion of past members of the GAA in Queen's University. John and I left him in the welcoming company of Fr Ambrose Macaulay and other members all in dress suits. I thought it was a sign of a new Ireland to see the GAA celebrate in the Great Hall of the university. Next morning the cardinal and John called for me at 6.30am at my sister's house in Glengormley. We had already said our private Masses in the early morning and so we sped off for the 8am ferry from Larne to Stranraer. The cardinal was in bubbling form recalling the speeches and personalities of the night before. Of course he had not gone to bed until 4 and so could only have had an hour's sleep; that was so often typical of his routine. On arrival at Stranraer we were met with a cold biting wind and flakes of snow. The bad weather did not daunt us. Sunday was to be a 'day off' when we would fit a bit of sight-seeing into our long journey down to Durham. The cardinal always liked to slot in a visit to an historical place when on a journey. He had been reading about the excavations at Whithorn so we headed down through Glenluce into the peninsula taking the coast-road. Naturally we had the excavations to ourselves. We hopped around in the half rain and sleet reading the signs and tracing out the remains of ancient house sites. There was a Presbyterian church nearby. A few parishioners were still there after morning service so we chatted with them and studied the list of ministers from Reformation times. Then we were off and apart from stopping for dinner on the way made no delay until we reached Durham. There wasn't much traffic on account of the bad weather. The countryside, whitened eerily in the dark by snow, seemed lonely and desolate. I was delighted when the cardinal pushed in a cassette and broke into song, inviting John and me to join in the chorus.

It was quite late when we arrived at Durham. Luckily, our hotel, the Royal County, Old Elvet, was near the Women's Prison. In the morning we said Mass at St Cuthbert's and walked to the prison where we were scheduled to begin our visits at 9.30am. The authorities in all the prisons accommodated us in every way and were most courteous. The cardinal brought gifts of chocolate and cigarettes to each prison he visited

Durham is an old prison. I think I remember an officer saying that they were about to spend a million pounds in urgent repairs. I was surprised how cramped and small the wing was where we were to meet the girls, having been used to the space of the wings in Armagh Prison. Here we met Martina Anderson, Ella O'Dwyer, Judith Ward and Martina Shanahan. For me it was a reunion with Martina Anderson and Ella O'Dwyer. Martina had spent a month in Armagh Prison at one time and I had visited them both when they were in Brixton. Our visit was held in the tiny chapel. Judith Ward brought us tea and cakes. She was in ebullient form and very proud to act as hostess. Martina Shanahan of the Winchester Three was tearful and very apprehensive of her coming appeal. The cardinal was very versed in the case and comforted her a lot pointing out all the weaknesses in the prosecution evidence. Martina Anderson and Ella were more seasoned prisoners, adapted to their situations, wary of their rights and had a programme laid out for their future prison stay. They were much interested in news from home and friends in prison in Ireland.

After Durham we soon saw that we would have to rush things to keep to our time-table. Finding Frankland Prison which was in Durham county was quite a problem, although I must say the cardinal and John Ward were excellent pilots. The cardinal was usually bent down over his maps giving directions. One had to deal with a lot of traffic; there are many roads under repair and construction in the midlands of England; but one must also remember that new prisons in England are generally located in the most remote areas; after our experience I was immediately struck on how difficult it must be for people on visits from Ireland to find them, especially when accompanied by small children and depending on public transport; imagine the suffering when told, as has happened, that their relative had been moved to a prison at the other end of England. At last we found Frankland, situated at a tiny village called Brasside. Here we met the other two of the Winchester Three, John McCann of Dublin and Finbarr Cullen of Maynooth. Finbarr's mother had lectured in history at Maynooth under the cardinal's professorship and Finbarr as a boy had served his Mass. Both young men were in good form and in a state of expectation as to the outcome of their appeal, Finbarr quiet and philosophical, John more extrovert, very talkative, his good nature shining in his face.

Both the cardinal and I knew John McComb from his letters; he is a prolific letter-writer and a keen observer of the political situation. He likes an argument. One could be at home with him right away. He wrote movingly in praise of the cardinal to the *Irish News* after the cardinal's death. Martin Foran impressed us very much. He has fought a lone battle for release; he has always maintained his innocence and maintains he was 'stitched-up'. He is not in good health. It is a pity both he and Judith Ward do not get more support from the general public.

We had quite a long journey to our next prison, Full Sutton. We were late but again the authorities were considerate. It is a new prison and is quite foreboding in appearance. The Anglican chaplain looked after us, and brought us coffee. He seemed very interested in us, partly, I suppose, because he was married to an Irish girl. We had a long happy conversation with Billy Power and Richard McIlkenny of the Birmingham Six. Everything seemed hopeful for them. There was still the euphoria at the release of the Guildford Four and one felt that 1990 would see the Six free. Both these men have a well-known reputation of being very spiritual. McIlkenny is known as 'the bishop'. I had visited him previously in Wormwood Scrubbs and I could see he was held in high respect by the officers there. This was our last prison visit of the day so we were no longer under pressure. The cardinal relaxed with his pipe and coffee and spoke at length to the men, filling them with hope and encouragement, relating details of events in Ireland which he thought would interest them.

It was dark of course when we set out for Leicester where we were to spend the night. One can imagine how tired and hungry we were when we arrived at our hotel. The next day's programme was just as hectic – Leicester, Gartree and Long Lartin. On our way to Leicester prison the cardinal had good fun using his car telephone, a gift he had lately received, contacting the prisoner governor to say we were on our way and ringing the chaplain, Fr Kieran O'Shea. Leicester is a typical city prison, nineteenth century Victorian style, dirty, gloomy and crumbling. Our visit there was to a very secure section where Gerry McDonnell, Pat Magee and Paddy McLoughlin, all of Belfast, and a few others were housed. You entered a small ante-room to the closed unit. Here a number of officers kept constant watch through a large heavily plated window which almost made up one wall of the room and looked into the wing. They were surrounded with television surveillance monitors and various electronic gadgets for opening and closing doors. The men inside were very critical of their conditions. They called it the Yellow Submarine – 'We all live in a Yellow Submarine ...' The only outlet they had to fresh air was a tiny little yard which itself was roofed with glass. Gerry McDonnell was one of the escapees from Long Kesh. He with Magee, Martina Anderson and Ella O'Dwyer had been picked up in Glasgow. Magee and McDonnell I had met before in Brixton. Gerry McDonnell is an indefatigable correspondent. I had known his late father for many years so we always kept in contact. The cardinal took time to talk to each man individually. In the prison I heard that an Armagh man (non-political) was held in another wing. I went to see him. No prisoners were in sight in any of the wings. They were all locked up. When the cell was opened up for me I was shocked to see that he shared the cell with many others. The overcrowding in British jails is, of course, a scandal. Then I couldn't help thinking – what a strange fate that a young man whom I saw grow up as a child in a little street in Armagh ends up in a cell in Leicester Prison!

Gartree, Market Harborough, was our next stop. As usual we had a hectic rush and then a search to find it. We had to wait to the afternoon as we arrived at meal time. We met Ronnie McCartney of Belfast. Ronnie is a model prisoner who has got a university degree while in prison. The prison authorities and the Board of Governors (some of whom we met) were in high praise of him and all were anxious that he be transferred to the north of Ireland which he desires. Every time he fulfils the regulations in this regard the Home Office makes excuses and keeps 'changing the goal posts'. One felt that their motive was vindictive and that the deterrent factor was unreasonably important to them. The cardinal had written letters supporting Ronnie in his request. Poor Paddy Hill was locked up in another section of the prison. The whole pressure following the release of the Guildford Four had got to him and he was 'very high'. The cardinal took a long time talking to him in gentle tones until he calmed down. It was wonderful to see his patience and compassion.

Long Lartin at Evesham, Worcester, was our sixth prison in two days. There was some satisfaction in the achievement but I will never forget the rush and tension trying to reach the prisons at speed lest we might overshoot a time factor and not get in. Three of the Birmingham men were in prison here. With the prison chaplain we saw Gerry Hunter and Hugh Callaghan in the chapel. Again this is a modern prison in the 'back of beyond'. Both men were in good form and hopeful of release. It is sad to think that a whole year has passed since our visit and they are still in jail. Surely their release must come with this new appeal. John Walker was in the visiting section so we made our way there and talked to him and his relatives. Walker is a very sympathetic type of man and has helped other prisoners a lot. With him at his visiting table was Vincent Hickey of the Carlswater Bridge case. It is a case that has featured in newspapers and television. Again a case of men protesting their innocence. Vincent told me that John Walker helped him a lot in prison.

From Worcester we set out on the last stage of our journey through Wales to Fishguard, somewhat exhilarated, relaxing from the intensity of the human problems and the depressing world of prison life. Once again the cardinal shoved in a rousing cassette and joined in the songs. We celebrated in Fishguard with a good meal. The town is literally a dead end. There was nothing to be gained driving round in the dark so we lined up in the queue for the boat and tried to doze while the wind and rain howled in from the sea. Ever solicitous the cardinal went to a little office to book a cabin, something which he pursued again on the boat. At least we got lying down. Rosslare appeared at last. The weather was good, the air fresh and the sun shining. We hit the trail for Armagh, stopping at Ashbourne for a meal. There the cardinal was reminded of a hilarious episode in the life of one of our late parish priests who had been a professor in Maynooth. We spluttered and laughed over the story. When we arrived back at Ara Coeli, the cardinal and John checked the mileage in the car. From Ara Coeli to Ara Coeli we had travelled 1,200 mile in a few days, a little indication of the pressures the cardinal worked under and the stamina needed for his work. But he thought it was worth it, just as the compassionate Christ did not spare himself. When the cardinal died these same prisoners we had visited sent messages of grief. The cardinal had showed himself a true friend to them. 'I was in prison and you visited me.'

This articles was first published in Creggan, *No. 5, 1991.*

Requiem for Cardinal Tomás Ó Fiaich

One of the pleasant things I enjoyed in the cardinal's history class my first year in Maynooth was his occasional foray into literature and art. I can still see him holding up his Carlton Hayes *Political History of Modern Europe,* turning the art pictures towards us and commenting on them, from Giotto to Delacroix and Goya. Many a student I'm sure was inspired by those occasional lectures to pace later in life the corridors of the Louvre and the Prado. I wasn't surprised then when he commissioned the *Cross of Life* by Imogen Stuart, this beautiful crucifix which dominates Armagh cathedral. I would like to meditate on the Cross for a few minutes.

First of all the simple reality that we all must die. And Jesus joined us in solidarity. God did not spare his own son. A stark reality, literally. 'My God, my God, why have you deserted me?' Everybody is welcome to lie before this altar in death. It is a simple common denominator, for saint and sinner, the one who loved or hated, young and old, rich and poor, parishioner and cardinal. Our liturgy then, first and foremost, is a powerful plea for mercy before it is a ceremony in honour and thanksgiving for the life of the person who has died. So our prayer for the salvation of Tomás, for the forgiveness of his sins and failures.

This crucifix is a distortion. It casts a shadow. 'I thirst'. The daily cross of the follower of Christ. Sickness. Tragedy. Pain. Whatever the mystery of suffering, Christ has taught us that it is vicarious, redeeming, salvific and medicinal. By his wounds we are healed. And St Paul has taught us we fill up what is lacking in Christ's suffering and that is redeeming too. The arms of Christ embrace us all from the Cross and Jesus has gathered up Tomás into that loving embrace. The new Adam restores everything in love.

> As the first Adam's sweat surrounds my face
> May the last Adam's blood my soul embrace.

I am sure Tomás, as every man, suffered. Whatever the blows from the sticks and stones of life or the burden of office this suffering is mingled with the suffering and forgiveness of Christ from the Cross –

'Father, forgive them for they know not what they do'. And that was a great virtue of Tomás. He forgave everybody. He held malice against no person.

But Imogen Stuart's cross is more than a distortion of pain. It is the Tree of Life. It is the tree of Paradise flowering once again. The white flowers underneath emphasise the new garden of heaven. A new creation. A new Adam. A new Tomás. Christ on the Cross is like a great bird poised for the flight to heaven going home to his Father. The Flight of Victory. And I can imagine Tomás, An Fiach Dubh, the Black Raven as his name signifies, winging his way to Heaven, home to God the Father, home to his parents and his brother Patrick, home to Patrick, Brigid, Colm Cille, Malachy, Kilian, Fiachra, Rónán and Oliver Plunkett.

Tá Tomás Ó Fiaich molta agus mé i mo thost. On Saturday night the Dean, his friend, paid special tribute to his personality and virtues. But just to say that I came from the same parish of Lower Creggan, that he inspired me in the direction of local history and the Irish language. He pointed out to me once that the Cross on his motto shield rises from the stony ground of Creggan. Tomás Ó Fiaich loved the stony fields of Creggan first. The rich tradition of our native parish led to his love for his country, its history, its folklore, its music and sport, its literature and above all his love of the Irish language. He was as much at home with Art Mac Cumhaigh, Art Mac Bionaid, Séamus Dall Mac Cuarta and Pádraig Mac Gioll 'Fhionduin as Patrick's *Confession,* Scotus Eriugena or *The Book of Leinster.* The local view in his philosophy broadens to a vision of Ireland, broadens to a European proficient in languages. He delineated these areas for us in the example of his life. He helped us define our nationality and gave substance to it. He will continue to inspire us in the future. The people of Ireland have come to pay respect to him. His funeral cortège was like the journey of Brian Bóramha to Armagh, as the Dean remarked, and he was a saint by acclamation like Colm Cille.

I am finished now except to say that he was an arch-exponent of the Irish language both in writing and speaking. I will finish in Irish. *Bhí fíorghrá tíre aige. Bhí sé íbeartach trócaireach. Bhí sé fial mórchroíoch le daoine. Saorfaidh Tiarna na gréine é.*

A Thomáis,
Má rinne tú caraid ariamh de Mhuire
Tiocfaidh sí chugat ar uair do bháis
Agus gabhfaidh sí go cruaidh do leithscéal
Go bhfágha sí maithiúneas ó Rí na nGrást.

Homily delivered by V. Rev. Raymond Murray, Administrator Armagh Cathedral, at a Requiem Mass for Cardinal Tomás Ó Fiaich in St Patrick's Cathedral, Armagh 14 May 1990. Published in The Furrow, *July/August 1990.*

The Birmingham Six, 1989

I am sure the case of the Birmingham Six will in due course be brought before the Commission for Human Rights in Strasbourg. Strasbourg is the outpost for Irish cases of injustice vis-à-vis the United Kingdom government. But such a move takes three to four years. We are anxious that the Birmingham Six will be set free before that. The campaign for their release must necessarily go along diplomatic and political lines.

While accepting the merits of the Anglo-Irish Agreement, one is realistic enough to see that the failure to obtain judicial justice is a factor in the erosion of 'nationalist' confidence in the agreement. All this injustice has been gathered together symbolically into two main cases, as if to say 'if we don't get justice here we will never get justice'. Firstly, the 1982 County Armagh killings of unarmed civilians by British forces – justice has been refused in the interest of what has been called 'national security'. It is not merely that the Irish government, as the weaker partner in the agreement, lost out to the power of the British government. Both governments represent people and the confidence of people in state justice has been badly damaged.

Secondly, the case of the Birmingham men symbolises not only the plight of people jailed for something they did not do but their long imprisonment symbolises also the suffering of prisoners and their families caught up in a cruel war. There is a moral burden on governments not to regard prisoners as 'hostages' to peace. It is clear that such a policy exists north and south and in Great Britain but it is not working. Thankfully in the north there are the first stirrings of consideration for prisoners of the 'Troubles' jailed for life; there have been some releases and dates given; hopefully more will follow. The Irish government, however, remains intransigent towards its long-term prisoners and has adopted a 'never, never' policy of release. The prisoners and their families are doomed. The Irish government should begin releases of some of its long-term prisoners in Portlaoise. Following that it can preach to the British government to release the Birmingham Six and other Irish prisoners who are far too long in British jails.

The Catholic Church has a vast diplomatic network throughout the world. One had hoped in the 1971–72 period of torture of detainees in Northern Ireland that it would have been used to a greater extent to bring pressure from abroad on the British government to stop the use of torture in interrogation methods. Amends can be made by our bishops adopting the case of the Birmingham Six and bringing it before the episcopal conferences of various countries in the world. Is not this also a real concrete case for various commissions for justice and peace? Practice of justice is more important than theory.

I would like to see the greater Irish family outside the island of Ireland taking up the case of the Birmingham Six. American-Irish should make their release a pre-condition for any kind of aid, grant or industrial venture. Such a policy is common in anti-apartheid and anti-colonial movements. The Irish in Britain should drag the Birmingham Six case into the political field and should inform all Conservative and Labour MPs that the favour of the political support of the Irish in Britain begins with the release of the Birmingham Six.

I gave the above talk at a meeting in the Mansion House, Dublin, organised by the Dublin Birmingham Six Committee, Friday evening, 17 February 1989. In 1975 Mgr Denis Faul and I we were alerted to their case by the late Fr Brian Brady and in 1976 visited their relatives in England with him to collect data. In 1976 we published a booklet, The Birmingham Framework, *proclaiming their innocence. This was followed by a pamphlet* The Birmingham Pub Bombing Case: Synopsis of the Forensic Evidence *written with the help of a solicitor, Mr Kieran Morgan.*

The Birmingham Six: The Truth Will Set You Free

Jesus was rejected at Nazareth when he proclaimed that he was the fulfilment of the prophecy – 'The Spirit of the Lord is upon me, because he has chosen me to bring the good news to the poor'. They dragged him out of his home town and took him to the top of the hill on which it was built to throw him over the cliff (cf. Luke 4:16–30). On another occasion people who had professed belief in him took up stones to throw at him when he described those who did not obey truth as slaves of sin – 'If you obey my teaching, you are really my disciples; you will know the truth and the truth will set you free' (cf. John: 8:31–59). These words of Jesus were unacceptable to many. He was sold for thirty pieces of silver, arrested, tortured and sentenced to death on false evidence by a fearful judge who was worried about his position. He was crucified and enclosed in a cell of stone. After three days he was raised by the Spirit of Truth to be the living witness of his own words – 'The truth will set you free'.

In our own time the Birmingham Six, the Guildford Four, and the Maguire Seven were delivered up by police in Judas fashion, condemned unjustly and locked away in tombs. For years only a few small voices cried out in the great wasteland of modern 'civilisation'. One half of the media was intimidated and the other half bought. Was it Pádraic Pearse used that phrase? The rich and powerful in Church and State were silenced by fear.

But truth is never killed. It walks through the middle of the crowd and escapes. It hides itself and leaves the Temple. It springs up and flowers like a seed in a tiny crack of concrete. It shines through a chink in the wall of the cell tomb. Man is a spirit. His word passes from spirit to spirit until it shatters the tombs of stone. The spirit of the Father passed to his dead son Jesus and set him free. Jesus had seen his own life ruined. He began with ideas of hope but on the cross his human heart sensed failure – 'My God, my God why have you forsaken me?' The Father did not forsake him, did not ignore his witness, his love and forgiveness. Truth dislodged the great stone rolled against the door of his sepulchre. The shining living Jesus emerged triumphant from the darkness.

The Jesus case was closed, or so the Romans and the Sanhedrin thought. But they had not effectively dealt with the witness of Jesus, with his love and forgiveness. That ensured his liberation and victory. Hugh, John, Richard, Billy, Paddy and Gerry, you and your families are disciples of Jesus. The rich and the powerful thought your case was closed and turned away from you and despised you. For a time truth was effectively muzzled and chained. You were abandoned in the interest of the politics of the powerful. But truth in the end set you free. The chink of light shone from under your cell doors. You emerged from your tombs resplendent, the truth shining in your faces.

In times of conflict the weak and the innocent are abused and imprisoned. In the clash of arms justice is denied. In the fever of anger and antagonism judges can become blinded to the truth and do injustice to the innocent. Do oppressed prisoners in their closed world then hear the voice of the universities or the arguments of distinguished lawyers and professors of law pleading for them? They have been blinded too. The leaders of government and commerce fall silent; the well-paid writers supply their wealthy bosses with the stories they want; high-ranking churchmen do not court risk. Still the truth emerges. Jesus said, 'Whatever is hidden away will be brought out into the open, and whatever is covered up will be found and brought to light' (cf. Luke 8:17). Don't say it can not happen in the Republic of Ireland. Is the Sallins Robbery case not relevant here? Why was the Barra Ó Briain Report ignored?

These six men have courage. There is no virtue the Irish admire more than courage, physical and moral. I thank God for the courage of the Birmingham men, their wives and children. I admire their statements and the statements of the Guildford Four supporting the liberation of other innocent victims. What a spirit of courage to see men and their families weakened but not broken by years of imprisonment! While these crucified men bend to the task with only the spirit of truth to support them, can the wise of this world be won over to the same task? Can the rich and the powerful be converted, like Simon of Cyrene, to take on the burden of the cross of the poor?

No one is perfect and no legal system is perfect; when people make mistakes they should be prepared to admit their mistakes and apologise to those affected. This is no less so when these people are trial judges, appeal court judges or even the Lord Chief Justice. The *raison d'être* of the legal system is to provide a service to the community, the service of curtailing certain specified activities which are seen as being harmful. At its basic its purpose is to convict the guilty and to acquit the innocent. If the legal system fails to acquit the innocent, then it fails to provide a service, which is a principal justification for its existence.

In the Birmingham Six case, six innocent men were abused in a police station, were wrongly accused of mass murder, were abused in prison, were wrongly convicted, were vilified by the courts and by the media and had to serve sixteen years of imprisonment before their innocence was accepted and they were released after a long campaign on their behalf.

At the trial, the trial judge, Mr Justice Bridge as he was then, now Lord Justice Bridge, told the six innocent men that they had been convicted on the clearest and most overwhelming evidence he had ever heard.

Later Lord Denning, then Master of the Rolls, refused an appeal by the six men to pursue a claim for damages and told them that if they were successful in their claim it would open an appalling vista of police conspiracy and perjury.

At one of their appeals the Lord Chief Justice Lord Lane told the six innocent men that the longer the appeal went on, the more convinced he became of the correctness of the original verdict.

At the third appeal the six innocent men were finally vindicated and the appeal court judge simply told them they could go.

No apology then from the three court judges; no apology since from Lord Lane, the Lord Chief Justice or from Lord Justice Bridge.

In the Birmingham case when the legal system failed and failed for so long in its most basic function of acquitting the innocent, an apology by Lord Lane, by the appeal court judges and by Lord Justice Bridge to the six innocent men, to their families and to the community which the legal system serves would seem to be appropriate and overdue.

The most severe suffering, as it always is with the innocent, was the organised and deliberate attempt by leading practitioners of the law to wound and smear them by lies and innuendo and by the tremendous energy exerted on damage limitation. The priority was preserving the reputation of the legal system. The image, the false image as it has been shown, was that it could not commit and perpetuate an injustice on the scale of the wrongful conviction in the Birmingham case. It reminds me of similar damage limitation related in St Matthew's Gospel (*cf.* 28:12–14) – 'The chief priests met with the elders and made their plan; they gave a large sum of money to the soldiers and said, "You are to say that his disciples came during the night and stole his body while you were asleep. And if the Governor should hear of this, we will convince him that you are innocent, and that you will have nothing to worry about."' The bright shining lie did not outshine the Light of the World. It did not outshine the innocence of the Birmingham Six.

The truth will set us free. But can justice prevail in this life? Love and justice are the foundations of peace, in social life, in community life, in national life. They should be our greatest desire because they are what God requires. We fall short. Jesus realised the difficulty. The real compensation will be paid in heaven – 'Happy are you when people insult you and persecute you and tell all kinds of evil against you because you are my followers. Be happy and glad, for a great reward is kept for you in heaven'(*cf.* Matthew 5:11–12).

Let us in this Mass express our belief in Jesus. If we follow him, we will have the light of life and will never walk in darkness. Jesus says to those who believe in him, 'If you obey my teaching, you are really my disciples; you will know the truth, and the truth will set you free' (*cf.* John 8:31).

I preached this homily at the Mass of Thanksgiving for the Birmingham Six in the Pro-Cathedral, Dublin, Friday 17 May 1991, 8pm. It appeared in The Furrow, *July 1991.*

Release of Prisoners, 1995

I ministered in the City of Armagh from 1967 to 1993 and from 1967 to 1986 was chaplain to Armagh Prison until it was shut down in 1986 when the prisoners were transferred to Magaberry Prison. My work by its very nature brought me into contact with prisoners and their families. It broadened to include problems of human rights and indeed meant involvement in the consequences of the web of violence – violence of republicans, loyalists, and the state. Truth, justice and charity are still important in the present transition period of the peace process.

During the twenty-five years of virtual war there were many times when people in Ireland must have asked would the 'Troubles' ever come to an end. There was a mountain of suffering and a mountain of prayers for peace. And now peace has come to the north and for that matter to the south and to Britain following the inspirational peace settlements in South Africa and the accords in Palestine and Bosnia. So peace is possible. The joy of the crowds who greeted President Clinton in Derry, Belfast and Dublin was a tribute to his concern, help and the charisma of his personality. But I think it was also a celebration of the people's own inner happiness, pent up in the past 16 months of peace since the ceasefires and spilling out at President Clinton's visit, a first great public opportunity.

At a distance it may be difficult for people in Britain to assess the depth and permanence of peace in Ireland, especially as they try to judge it from the public positions taken by governments, political parties and factions. Particular questions such as decommissioning of arms, radical reform of the RUC, release of prisoners, and possible ways of sharing power in government are much in the news. Let me give the sincere and strong opinion of a person who is not only on the ground in the north of Ireland but is in touch with the 'jungle' behind the public scene. I believe that peace will be solid, permanent and indeed buoyant. I can say that honestly from my personal contacts with leading republicans in Derry, Belfast, East Tyrone and South Armagh. Beyond the political bickering, marching seasons, and punishment beatings that sometimes characterise Northern Ireland there is a commitment to peace. Do not be deceived by occasional signs of despondency and apparent set-backs. What is a year, what is two years for people to dialogue? The Irish government and the British government will continue to give the peace process appropriate nudges – they have gained a lot of discernment over the years and they will move things prudently. The only criticism voiced is that they should speed up the momentum. The general populace will sustain the peace – after all it is our small communities who have suffered most – over 150 for instance killed in my own little community. Many of the grievances, social and political, that led to the civil rights movement have been solved – the discrimination in housing ended in the 1970s, there are constant efforts to off-set the deprivation of dignity suffered by generations of unemployed, and there is legislation which hopefully will whittle away discrimination in job opportunities and promotion. The general oppression of the culture of Catholics, be they nationalists or republicans, is ending. Furthermore, both Britain and Ireland have been overtaken by the external influences of the new Europe and the end of the Cold War – the single common market is bearing fruit in Ireland as border towns return to natural hinterlands and economic unity is fast becoming a reality – hundreds of thousands of people from the south of Ireland, as far away as Galway and Dublin, are crowding the Belfast shops daily for their Christmas shopping. Armagh is only seven miles from the border and is linked socially, economically and culturally with neighbouring County Monaghan in the Irish Republic. Clones is the central mecca for the big Gaelic football matches of the nine-county Ulster. Local government in Northern Ireland, apart from Belfast which drags behind the rest, has seen a miracle of co-operation of all parties with a conscientious sharing of traditions. You can hear programmes in Gaelic from Radio Ulster; historical societies embracing people of every background have mushroomed – a sign that people have been asking 'who are we?' 'what are we?' – 'are our traditions necessarily opposed?' A lot of soul searching has led to a change of heart and attitudes of many people, and new beautiful friendships have blossomed. Ecumenism too is improving in this general quiet revolution. The physical aspects of the war are disappearing – military vehicles and foot patrols, security barriers, closed border roads, observation posts; the reduction of expenditure on security, just announced, means transference of resources to more fruitful causes.

In this context let me say that the release of prisoners has an amazing effect on the good will of relatives and friends. That has always been the case but is even truer today. My colleague Fr Denis Faul and I, even at the worst of times, have often called the release of prisoners the key to peace. A softer compassionate line towards prisoners is a healing remedy to both sides of the community in Northern Ireland. Out of the thousands of ex-prisoners very few have reverted to paramilitary activity in the past twenty-five years. In fact I have been amazed to see over the years how ex-prisoners in the border counties of Armagh and Monaghan have slipped quietly back into the community. They have a lot of life to catch up on and many have little time for politics again; they are little seen or heard. At the present time there is absolutely no question of ex-prisoners resuming a paramilitary rôle. The Irish government has recognised the good effect of the release of prisoners. They have steadily released them over the past year. The Northern Ireland Office has by act of parliament enabled the restoration of 50% remission so that almost a hundred prisoners will be released at Christmas. We hope for a similar softening attitude from British prisons – better conditions for Irish prisoners and releases to their homes in Ireland. That to us is the best rehabilitation. The harsh treatment of a prisoner like Paddy Kelly shocked the Irish members of parliament of all parties from Dublin when they visited here and they expressed their resentment in the media when they returned home. A rigid attitude in Britain jars with the situation at present in Ireland. A quiet even happy atmosphere pervades the prisons north and south – there are now excellent relations between officers and prisoners.

People got involved in the IRA for various reasons at various times. Because of the complication of various contexts and the varied temperaments of persons involved in the IRA one should be careful not to impose a general stock condemnatory judgement on individual republican prisoners. There has always been room for change in the inner attitudes of people. I would have to say also that republican prisoners have been noted for honouring their word – they have always obeyed parole conditions to the letter. Prison officers in Ireland know that if they say they are not going to be involved again in a military way that they mean it. Certainly now the context is one of a revolutionary peace process. Republicans have been building up political power since the hunger strikes of the early 1980s. This political movement of republicans has now definitely taken the upper hand; the energy of militants is being educated and moulded into democratic politics. Witness the acceptance of Irish republicans by Dublin, Washington, the democratic nationalists of the north of Ireland and the cautious Northern Ireland Office. It has gone beyond the formal handshakes. The competence of political leaders like Gerry Adams, Martin Magennis and Mitchel McLaughlin is recognised. Everyone in the United States is familiar with the charismatic figure of Gerry Adams whereas the Secretary of State Sir Patrick Mayhew is hardly known. Such a wry remark was made to me by a smiling high-ranking official in the Northern Ireland Office. It would be impossible now for republicans to forfeit their political progress and lose a figure like Adams. A number of happy circumstances have brought about the peace process. Republicans are realistic to know that these will never occur again. I can not imagine that the governments in Dublin and London will allow Irish republicans to be humiliated or isolated. It seems counterproductive to Irish people at home that republicans continue to be held for long long years in prisons in England. Deterrence is not now as important as formerly. In the new peace process context Irish republicans are respected. There will be a place for them in society, in government and even in security as compromises are worked out. It is logical that it should no longer be a black mark in peace time for a prisoner in Britain to hold Irish republican democratic principles. To record a prisoner's adherence to such principles as an obstacle to release seems outdated. Happy to say that a tolerant official attitude now exists in the prisons in Northern Ireland and in the Republic of Ireland.

Personally speaking as a former prison chaplain and priest active during the conflict, I believe that long term prisoners are entitled to a new beginning in their lives. Republicans and loyalist leaders have expressed public regret for their atrocities and crimes. I can say that some prisoners will express privately to ministers of religion their sadness that people have suffered at their hands while they are often reluctant to say the same things to prison officials. On the other hand government bodies have lacked the humility to express regret for state crimes. Moderate Catholic opinion in Ireland was appalled at the injustice done to the Birmingham Six, the Guildford Four, the Maguire Seven, the torture and ill-treatment in interrogation centres, atrocities like Bloody Sunday and the 150 unjust killings and murders of innocent and unarmed people by security forces. There has not been fair play and justice for the relatives of victims, some of them children, who have been killed by the lead and plastic bullets of security forces. A few soldiers only, and no RUC men, have been sentenced for these crimes. The few soldiers who have were released after a few paltry years. In contrast, Irish prisoners have been held in harsh conditions in English prisons for extremely long periods; moderate opinion in Ireland regards that unequal treatment as contrary to fair play and justice and harmful to the name of police and judiciary and some people even view it as revenge.

An abbreviated version of this statement in favour of an Irish prisoner was submitted to the Parole Board of Full Sutton Prison, England, in 1995. I appeared before the board on his behalf.

V

RUBBER AND PLASTIC BULLETS

The Death of Stephen McConomy, 16 April 1982

Seventeen people have been killed by rubber and plastic bullets in Northern Ireland. Eight of them were children and one was a woman. Hundreds of people have been seriously injured. There has been widespread indiscriminate use of them and they have been used in non-riot situations. Despite two international tribunals of enquiry into the deaths and injuries caused by them, 3–4 August 1981 and 16 October 1982, organised by the Association for Legal Justice, they are still in use in Northern Ireland. All the fatal casualties except one have been Catholics. Their deadly misuse has been chronicled in *British Army Terror: Brian Stewart* (by Brian Brady, Denis Faul, Raymond Murray, 1976), *Rubber & Plastic Bullets Kill & Maim* (Denis Faul, Raymond Murray, 1981), *Plastic Bullets – Plastic Government* (Denis Faul, Raymond Murray, 1982), *They Shoot Children* (Liz Curtis, Information on Ireland, 1982), and *A Report on the Misuse of the Baton Round in the North of Ireland* (Submission by the United Campaign against Plastic Bullets to the Mitchell Commission, 1996).

STEPHEN MCCONOMY

On 16 April 1982, the sun was shining in Derry. Mrs Maria Mc-Conomy, mother of three little boys, was up early and got all her housework done. On account of the good day she thought she would make an early dinner. She went down to the Market Flats to collect her eldest son Stephen. Stephen, somewhat of a loner, was standing at the wall. He was eleven years old but perhaps made a little older by life itself, almost acting as a tiny father figure in the family, since his father and mother were separated for the past four years. All came in and had their dinner.

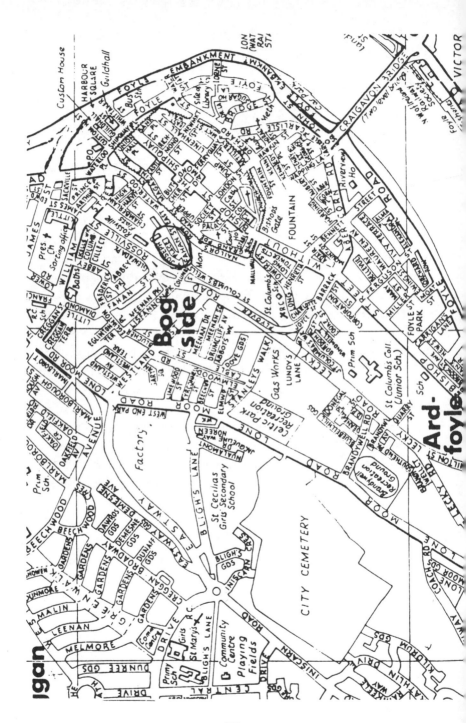

After dinner Stephen lay around the sofa waiting for his mother's permission to go out again. The mother, who was very close to him and often shared her secrets with him read his mind. 'Son,' she said, 'you want to go out again?' 'Aye, Ma', he said. Outside the house he turned back and opened the wee window of the kitchen to say a few words to his mother. 'Ma,' he said, 'I'll be in at half-eight'. Her little boy, or her 'Wee Un', as Derry folk are wont to say, had a lovely face. People always remarked how his whole face lit up with a smile. She never saw him alive again.

That evening between eight and half-past eight, just the time when Stephen would have turned from his play to head home, he was at Fahan Street which lies under the shadow of Derry Walls and runs down from Butcher's Gate. The Rossville Flats tower over the area. There is a lower group of dwellings called Joseph's Place at an elevation and there a balcony and ramp run to connect up with the roadway.

Around eight o'clock, Martin Moore went to Donagh Flats in the Rossville Flats to visit his girlfriend, Elaine McGrory. On his way he saw a saracen parked on the slip roadway running down from Butcher's Gate. There was a bomb scare up at Butcher's Gate. Things were quiet as is usual when there is a bomb scare. RUC men were stationed on the wall above Fahan Street. He saw five or six children playing around the saracen. The remarkable thing was that they had a tri-colour and they were placing it over the front of the jeep. A 'game' was going on between the soldiers and the little boys. He remarked on this when he went in to the McGrory flat. Elaine, Rosemary, Mrs McGrory and Martin went to the window to look out. The windows are very big and there is a fantastic bird's eye view from the big windows. The flat is on the eighth storey.

On the same evening, James Meenan of Lisfanan Park was coming from his home to the Rossville Flats. He saw the saracen parked halfway down Fahan Street. He saw the children throwing a few stones at the saracen, four or five children, he thought, about 10 to 12 years old. He walked up to Joseph's Place which meant he was standing above the saracen. He noticed Stephen at the front of the saracen. He was wearing a brown bomber jacket. A friend, John White, joined James at this time at Joseph's Place. Both of them were watching what was going on.

High up in the Donagh Flats, Mark O'Donnell was also watching the scene from his window. This was at 8.05pm. He noticed the saracen starting and revving as if to charge the youngsters. He noticed one boy with a stick hitting the saracen. James Meenan says he saw four or five boys at the back of the saracen and one was trying to pull the shields off the sides of it. All those who were watching saw the latch come down on the driver's side. They were frozen with apprehension when they saw the plastic bullet gun coming out. Four or five of the boys turned to run towards Rossville Street. Stephen was at the front. He had been watching them trying to tear the shields off the side of the saracen. Stephen turned as if to go away, his two hands in his pockets. He mounted the footpath. Then the bang. The force of the shot lifted him on to the grass. He lay lifeless.

James Meenan and John White ran down the ramp to where he was lying. James shouted at the driver of the saracen, 'Can we get the Wee Un?' He did not answer but kept the plastic bullet gun out. He shouted again, 'Can I get the child?' The driver said, 'Go near him and I'll shoot you'. People were shouting, 'Can we go up?' They still did not answer. The soldier who fired the plastic bullet had a grin on his face.

James describes how they got him to the hospital:

'Two or three minutes later, the passenger soldier in the "Pig" said, "You can go up and get him now". My friend and I ran up and we were crouched down with our hands over our faces because he

View of Donagh Flats. Figures from left to right mark where Stephen lay, where he was hit and the position of the saracan

still had the plastic bullet gun out of the hatch. I lifted Stephen and carried him towards Joseph's Place. We were in the car park and an RUC jeep came around. My friend John White banged on the side of the jeep and on the side door and they told us to put him in the back. Both of us placed him in and went with him. The RUC said the ambulance was meeting us halfway across the bridge. We went to Altnagelvin Hospital and there was no one to meet us. I carried Stephen into casualty and I laid him on the bed in the casualty. The nurse told me to take him into the next room and lay him on the bed. We walked out then and waited. CID men came up about twenty minutes later and asked me and John White to go to the barracks. I said I wanted to stay and see how Stephen was doing. They said they would bring me back but they did not. When I lifted the boy, I noticed he had been hit on the back of the head. In the jeep I held my arm under his neck and blood went through my jacket, jumper and shirt. At times he was not breathing; other times he was breathing in thick jerks; he was unconscious the whole time.'

Mrs McConomy heard the news at her sister's when a little boy came knocking to say the he had been 'hit with a plastic'. Then followed the traumatic visit to Altnagelvin and the watching by his bedside at the Royal Victoria Hospital, Belfast. There was no hope for Stephen. His head had been cracked and his brain damaged. He died on Monday afternoon.

There was strong reaction to the death of Stephen. There was some rioting in Derry. Angry mothers staged a protest march from the Bogside to the Guildhall. Bishop Daly said, 'There have been too many deaths and serious injuries in Derry and elsewhere in the north in recent years through the use of plastic bullets. The whole question of their use should be subjected to the most careful scrutiny. This supposedly non-lethal weapon has caused so many deaths and serious injuries that it should not be used again whatever the circumstances before a detailed inquiry takes place'. His words were voiced by many others.

More than a thousand people attended the Requiem Mass for Stephen at Saint Columba's Church. Among the congregation were children from Saint John's primary school where Stephen had been a pupil. During the Mass the school choir sang the hymns and members of Stephen's class read the lessons, the prayers of the faithful and presented the offertory gifts. Bishop Edward Daly presided at the Mass which was celebrated by Fr Michael Collins and Fr Séamus Kelly.

The RUC promised an urgent investigation. On 16 August 1982, the RUC confirmed that the DPP had decided against making charges against the soldiers who fired the plastic bullet which killed the boy. This brought an outcry from Churchmen and Catholic politicians. Bishop Daly said he was dismayed at the DPP's refusal to prosecute. He called for clear answers to the question why charges had not been brought in a case where there was an apparent lack of military regulations and death had resulted. So distraught was Mrs Maria McConomy and her sister Rhona that they threatened to go on hunger strike. On 4 July 1983 nine bishops of the northern province issued a statement calling for the withdrawal of plastic bullets as a riot control weapon:

'Many people have been killed by these weapons, some of them very young. Each of these deaths has caused deep grief in the family of the victim. The deaths have generated resentment throughout whole communities and have been the cause of growing alienation among wide sections of the population. The most recent inquest on such a victim, a boy of 11 years old, made the following findings:

1. It was found that there was insufficient evidence to suggest that Stephen McConomy was rioting when he was shot.

2. It was found that he was shot from a range of 17 feet when the minimum recommended range is 60 feet.

3. It was found that the riot gun from which the plastic bullet was fired was faulty.

Rioting is morally wrong but the methods used to control it must also be subject to the moral law. There cannot be one law for the security forces and another for the public. The use of plastic bullets is morally indefensible. The plastic bullet should be withdrawn as a riot control weapon.'

Blinded by Rubber Bullets

RICHARD MOORE

My parents are William and Florence Moore. I was born on 12 July – what a date! – 1961 and live at 42 Malin Gardens, Creggan Estate, Derry. There are twelve in our family – Lily, Margaret, Liam, Jim, Pearse, Bosco, Noel, Martin, Deirdre, Gregory, Richard and Kevin.

On Tuesday 4 May 1972, I was at St Eugene's Primary School. I was ten years old. We got out of school at 3.30pm. There are two schools parallel with one another facing up into Creggan, the primary school and St Joseph's Secondary School. A field, the football pitch of St Joseph's School, runs between both schools. There is a British army base, two army sangers, observation posts, facing up between the two schools at Creggan; they guard Rosemount RUC Barracks.

I got out of school at 3.30pm. Me and my mates began to run up the field. There are various levels in the field, slopes and that. We passed the first army post and I began to slow down and my mates began to run on, you know a matter of yards.

The next thing I remember is waking up in one of the canteens of the school, on the table. That's when I was shot – in that field. I was only four yards away from the sangar when it happened. My brothers and members of the *Derry Journal* later measured it. Mr John Hume was there too. He was a local community leader at that time.

On the table it was more or less pain I felt – so extensive that I did not feel it! – hard to describe it – a massive headache like an illness, and I wasn't fully conscious. I remember a man saying, 'What is your name?' He was Mr Doherty, my music teacher. That's how bad a shape I was in. He didn't recognise me. When I told him my name, I must have drifted off into unconsciousness.

I remember waking up in the ambulance – heard the sirens, that's how I know – and my father and sister were beside me. In the meantime, when I was lying in the canteen, and it was only a minute's walk from my home, they had got down in time to get on the ambulance. They more or less just asked how I was.

So then it was the hospital. I don't remember much about the hospital. I don't remember when I fully gained consciousness to know

135

where I was and what I was doing. In fact until recently I thought I was shot on 5 May, so my calculations must have been wrong at the time.

On the day it happened I saw no rioting at all. There were two ways home from school. There was no advantage in either of them and what way you took was a matter of chance. In fact I never saw rioting at that post any day. It was of no significance at all. I never went that way on a regular basis. It was just a way home from school. The army later claimed there was rioting. They spoke about twenty hooligans after the incident. I was one of the oldest in my group – ten years old – so they could hardly talk about the primary school children rioting. They tried to insinuate that older boys from the secondary school were already out. But I was already on the table shot at 3.40pm when the secondary school got out.

A point that I find amazing was that I was supposed to block the army's view into Creggan and the danger was, it was claimed, there could be shooting from there at the post. They cleared the view by shooting me with a rubber bullet.

I was two days in Altnagelvin Hospital and was then sent for convalescence to St Columba's Hospital, Derry. There is an eye department there. My right eye was removed. I got fifty-four stitches in the face. My face was badly swollen. My brother Martin described it as looking like a blown-up tube. He said he couldn't see my ears and my face was a mass of blood. The bandages were changed on the hour. At one time they spoke of removing the left eye. It had been closed over with four plastic stitches, the ones that dissolve. However, the sight did not return to my left eye. I also lost my sense of smell.

After two weeks, I was let out home. I travelled to specialists in Dublin, several times to Belfast, partly to do with my case. In January 1973, I went to Worcester, near Boston, with my mother and my brother Kevin. We were guests of Daniel Herlihy, chairman of the Worcester Area Committee for Justice in Northern Ireland. Mr Herlihy had been contacted by Dr Raymond McClean. Donations had been raised by them and people at home. Ulick O'Connor had written a story and there was a response to that. People in the south were very kind. They also ran a big do for me in Worcester. I was examined by Dr Charles D. J. Regan at the Massachusetts Eye and Ear Infirmary,

Boston. There was nothing he could do for me. He would not take any fee. He said I would not see again.

For a while I thought it was the pads on my eyes kept me from seeing. After I came out of hospital, my brother Noel took me out for a walk and told me I wouldn't be able to see. My father and mother were in despair. My brother knew the news had to be broken. Looking back, there were a number of things helped me to accept. Number one – my family. They took me out, runs and walks. My father and mother went to the chapel every morning. We went to a holy well in Dublin. My mother had my breast pinned over with holy medals. My father and mother had great faith. My father used to take an odd drink, but he even give that up to offer up for me. Number two – also the way I was treated in the area, neighbours coming to meet me and see me. A lot of mates. People were very kind to me. Even to this day, my mother still writes to people who helped me and wrote to her. An army captain in England, for example, is a person who was very kind to me.

So I got over the worst stage. Music then too gave me an outlet. At Martin's wedding, Lorny Deane, Marty's brother-in-law, was playing the guitar. This was in July after I was shot. I mind going up to Lorny and he sat the guitar on my knee. I wanted to learn to play. My family was afraid that, if I failed at the guitar, it would be a great disappointment to me. My mother was naturally protective. I remember waking up at night and hearing my mother crying aloud as she was praying. She used to pray long into the morning. She used to watch out the bay window and thought I was lonely. The real thing I missed was football! It seems strange to say that. I missed football!

I eventually learned the guitar and the mandolin and I now run the Chapel Folk Group in the Long Tower church along with my girl friend, Rita Page. That played a big part. I was able to make my own friends and so grow more independent of the family. Once I was Richard Moore blinded by a rubber bullet, then I was Richard Moore the musician.

One of my aims was to remain normal. I did my CSE, five subjects, and then my 'A' levels. I was under extreme pressure to go to a school for the blind. I just continued going to the same school. Mr Armstrong, head-teacher, and the teachers accepted me and made allowances for me. Sometimes I taped the class. Teachers recorded textbooks for me. Miss Maguire taught me Braille. Mrs Donnelly taught me typing. Kevin McCallion taught me general knowledge, more private tuition. All went out of their way.

Now I am at Coleraine University and studying social administration. Again I find the lecturers especially helpful. At the Galway Mass I met Pope John Paul II and took part in the Offertory Procession.

We took a civilian action case. It lasted five years, until 28 February 1977. It was settled out of court and I was awarded a substantial sum. Trouble is my father lost allowances and this was awkward because I wasn't to receive it until I was eighteen years. My father was on the 'bureau' at this time and was penalised. I too was penalised, only receiving a minimum grant at the university when we fought the case, and receiving no blind allowance during holidays.

My father died in 1978. My mother's brother, Gerald McKinney, a good family man and good to our family, was shot dead on Bloody Sunday in Derry with his hands up. That was very hard on my mother – two incidents in the one year. My parents were brilliant.

EMMA GROVES' STORY

It was on 4 November 1971 and the British army was in the district raiding houses. It was in the early hours of the morning, which was the normal time when they raided houses. All my children had to be taken from their beds. I am the mother of eleven children; the youngest at the time was five years of age. It was very annoying and upsetting for the children to sit and watch the British army ransack their home and pull everything apart. They had been arresting some men in the street and one of those arrested was a neighbour of mine. He was the father of four young children and his wife was in a very distressed state. I left my house and went to comfort her. I made some tea, got the children dressed and gave her a tablet to try and settle her down. I tried to assure her that her husband would only be held a few hours. As it turned out, he was held for several years. I heard someone shout that the paratroopers were coming into the district, so I returned to my home.

Everyone in the area was put under house arrest, which meant a soldier was put in every doorway and no one was allowed in or out. The paratroopers were in a very aggressive mood and were pulling young men and boys from their homes, some in just their bare feet, some with just their shirts and trousers on.

I had pulled up my venetian blind and was looking out the window. What I saw was very frustrating. I didn't know whether to scream or cry. The very last thing I ever saw was a young man having his head banged off a saracen. I told my teenage daughter, 'For God's sake, put on a record to boost our morale.' She put on 'Four Green Fields' and, it had only been playing a few minutes when a paratrooper stepped in front of my window and fired directly into my face. This happened in front of my children who were by this time in hysterics. I was told later my face was in a terrible state and the blood was everywhere. My husband threw a towel over my face and tried to get me out to the car to get me to hospital. One of my neighbours from across the street ran out to help and the soldiers threatened to shoot him. He told them to go ahead but he was going to help me no matter what. They at first refused to let us leave the district but my husband pulled the towel away to show the terrible injuries and they finally let us go.

At the hospital, my eyes were so badly damaged they had to be removed. I now wear artificial eyes and had to receive plastic surgery to build up the bridge of my nose. After my eyes were removed, my family couldn't bring themselves to tell me I would never see again. Mother Theresa of Calcutta was in Belfast at that time and it was she who came to my bedside and told me my eyes had been removed. I went into very deep depression and just wanted to die. When you are the mother of eleven children and a very active person, it was very hard to accept.

I was taken home and remained in my bedroom for a very long time. My eldest daughter was taken out of school and had to be mother and housekeeper to the rest of the family. Eventually, after a lot of help and prayers, I realised that I would have to come to terms with my blindness. It was very hard. I missed seeing the children's faces and the colour of the trees and flowers, and going out for walks, doing the shopping.

The rubber bullet that had shot me was then replaced with the plastic bullet. Many children were being killed and injured. I decided

I would have to get involved in trying to have these lethal weapons banned, so I joined The United Campaign against Plastic Bullets. With other members I have travelled the world to tell people my story and enlist their support in our campaign.

I received compensation for my injuries but to this day I couldn't tell you the name of the soldier who shot me. He was never prosecuted. I never received the justice I desperately wanted, for him to appear in court and tell me why he shattered my life that day.

To date seventeen people have been killed with rubber and plastic bullets, eight of them school-children, and hundreds more have been severely injured. Over a million pounds has been paid out in compensation, but only one member of the security forces has ever been charged in connection with the deaths and injuries, and he was acquitted.

Plastic bullets are still being used in Northern Ireland and have been fired on several occasions since the ceasefire.

Many people have been seriously injured by rubber and plastic bullets. Some of the early injuries were described in the British Journal of Surgeons, *Vol. 62 (480–486). The above are the personal recollections of two people blinded by rubber bullets.*

On 30 June 1981 Richard Moore of Derry and his brother Martin visited me in Armagh. The above story Richard told me. It was first published in Denis Faul & Raymond Murray, Rubber & Plastic Bullets Kill & Maim.

Mrs Emma Groves, Belfast, active in The United Campaign against Plastic Bullets, gave this account at the Forum for Peace and Justice, Dublin Castle, 11 April 1995.

Teachers and the Sacredness of Human Life

In 1982, the late Pat Canavan and Larry Burns founded the Organisation of Concerned Teachers after reading a letter I had written calling on all responsible adults to make public their opposition to the use of plastic bullets. On 13 May 1982 the European parliament voted for the banning of plastic bullets in all ten Common Market countries. Three hundred teachers signed a declaration against their use which was published in various languages in European countries, North and

South America, Japan and the Arab world. On 24 June 1982 I gave the following lecture to the Organisation of Concerned Teachers in Belfast. It was written with the assistance of Mgr Denis Faul.

INTRODUCTION
All human life is sacred. This statement must be analysed. Does it mean only that the processes of reproduction and birth must be sacred, or does it mean that the killing of a person draws attention to the fact that this life is sacred?

Must we not assert that every phase, indeed every moment, of a human life is sacred? The human person has the continual potential to love God. That is why human life is sacred. A person is holy to God. But a person can only exercise love of God from an environment where human rights are respected as absolute. If the human person is degraded by racism or religious bigotry or an unequal application of the law, or by being subjected to material wealth such as money, oil or gold, then the sacredness of human life is being destroyed.

TEACHERS AND THE GROWTH OF HUMAN LIFE
In the Republic of Ireland, when a child goes to school, he is registered in a new name. Patrick Sweeney, he learns, is also Pádraig Mac Suibhne. He gets a new identity symbolised by a change of name. It is as if the state took on a propriety right to provide for his education, introduce him to human rights and develop his potential.

Teachers have a particular important part to play, not only in fostering in the young mind the sense of the uniqueness and sacredness of his own life, and the respect and reverence due to the life of others, but also the teachers must defend the lives of the children entrusted to their care. Parents will feed and protect their children out of love in most cases, out of maternal instinct in the rest. I think, however, that the child's first contact with the outside world is with the 'state', the 'government', the 'civil power', the 'law', when he goes to school. In an ideal situation the child should see all these powers as benign and protective of his existence in human rights. What a tragedy if the schoolchild sees them as hostile, as murderers and deceivers who blow off the heads of his tiny companions with plastic bullets and cover up the crime? Surely the child, in his own way, perplexed by the hatred and hostility from public life and the authorised agents of the government, will turn to his teachers and say, 'Make it right! Make it right!' Most of the injuries from plastic bullets have been children. In the words of the International Tribunal in Belfast last year, 'Their injuries approach in severity those that would occur in war'. I will never forget the fourteen-year old boy who moved like a crab across the floor to testify at that tribunal. Surely the message of the deaths and injuries of these children by plastic bullets is, 'Destroy the iniquity and the evil. Restore publicly the love and protection of family life'.

The teachers of Belfast and Derry have seen ten of their children killed by the state in a hostile and brutal fashion. No explanation is forthcoming. In each case the crime has been covered up. Some people give the impression that a child is expendable – 'only a child' they say, as if the children of the city streets do not count, as if their lives were less valuable. To teachers this is doubly hurtful because they realise the potential that is there. This is the great fulfilment and satisfaction in the world of teachers – their nearness to potential and the springs of life in children. Despite last year's International Tribunal, despite the fact that the European parliament voted overwhelmingly to ban the use of plastic bullets in all ten European Common Market countries, the Secretary of State, Mr Prior, Lord Gowrie and Sir John Hermon insist on retaining them for use against Irish children. They will be brought out again. More children will die. People said the plastic bullet was used in vengeance in the hunger strike period and that it would not be used after that. People with power and influence in Church and State withdrew. Then Stephen McConomy, aged eleven years, was killed.

Teachers have to face a death culture which is the opposite of the living imaginative culture they are called to promote and enjoy in others. Teachers watch their children grow and express themselves in art forms, life, joy and liberty. That should be the way, but they face the death culture – like the Ballymurphy slogan, 'Is there a life before death?' It is the state, who should be the upholder of law, who is promoting the death culture as well as the 'outlaws'. Take a look at west Belfast. On one side of the M1 lies Boucher Road with its splendid factories and on the school side of the M1 is colossal unemployment. The Milltown and City cemeteries are more than symbolic.

Teachers of west Belfast are faced with a death society.

THE CHURCH

The pro-life constitutional amendment in the Republic of Ireland is current news. The Church supports it because the Church regards human life as sacred from the first moment of conception. The Church has also been very clear in its condemnation of murder, but the intensity and directness has sometimes appeared to vary with the social importance of the person murdered. Can it be said that the re-action to some murders, and I mention here the fourteen rubber and plastic bullet deaths, and the slaying of Danny Barrett, aged fifteen years, suggests that the Church is strong with the weak and weak with the strong? Carol Ann Kelly, Julie Livingstone and Danny Barrett have been largely forgotten by the people who took responsibility for them when they passed outside the family home, namely the schools and the Church. The ghosts of these children are knocking at the doors of the people who said, 'We will be responsible for moulding you and upholding your potential and your talents'. The ghosts of these children are asking, 'You people who took responsibility for our growth, why are you not speaking publicly and effectively about the way in which the growth of our young lives was cut off?' The motto of the Christian Church should be, 'Don't take me for granted'. The day that the state, the government, the army, the media can smugly predict that the Church will react within the ambit of their power will be a day of death for the Church. The Church must always be ready to do the unexpected, to take the path of greatest loss to defend the 'little ones'.

Jesus told a parable about children: 'See that you don't despise any of these little ones. Their angels in heaven, I tell you, are always in the presence of my Father in heaven. What do you think? What will a man do who has one hundred sheep and one of them gets lost? He will leave the ninety-nine on the hillside and go to look for the lost sheep. When he finds it, I tell you, he feels far happier over this than over the ninety-nine that did not get lost. In just the same way your Father in heaven does not want any of these little ones to be lost.'

Mr Kevin Boyle, Professor of Law, Galway University, will be bringing the cases of the deaths by plastic bullets here to the European

Commission of Human Rights in Strasbourg. The Association for Legal Justice, Fr Denis Faul and myself appreciate the support in this action from the Organisation of Concerned Teachers. Young people often say that they cannot see a way to justice except by violence, that the violent only yield to force and violence. The Church's call to a peaceful political way to justice is just hollow words unless it provides the practical alternative. It must be seen to identify and work with the unemployed, the poverty line, the plastic bullets' victims, to leave the ninety-nine grazing and go after the 'little one' that is lost.

VI

STATE KILLINGS AND MURDERS

Killings by British Security Forces, 1969–76

The second man to die in the Northern Ireland 'troubles' was John Gallagher, a young married man from my own parish of Armagh, the night of 14 August 1969. I live in rooms three storeys up and I had been watching a loyalist crowd massing in the street outside the City Hall where a civil rights' meeting was taking place. The leaders of the meeting, sensing the build-up outside and the heavy concentration of police, told the crowd to leave and disperse to their homes quietly. The crowd were directed to the left by the police when they went outside. A short distance away the street had a left turning. Some of the crowd who turned down this street, Cathedral Road, were met by a party of B Special police who fired killing John Gallagher and wounding some others. The Scarman Tribunal into Violence and Civil Disturbances in Northern Ireland in 1969 was satisfied that the police did fire and that one of them did kill Mr Gallagher while others wounded Mr McParland and Mr Moore. After making allowances for the strange, difficult and frightening situation in which the police found themselves, the report said that there was no justification for firing into the crowd. The tribunal placed a measure of responsibility on a police inspector who put an untrained party of police from a country area into an alarming town riot without briefing or leadership. No RUC man has yet been charged with the murder of John Gallagher. On 22 August 1974 I wrote to Mr Merlyn Rees, the Secretary of State, 'On 14 August, 1969, John Gallagher, one of our parishioners, was shot dead in Armagh. Are police investigations still continuing into this fatal shooting?' The reply was that investigations had closed but would be re-opened if fresh evidence was obtainable.

The Scarman Report also found unjustified the killing of Patrick Rooney, a boy of 9 years, by the police in Belfast. The report states, 'We are unable to justify the shooting from the Browning machine-gun which was responsible for the death of Patrick Rooney'. On 19 April 1969 police entered the home of Samuel Devenney on a day of rioting in Derry and beat him up in front of his children. He died in hospital in Belfast on 17 July 1969. He was 42 years old. Following an inquiry conducted by Scotland Yard detectives on the instigation of Sir Arthur Young, Chief Constable, Sir Arthur made a statement. He attributed lack of evidence to a 'conspiracy of silence'.

I mention these deaths at the beginning of the present crisis because it is there the rot set in. You could be shot dead on your own street by the British army or the police and nobody would be made amenable for the killing. Since that time some 60 innocent people have been killed in an unjustifiable manner by British government forces – 14 in Derry on 30 January 1972, 6 on the New Lodge Road, Belfast, 3 February 1973, and so on.

On Saturday 15 June 1974, a 22 year-old man, John Pat Cunningham from my parish, really a retarded boy who had the mentality of a 10 year-old child was shot dead by the British army. He was afraid of the soldiers, having been beaten up by them on a previous occasion. The army said they called on him to halt before they fired. There was no independent inquiry into his death. He was shot at 120 yards. The officer said he had his hand in his pocket. If he was a gunman, what use would a pistol be at that distance?

Fr Faul and I documented the cases of Leo Norney aged 17 years gunned down by the Black Watch Regiment 13 September 1975, Majella O'Hare aged 12 years gunned down by the Third Parachute Regiment 14 August 1976 on her way to church, Brian Stewart killed by a rubber bullet October 1976.

By their actions in killing 60 innocent civilians, the British army have violated human rights spelled out in *The Universal Declaration of Human Rights* and *The International Covenant of Civil and Political Rights*: 'Everyone has the right to life, liberty and the security of the person' (Article 3 of *The Universal Declaration*).

'Every human being has the inherent right to life. This right shall be protected by law. No one shall be arbitrarily deprived of his life'

(Article 6 (1) of the Covenant).

Not only were these innocents – people like Patrick McElhone, Pomeroy, County Tyrone, taken out and gunned down in the field in front of his aged parents' house and Brian Smith gunned down by the paratroopers while he stood chatting to friends in Ardoyne – deprived of their lives, but they were slandered by malicious lies promulgated by dishonourable officers that they were gunmen.

Why can agents of the British government kill people manifestly innocent in very suspicious circumstances and never pay any penalty? Are they really operating under the law if they are never effectively made amenable to law? Are they above the law? Is there a conspiracy to make them immune from effective prosecution?

On 7 January 1976, the British Prime Minister Harold Wilson announced the use of the SAS, the Special Air Service Regiment, in Northern Ireland plainclothes irregular units. What the real motive of the British authorities was can only be guessed at but the general idea seems to have been to terrorise the people by assassination, by highly unorthodox and criminal methods contrary to Hague Regulations and Geneva Conventions. Fr Faul and I chronicled the shooting of Peter Cleary taken out from the house of his girlfriend and her relatives and killed in a nearby field. So far in the past year the SAS have gunned down 8 people in cold blood – Colm McNutt and Denis Heaney in Derry, Paul Duffy in Cookstown, John Boyle in County Antrim, Jim Mulvenna, Dennis Brown, William John Mailey and a Protestant, William Hanna, in Belfast. This is known as the 'kill, don't question' security policy and is a massive breach of the rule of law.

This is part of a speech delivered by me to Congressmen in Washington DC, 3 October 1978, and to the Ad Hoc Committee for Human Rights in Northern Ireland, Philadelphia, 7 October 1978.

The Death of Patrick McElhone, 7 August 1974

On 7 August 1974 Patrick McElhone spent the whole day from early morning working with his tractor in a field of his farm at Limehill near Pomeroy, County Tyrone. He was disturbed at his work before five o' clock by a soldier with blackened face, armed with an SLR rifle and pistol, who asked him his name. There was some cross-difficulty due to the accents of the men. But Patrick gave his name and when asked about some man in the area he said he did not see him. Patrick McElhone himself aroused no suspicion. He was just an ordinary farm labourer going about his ordinary work, dressed in old farm clothes, a pair of wellington boots and old hat. The soldier who had left his section and come into the field was Lance Corporal Roy Alun Jones.

Roy Alun Jones had been ten years a soldier. He had been two and a half years at an infantry junior leaders' establishment, had gone to Hong Kong with the South Wales Borderers, then served in Kent and in Aden in 1967 where he carried out service in an urban guerrilla war situation. Lance Corporal Jones first came to the north of Ireland in 1969. He served on the Falls Road and about a year later served again there. His final tour in Ireland was a long one of more than eight months.

On 6 August, Major C. B. Jones of the Royal Regiment of Wales, stationed in the Pomeroy area, detailed operations to a platoon to operate there. He had in his possession the information folders from the previous regiment there, the Life Guards. He instructed Sergeant Harrye to search out-buildings and farms and to talk to local people regarding information they might have regarding 'terrorist' activity. As guide lines, they were given a briefing by Major Jones on previous 'terrorist' activity, a list of names provided by the Life Guards of 'terrorists' in the area and of those wanted for criminal charges by the RUC. There was no information at all on the McElhone family. Patrick McElhone was above suspicion. This was the first time the platoon operated in a country area.

At 3.40pm the day before the killing of Patrick McElhone, the operation in the countryside began. Sergeant William Harrye was in charge of the platoon. He briefed the platoon sections. He explained to them the area they were to cover. He told them that within this area they were to search cars and vehicles, do spot checks on people and on out-buildings but not to enter dwelling houses. He had a folder with a history of activities in the area.

On 7 August, Lance Corporal Jones was in a section under the command of Corporal Bridgeman. After he had questioned Patrick McElhone, his section moved to join the other section who had been at another farm. The two sections formed into one platoon and proceeded to the McElhone farm. That was in the late afternoon. Three people lived on the farm, the aged couple, Peter McElhone and his wife Margaret and their son Patrick. Corporal Wood and his section went to the road junction below the farm, while Jones' section remained in the vicinity of the farm. The NCOs deployed the private soldiers. They themselves, along with one or two of the members, continued to search the farmyard area and the out-buildings. Sergeant Harrye was in command. Corporal Bridgeman was second-in-command. Lance Corporal Jones acted as a senior soldier. Sergeant Harrye asked Mr Peter McElhone's permission to look around the out-buildings of the farm. He agreed to the request. There was no disagreement with the elderly McElhones.

Mrs Margaret McElhone, mother of Patrick, had lived on the farm since her marriage. She had two sons. Michael was in England. Patrick worked on the farm at home and looked after his old parents. It was a mountain farm. The family was not well off. Patrick's interest was playing Irish music.

Mrs McElhone remembers the soldiers arriving at the farm with blackened faces. She was in the house with her husband when they came to ask permission to search. At 6.10pm, Patrick came in. He was very hungry after working all day. He was anxious to get his tea and go out again to finish his work. His mother was in the kitchen, the middle room, when he came in. He sat down at the table in a gesture to hurry her up. She put on the kettle to boil while he was waiting. The kettle was just coming to the boil, the kitchen door lay wide open, she looked out. Two soldiers came to the door. A soldier waved his finger at Paddy. He got up at once and went out.

The soldiers closed the door when they got Patrick on the steps.

Father and mother were left in the house. Mrs McElhone went down to the lower room. The top part of the window was open. She looked out. She saw the soldiers with Paddy on the road at the gap of the house. Two took him out on the road and began to question him. Paddy was standing in the middle. The soldier on the right was shaking him. She never heard his voice. She thought Paddy must not have answered him. She heard a soldier say that he was not helping the British army very much. With that they ran up the road out of her sight.

Mrs McElhone then came down to the kitchen where her husband was sitting. After Paddy had gone out of her sight she heard very loud talk. She told her husband that he would have to go out and see what they were doing with Paddy. When he was out a few minutes, as she was crossing the kitchen floor, she heard one shot. She was ready to faint. She said, 'Surely they didn't shoot Paddy'. She went out on to the street. She could hear her husband coming screaming and crying down the road. 'Maggie,' he cried, 'poor Paddy is after being shot dead.'

Peter McElhone said that when he went out he saw two soldiers with Paddy. One of them had him by the collar of the coat. He could not understand the soldiers' accent but he noticed that Paddy didn't answer them. They made Paddy run and followed him up the road into the hay field. Peter McElhone was not expecting his son to be shot. He did not see the soldier raise his rifle and shoot him. The second soldier turned and ran up past him. The other soldier shoved Paddy into the field. Peter at this time was standing on the road looking down into the hay field. He heard the shot and saw his son falling. He said to the soldier on the road, 'What did you shoot my son for?' The soldiers told him they would shoot him too if he didn't go into the house. They wouldn't allow him into the field.

According to Lance Corporal Jones, he went to the door on his own initiative to ask McElhone to come out and talk to Sergeant Harrye. He brought him to the sergeant and went off about his business, taking no further notice. According to Harrye, McElhone gave his name as Michael. None of the soldiers heard raised voices. Harrye says he let him go. At that stage Jones came back and asked, 'Have you not run a "P" check on McElhone?' Harrye said he hadn't. He asked Jones to go and fetch McElhone again.

Jones said that McElhone walked up the road away from the house and went into the field. He shouted something like, 'Will you halt,' or 'Halt a minute'. He said that McElhone did not react; he may not have been able to hear him because of the wind. McElhone walked on and entered the field. Jones was catching up on him. When Jones got to the gate, he said he shouted 'Halt'. He said McElhone looked over his shoulder. He was six to seven yards away. He said McElhone made a break to run. Jones already had his rifle up. He said he fired from a distance of ten to twelve metres, a snap shot, and that it was the only way to stop him.

The weapon used in the shooting of Patrick McElhone was an SLR rifle. It has an effective range of 600 metres. One normally engages an enemy at 300 metres. To discharge at 25 yards would probably be fatal. Patrick McElhone was shot through the right scapula. There was a large exit wound over the heart. There was a very big pool of blood underneath the body. He lay face down on the field dead.

On 24 March 1975, Roy Alun Jones, on a Bill of Indictment 748/74 was charged with murder. It was alleged that on 7 August 1974 in the County of Tyrone that he murdered Patrick Anthony McElhone. He pleaded not-guilty to the charge. On 27 March 1977 he was found not guilty.

My account of Patrick McElhone's death first appeared in Malairt, *No. 1, Winter 1977, an Irish language magazine, Queen's University, Belfast. It also appeared in English in a pamphlet* The British Dimension *published by Fr Denis Faul and myself in 1980.*

A Paratrooper Shot Majella O'Hare, 14 August 1976

The 14 August 1976 was a day of special remembrance for Nurse Alice Campbell of Crossmaglen, for it was on that day she was to be married to Brian Reavey of Whitecross. Alas Brian Reavey and his two brothers John Martin and Anthony were assassinated in January 1976. On the fourteenth morning of August 1976 Séamus Reavey, Brian's brother, collected her from her work at Daisy Hill Hospital, Newry, at

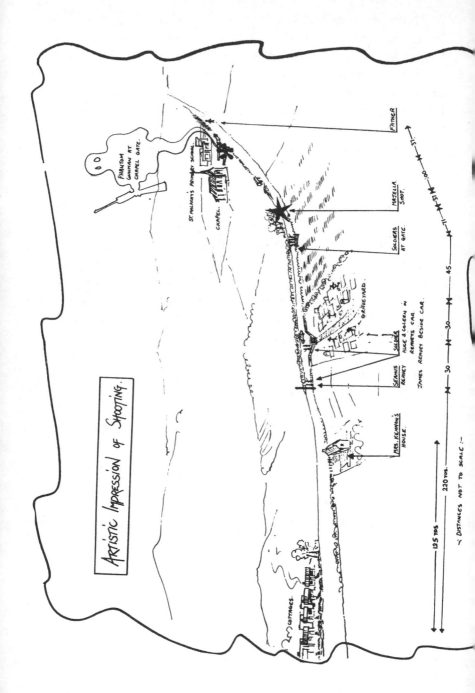

ARTISTIC IMPRESSION OF SHOOTING.

PHANTOM GUNMAN AT CHAPEL GATE.

ST MALACHY'S PRIMARY SCHOOL.

CHAPEL.

MRS. KENTON'S HOUSE.

COTTAGES.

GRAVEYARD

FATHER

MATELLA SHOT.

SOLDIERS AT GATE.

SOLDIER

ALICE & COLEEN IN KENNY'S CAR.

JAMES KENNY BESIDE CAR.

SEAMUS KENNY

125 YDS.

220 YDS.

- DISTANCES NOT TO SCALE :-

9am. They bought a wreath and went to pick up the father, James Reavey, and little Colleen his eight-year old daughter. They cut roses from the garden at the old Reavey home at Greyhilla, Whitecross, where Brian was assassinated. They arrived at Ballymoyer graveyard about 11am. Séamus noticed a group of soldiers in the hay-cut field beside the graveyard. By the time they were half-way down the path of the cemetery, the same soldiers had entered at the bottom left of the cemetery and met them on the path. The paratrooper in charge told Séamus Reavey that he wanted to see him when he was finished.

They delayed in the graveyard some twenty minutes, thinking the soldiers might move off and leave them alone. But when they came out and Séamus unlocked the car door for the others, the paratrooper called Séamus in the foulest of language. This was witnessed by Hugh Kennon who had been stopped on the road by the British army. He remarked on it. The paratrooper kept Séamus about half-an-hour at a telegraph pole some thirty yards above the graveyard. There he put Séamus through deep agony, insulting the memory of his dead brothers. To the stranger this inhumanity is incredible but it is a common attitude of the British army to the oppressed Catholic community.

While they were talking, a group of children went by. Séamus Reavey says they looked happy. They were a group of ten children who were heading for their sodality Confessions at Ballymoyer chapel, some five hundred yards down the road. Mrs Murphy of the Orlitt Cottages, from where most of the children had come, had warned the bigger ones before they left not to pass any remarks to the British army. The four soldiers at the gate of the cut hay field, about forty-five yards below the graveyard gate, shouted some taunts, to which the children hardly replied. One of these soldiers lay on his stomach manning a machine-gun. This was the gun that killed Majella O'Hare.

At this stage two little girls aged eight and seven were some distance in front. They were followed by a boy of thirteen and the girl of sixteen. The rest of the eight children were stretched across the road, two of these lagging a little behind. Majella was second from the left-hand side of the road. She had the youngest child (three and a half) by the hand. There was a loud bang and Majella fell.

All the civilian witnesses are agreed that there was one single bang. They describe it as 'loud', like an 'explosion'. Mrs Teresa Murphy says, 'I heard the shot, a bang with a tail on it, not a sharp clear sound, but very loud.' This is an accurate description of a firing from a machine-gun which can fire 800 rounds a minute. The lightest touch will discharge 3 shots. And this is what happened. The paratrooper discharged 3 shots. Two of the bullets penetrated Majella's back and came out through her stomach. The bullets ploughed up the heap of gravel in front of the trailer which was parked on the road verge.

On the day before, Friday, Majella and some friends had spent the day at Gyles Quay, a favourite seaside spot near Dundalk. She intended going back to spend the weekend there with neighbours. So she refused the offer of a day's shopping with her mother and her brother Michael in Newry. She had waved goodbye to them at 10.30 that morning. Before she set out for Confessions, she left a note for her mother saying that she would be back from Gyles Quay on Sunday night.

James O'Hare, Majella's father, had gone to do some work at St Malachy's school which is beside the chapel at 10.00am. There were no soldiers then. But some time later six soldiers came out of the Rectory Lane opposite the chapel gate. They went up the road towards the graveyard. He had seen the Reaveys up the road and was worried for them when they were stopped by the soldiers coming out of the graveyard. He was keeping an eye out as he worked on the grass verge in front of St Malachy's school. He saw the children coming down the road to Confessions. Below the height he was able to make them out and he recognised Majella among them.

Then he heard a bang and saw a child fall. He ran towards them and found the little girl dying. Majella was the darling of her parents' heart. She had been born some years after the other members of the family, Michael, Marie and Margarita. She was the love of their home. While comforting the child he was badly abused by some of the paratroopers.

When the gun was fired there was a lot of confusion on the road. The children were screaming. The soldiers were shouting. One of the paratroopers ran down the road. Another soldier, a marine, came out of the bushes near where the child lay. The Reaveys and Alice Campbell took cover with the rest. Una Murphy, the sixteen-year old girl who was the eldest in the party of girls described the incident, 'When we crossed the brow of the hill, the soldiers were lying at the gate of Hugh Kennon's field on our right, three maybe four, two on their stomachs, two sitting back. They had guns – one was black with a thick barrel, then thin. We did not speak but they spoke to us. One asked were we going for Communion – to visit our God. This man had very brown eyes and black hair. He was sweating a lot. We ignored them and then they said, "You don't speak to the likes of us". We pretended to be speaking among ourselves.

'We walked down the road. Then there was this big bang. Stones started to fly up from up in front of us. The young ones started to scream and Majella gave a scream and fell. She fell on her stomach. She was wearing a nylon blouse and skirt. A hole appeared in the blouse on the right hand side of her back. We all stood there looking at her. We did not know what to do. A paratrooper came running down the hill and Jim O'Hare came running up the road from the Chapel. He knelt on the road and put his arms around her. The soldiers told Jim to take his fucking hands off her. Jim said, "This is the only wee girl I have left". The soldier said, "I don't give a fuck" and he told us to get up the road.'

When there was no more firing, the Reaveys finally persuaded the soldiers to let Alice Campbell, a nurse, attend Majella. She did all she could for her. Fr Peter Hughes had arrived just before twelve for Confessions. When he heard from a soldier that a little girl was shot, he rushed to spiritually attend her.

Alice Campbell describes the rough treatment towards Majella in throwing her into the helicopter with her legs dangling out, and indeed she was almost falling out when the helicopter lifted. Here is part of Alice Cambell's statement:

'As Séamus was putting his keys into the door of the car, a paratrooper roared at him, "Come up here Séamus Reavey or I'll knock the fucking head off you." Séamus said, "No need to shout, I'm not going away." I put Colleen into the back and I got into the passenger seat. Séamus went over to the paratrooper who was standing at the pole at the right hand side of the road in the direction of the chapel. I was crying in the front of the car after coming up from the grave. The car was pointing away from the chapel. Mr Reavey was standing at the passenger door.

'I heard a loud bang from behind me. I thought it was an explosion. Then I thought they had shot Séamus. I heard Séamus roar, "Duck!" I pushed Colleen down in the back and I lay down in the front. Séamus then crawled down and opened the door of the car and told me to crawl out and lie alongside the wall beside Mr Reavey and the soldier. This soldier shouted, "That's an Armalite". Jimmy Reavey said, "But there's children away down that road. Let me go down." The soldier roared, "No! lie where you are." He pleaded with him once more but he still insisted on him lying where he was.

'One of the soldiers from the lower part of the road came up and said, "There's a child been hurt". I then said to Mr Reavey, "Perhaps I could do something for her". Mr Reavey asked the soldier to let me go down but he would not. Mr Reavey said I was a nurse. After five minutes the soldier took me down by the hand to where the child was lying on the road. Someone had taken the father to the side. The child was lying on her back. A wound was visible on her abdomen (exit wound). I tried to deal with this. She was semi-conscious and groaning. I was tilting her chin with my hand to give her more air and she pushed my hand aside and muttered, "Don't do that". The soldier who was assisting me kept saying. "That is your fucking Provos for you".

'Fr Hughes arrived and came out of his car. The soldier that was assisting me said, "There he is again. He is always stuck in it." Fr Hughes said prayers over her. A local man, Barry Malone, was driving past. The same soldier, who was hysterical, gave an unmerciful yell and said, "There's what your fucking Provos do, there it is for you – look". Then he thumped the top of the car and said, "Drive on to fucking hell".

'About ten minutes later the helicopter arrived. The father was put in first. The girl was put in head first with her legs dangling out. I was kneeling with my red trousered legs out of the helicopter, holding on to a strap. With the help of the father I tried to get her head up. I thumped the soldier on the back and told him to bring the child's legs in and he did so. He said, "It'll only take five minutes. We have a doctor standing by". I started to give her the kiss of life in the helicopter and I told the father to start saying the Act of Contrition.

'When we landed I saw a surgeon and called him. I carried Majella into the casualty department. There were three doctors present. One put a stethoscope to her heart and got a heart beat. Another doctor applied a stethoscope and said, "She's gone off". I went to the main entrance and I met Mrs O'Hare, Majella's mother and she kept saying, "Tell me please, honest, is she dead, is she dead?" I couldn't tell her. Fr Hughes came on the scene and told her.'

After the helicopter had left the scene an ambulance arrived. Fr Hughes had followed it to the casualty ward, Daisy Hill Hospital, Newry. Majella was dead. Michael and his mother had met the ambulance and car on their way home from shopping in Newry. They asked the people who were gathering in groups in Whitecross what had happened. They were told Majella was shot. They went to the hospital. Fr Hughes broke the sad news. Newspaper reporters have written up this story and politicians have commented on it. Significance has been attached to the various reports from the British army headquarters at Lisburn. David Blundy outlines them in a special report in the *Sunday Times,* 22 August 1976:

'Majella was shot about 11.45am. According to the first report of the incident issued by the press desk at the army HQ in Lisburn, it seemed that yet another child had been the victim of terrorist violence. The report, issued at 12.14pm, said that a gunman had opened fire on an army patrol in Whitecross, near the border in County Armagh, and a 12-year-old girl had been hit. It seemed that the army had not returned fire. This report was carried by Belfast's local commercial station, *Downtown,* in its news bulletins at 1pm and 2pm that day.

'But just after 2pm, the army's story began to change significantly. The second report said that a gunman had opened fire on the army patrol, and it was "believed" that the army may have returned fire. By 3.30pm, the army press desk said it was then certain the army had returned fire, but had failed to hit the gunman. Majella O'Hare had died in the crossfire.

'Last week, one of the senior army public relations officers at Lisburn said he didn't have the faintest idea why the army had initially denied opening fire. "We were under pressure from the press to get a statement out," he said, "perhaps it is over-enthusiasm to get a statement out quickly." The confusion is puzzling, however, because the one fact the army patrol could have quickly and easily ascertained was whether or not one of the soldiers fired his gun.

'The next day, after the post-mortem report on Majella, the Royal Ulster Constabulary issued a statement "confirming that the fatal bullets probably came from an army weapon. A report that the army came under fire is still under investigation." The post-mortem revealed that Majella had been hit by two bullets, both of them believed to have been fired by one of the army's general purpose machine-guns.

'But there are still serious doubts about the army's claim that the patrol was fired at by a gunman. Eye-witness reports do not confirm this claim, and unofficially, police investigating the case refer to the army's "phantom gunman".

'In fact, police say that the army fired at least three rounds. Majella was hit by two bullets, and these have been found to be army ones. So far they are the only bullets to have been recovered. One short burst from a general purpose machine-gun would not make individual explosions, but because of the speed of fire, might sound like one bang.

'Neither the army nor the police would comment further on the shooting last week. The army repeated the statement put out at 3.30pm on the afternoon of the shooting that an army patrol came under fire from a gunman and shot back.'

From the statements of witnesses some important points can be made in reference to some of the issues Blundy raises. There were many soldiers on the road and under cover that day. When Séamus Reavey drove down and stopped near Majella after she had been shot, there were about 15 soldiers in the vicinity. They had come from the hilly bushy left hand side of the road and the cut meadow on the right. The meadow was impossible territory for a gunman. A soldier was seen to emerge from the hedge on the left. There was no gunman there. Some of the soldiers adopted positions in anticipation of a gunman behind the chapel wall, the 'phantom gunman'. James O'Hare was working near there. He saw no one there and heard no shot there. Witnesses on being questioned say some of the soldiers were afraid but the paratroopers didn't seem to be afraid. One thing seems certain – the paras and a few marines, as distinct from the general body, had a story prepared for a shooting incident, that they were fired on by an armalite rifle and they fired back. There was a lot of insistence to get the children, the people of the cottages, and the Reavey group to say that they heard a number of shots, variously reported 4, 5, 6, 8, 9. The blonde marine, who lay on the ground beside the Reaveys, declared it was an armalite right away. The first thing the soldier said to Fr Hughes when he arrived to attend Majella was, 'Isn't that a terrible thing to see a little girl shot by an armalite rifle?' The dark brown-eyed para's attitude was sinister in the extreme. He tried to bully the many shots story all round. The blonde marine tried to force the exchange of shots theory on Séamus Reavey at 5.15pm that day – even saying that he fired back himself – an utter lie since he lay beside Séamus Reavey and fired no shots.

The paras who burned down people's houses in South Armagh and shot two men recently there in cold blood had prepared another 'incident' for Ballymoyer. The irony is that things went wrong. They shot poor little Majella O'Hare, whether by accident or intent, and the killing was quickly fitted into their prepared trap and the theory of the armalite weapon, weapon of the Provisional IRA, went ahead.

For once the press desk at army HQ, Lisburn, can not be blamed for the initial story. They accepted the report sent by the para officer in command on the scene at Ballymoyer. He told them that a gunman had shot Majella. This was very shortly after Majella was shot. Una Murphy says in her statement, 'Sometime later the soldiers came up to the gate of the house and were speaking across the radio. They said there was a couple of shots believed to be from an armalite rifle'. No doubt they thought this would deal a great blow against the Provisional IRA, following the media coverage of the tragic deaths of the Maguire children. And this worked. The report was scooped by politicians and the *Belfast Telegraph*. The para commander was sure he could bully some evidence from local residents and confuse them. What upset his cover-up? The RUC arrived on the scene. They demanded that the machine-gun be handed over for forensic inspection. The para refused because his story would be blown. The RUC insisted and it was handed over. Army HQ press desk at Lisburn began to change its story significantly.

At 2pm they now said it was believed that the army may have returned fire. By 3.30pm some thinking had been done. They would certainly admit the army returned fire. They knew the RUC report would say their gun killed Majella. But they still covered up – they failed to hit the gunman. Majella died in crossfire! They have failed to retract this lie.

A British army soldier, Private Michael Williams, was charged with the murder of Majella O'Hare. The charge was later reduced to manslaughter. He was acquitted of this charge at his trial at the Belfast city commission in April, May 1977. At the trial Williams said he had opened fire on a gunman who had appeared at a gap in the hedge just after the girls passed. An RUC detective said that the only ammunition cases found in the vicinity of the shooting came from the soldier's gun. Majella was struck by two bullets fired by Williams. Williams said he was guarding other soldiers at a checkpoint near the church. He said he saw a man in the hedge. 'I shouted "look out" and fired my weapon. The man was dressed in a brown jacket. He was in view for just seconds. As soon as I fired he disappeared'. Williams said there was a 'crack' before he fired and added 'I did not see the children in front of me when I fired'. He said he could not accept the suggestion that there was not a gunman in the hedge. He said he saw a gunman and that was why he fired. He said there was no way the gun could have gone off accidentally. On 2 May 1977 the *Belfast Telegraph* reported Williams's acquittal. Judge Gibson said, 'In view of all the evidence I have come to the conclusion that there probably was a gunman and the accused saw him raise the gun to the firing position and that each of them opened fire simultaneously. The gunman made his escape during the confusion. If this is what happened the accused was entitled to shoot as the only way to prevent further shots being fired at the patrol and apprehending the terrorist ... I find the charge of recklessness is unsubstantiated and I do not accept the suggestion that the accused weapon was discharged by accident'. The judge said the opportunity that Williams had for accuracy was minimal. 'He took the risk and Majella O'Hare was killed, but whether it was gross negligence is not to be judged from the outcome but by the chance that some fatality might occur.'

James O'Hare, father of Majella, died on 5 December 1992. On the way to the hospital in the helicopter Majella had lifted her head once and just said, 'Daddy'.

This is an expansion of my account in the pamphlet Majella O'Hare *(1976).*

The Shooting of Michael McCartan, 23 July 1980

Michael McCartan, 16 years of age, an innocent unarmed Catholic boy of Lower Ormeau Road, Belfast, was shot by the RUC on 23 July 1980 and died early on 24 July. I wrote this account in a pamphlet on the killing by Fr Denis Faul and myself, published in 1980. An account of the trial of Constable Robert McKeown for his murder has been added. McKeown was acquitted.

Friday 25 July 1980 was an important date for the McCartan family who lived in Artana Street, off the Ormeau Road in south Belfast. Their son Seán, aged 15 years, was expected home from his holidays in the United States. There was an air of excitement as the day drew near. Nobody took it more serious than his father Charles McCartan, who is invalided and suffers from nervous trouble after an explosion, and his eldest brother Michael. The idea was to have the house looking nice for Seán coming home.

On Wednesday 23 July, Michael helped his father paint and decorate. He cleaned the pictures. The parents had bought a new unit which was placed against the wall near the front window of the living room in the little terrace house. It looked nice, ornaments, glass, books and records proudly arrayed. Michael was in and out of the house all day, but he wanted to stay in that evening and polish the unit. So he left word to say to his mates, when they would call, that he was asleep. His day's work, however, got the better of him and the affection for his mates finally drew him out about 8.30pm or 8.45pm.

Michael was born on 4 March 1964. His mother smiles whimsically when she recalls that his full name was Michael Hugh, but he liked to call himself Michael Séamas. Charles and Molly McCartan have just turned forty. Besides Michael, they have six other children, Seán (15), Dermot (14), Marie (12), Martin (10), Róisín (7) and Conor (6). Michael went to St Augustine's Secondary School, Ravenhill Road. He left school in May. His uncle Neill had set himself the task of getting Michael an apprenticeship in joinery or plastering. There is little prospect for Catholic teenage boys in the Belfast of the 1980s. Michael went around with some half-dozen lads of his own age. The others liked him. He was a little quiet, fond of dogs, some hunting, some fishing, discos sometimes, dandering about with his friends, playing cards in a nook under the Ormeau Road Bridge beside the river Lagan near his home. That was life.

Seven lads altogether assembled to play cards under the Bridge after 8.30pm on Wednesday night. They were all mates – Jim Morrison (16), Thomas Smith (16), Martin Robinson (17), Samuel Caskey (18), Victor Gargan (15), Bobby Harvey (17), and Michael McCartan (16). Smith, Robinson and Morrison had called for Michael. They started to play poker. A short time later Victor Gargan and Sammy Caskey came and they stood watching the game. Usually four played at a time. Then Bobby Harvey came down and asked Marty Robinson to go to the house with him. Those two left. They then let Victor and Sammy play. After Bobby Harvey and Marty Robinson came back, there was some talk about paint. There seemed to have been some exchange of conversation like, 'Are you going to get that paint?', 'Let's go and write our names on the wall'.

There was plenty of light to play cards, even at this time, and the huge street lamps were very bright. It was around 10pm. Some of the group were tired playing cards and the paint episode was a welcome change of scene. Four left: Harvey, Smith, Robinson and McCartan. The other three remained under the bridge in the nook playing cards. Michael's mother recalls that Michael came to the back door about 10pm. He said, 'I want a cheese sandwich, no tea. I'll be back in a minute'. His mother gave him the sandwich, went out to the entry and shouted after him, 'Don't you forget to come back. Your tea is ready.' That was the last she saw of him, in the middle of the entry.

A few minutes would take him back to the waste ground beside the river where once an old factory stood. That was only another street away. Artana Street and the street next to the waste ground, Dromara Street, run parallel to it. There are entries behind each street and then cuttings or narrower entries across from one street to another. People also called the strip of concrete pathing running behind Dromora Street, beside the open waste ground, an 'entry', although it is now open on one side. Michael would have been back to his mates in a few minutes, having grabbed his snack. He may also have picked up the tin of paint and the brush from the window-sill, unknown to his

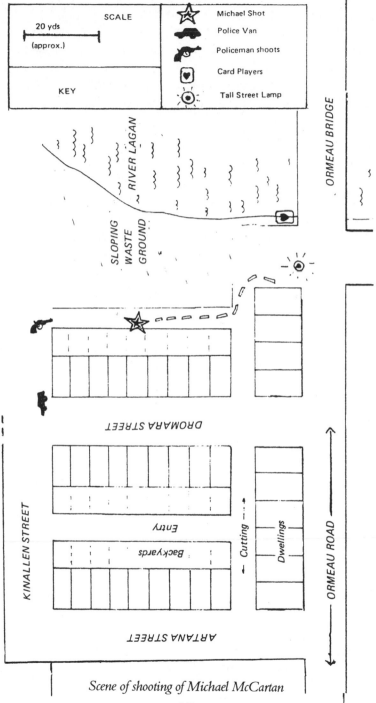

KEY

SCALE — 20 yds (approx.)

- Michael Shot
- Police Van
- Policeman shoots
- Card Players
- Tall Street Lamp

ORMEAU BRIDGE

RIVER LAGAN

SLOPING WASTE GROUND

DROMARA STREET

KINALLEN STREET

Entry

Backyards

Cutting

Dwellings

ARTANA STREET

ORMEAU ROAD

Scene of shooting of Michael McCartan

163

mother, when he called for his sandwich.

Michael rejoined his companions and started writing the word 'Provos' on the wall beneath the hoarding, which is on the gable of a row of houses on the Ormeau Road, between the waste ground and Dromora Street. The three other lads were standing beside the tall lamp. It is sixteen yards from the lamp post to the paint daubing. There are numerous lamps on the bridge and on the river banks which throw such good light that the boys could even see the cards when under the bridge. The three lads then saw a dark green van coming out of the Stranmillis Embankment, the road directly opposite the waste ground. It halted at the main road. There were two policemen in plain clothes in it. This van was well-known to the inhabitants of the district as a police vehicle. Certainly it was known to these lads. Some of them had been stopped several times by it and questioned by the occupants (not necessarily the same men as the night of 23 July). Some were arrested by plain clothes police the previous year from a similar van and were brought to Donegall Pass RUC Station. They were not charged with any offence. After passing, the van turned left down the Ormeau Road. The boys told Michael to put the paint down, 'It's the Peelers'. He set down the tin and brush and walked over to them. Michael then went back to the painting. The other lads stayed beside the lamp. The van went down the road but they did not know where it went. They did not watch it very long. Then they saw the van coming up the road. It turned down Dromara Street. The lads told Michael to put the paint away, but he kept on painting. He was now painting 'Provos' on the hoarding. Maybe he did not believe them, or just stubbornly kept on painting to finish the word. The van went to the bottom of Dromara Street and turned right on to the waste ground which used to be part of Kinallen Street; there are no houses there. Kinallen Street is now waste and runs from the bottom of Artana Street, past the bottom of Dromara Street towards the river. The lads went to the bottom of Dromara Street and they could see the back of the van jutting out at the bottom of the street. They went back and told Michael the 'Peelers' were there. Michael would not be able to see the van from where he was at the hoarding. They left him walking down the concrete strip they called an 'entry' on the waste ground running at the back of Dromara Street. It is flanked by the back yards'

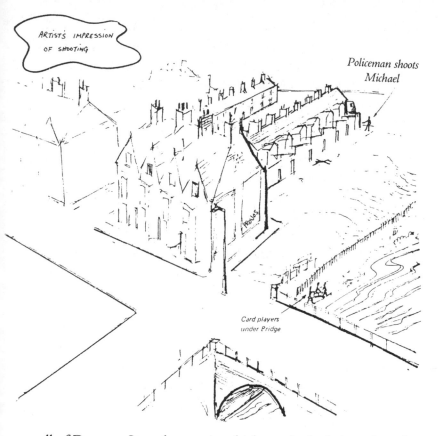

ARTIST'S IMPRESSION OF SHOOTING

Policeman shoots Michael

Card players under Pridge

wall of Dromara Street houses, in which are the back doors into the yards. It is forty yards from the 'paint' hoarding to where Michael's body lay at one of the back doors. It would seem that he was shot from the corner of Kinallen and this concrete strip, a distance of thirty yards. Before Michael headed down the 'entry', he ran towards the nook of the card players, stopped, looked towards them, and then ran back to the waste ground.

One policeman had left the van and walked eighteen yards to this corner. He then shot Michael coming walking down the strip with tin and brush in his hand. Michael seems to have staggered, dropping the tin. There are three white splashes of paint over a few yards. Then he fell at one of the back doors (where people saw a spot of blood), half-way down the 'entry' or concrete strip. Just before the shot was fired, the other policeman reversed the van. The boys were watching the van from the top of Dromara Street at this time. Just as it was coming up the street, they heard the shot. The other three lads, still under the bridge, heard the shot also but disputed among themselves as to whether it was a shot or the backfiring of a vehicle. They remained on playing cards for about fifteen minutes. None of the six lads heard a 'halt' call or a challenge. An experiment carried out by the Association for Legal Justice with Fr Murray showed that a challenge call would be heard under the bridge where the card players were, despite traffic, from the point where the shot was fired, or where the body lay, or at the cutting near the top of Dromara Street.

The policeman who fired the shot joined his companion who had stopped the van at the top of Dromara Street at the entry of the cutting running back into the waste factory ground. Mrs Kelly who lives in 2 Dromara Street had seen the van going down the street between 10.20 and 10.30pm. She went into the kitchen and came back into the front room again. She saw the two men in the van; the policeman who fired the shot had rejoined his companion. She then saw one of them get out and go up the entry (cutting) opposite her house. He came straight back again and spoke to the man who had remained in the van. The other man went up the entry (cutting) and the first fellow went up the street towards the Ormeau Road again. Mrs Kelly was suspicious of the strangers and feared they might be planting a bomb. She went back to the kitchen to get her key and walking stick, intending to go out and phone the police. When she got back to the front door, the police and army had just arrived and the ambulance came a short time later.

When the three lads at the top of Dromara Street heard the shot, they ran down to the Burger Man Chippie at the top of Farnham Street, two or three streets down and stood outside it. The three under the bridge emerged some fifteen minutes after the shot. They had their names taken by the British army. They heard Michael was shot but only knew the next day that he had died. The police give the time of the shooting as 10.33pm. This would fit in with the evidence.

The commotion in Dromara Street soon brought neighbours to the doors. Mrs Jessie Ross learned the news from her ten-year-old daughter who came into the house. She came out and spoke to a policeman. She saw the ambulance men with the stretcher and knew the boy on the stretcher to be Michael McCartan. She found out from a policeman that a priest had not been called nor had the police informed the parents. She phoned Fr Newberry who arrived on the scene and later went to the Royal Victoria Hospital. At first everybody thought Michael was wounded but not too bad. He died at 1.30am on Thursday morning 24 July.

Seán came home from America on Friday. Fr Newberry and the father went to meet him coming off the coach to break the news. It was a sad homecoming for him. He was carrying his presents for Michael, records and a shirt. Seán was in the United States with a party of Catholic and Protestant school children on a four-week trip to Milwaukee, Wisconsin, organised by Ulster Project.

Subsequent to the above account the *Belfast Telegraph* of 10, 15, 16, 19 June 1981 reported the trial of Constable Robert McKeown for the murder of Michael McCartan. It was stated that he was attached to the RUC dog handling section based at Stormont. It was detailed at the trial that the youth was shot at 10.30pm on 23 July and died at 1.15am on 24 July 1980. Crown counsel said a high velocity bullet would make a hole in clothing at the entry point, but not necessarily at the exit point; the only hole in Michael McCartan's clothes was at the back. The bullet was never found. The crown case was that the youth was therefore shot in the back and could not have been in a posture which would have made the RUC officer think he had a gun. A doctor and surgeon gave evidence that they believed he was shot in front, while a forensic scientist told the hearing he believed the bullet entered his body through his back. The scientist said he found the bullet entrance hole in the lower left side, and at the back, of the youth's blue denim jacket. He said, 'In my view there is no possibility of this being other than the entrance hole. The bullet residue indicates that the bullet travelled into the body from the back'. He added that there were corresponding holes in the back of the youth's shirt and red T-shirt and that there was no other bullet hole in his clothing. The accused McKeown claimed he thought the paint brush the youth was holding was a gun and that he opened fire to defend himself, believing he was about to be attacked. The other RUC officer, who was in the van with McKeown when they stopped, said that they had been alerted to keep watch for two armed and masked men travelling in a car, reportedly spotted in the Markets area. He said he did not see the actual shooting but heard McKeown shout a warning 'Stop! Police!' before he fired a single shot.

On 16 June an RUC detective-Chief Inspector read McKeown's statement in court, 'When I got to the corner of the wall I drew my Walther pistol and held it to my side. I was facing a situation I never faced before. I saw a youth whom I recognised as the one I had seen pick up a parcel a few moments earlier. He moved hurriedly past me. I shouted to him 'Police! Stop!' He started to run. I again shouted and he turned towards me'. McKeown said he thought the paint brush was a gun and that the youth was going to shoot him. 'I immediately fired my gun once and he fell to the ground. He was conscious and I asked him where the gun was but he made no reply.' No gun was found. It was stated that McKeown was about ten yards from the youth when he shot him. On 19 June the *Belfast Telegraph* reported the acquittal of Constable Robert McKeown. The judge, Lord Justice Jones, said the killing was 'a bona fide mistake' and that the RUC man's belief that the paint brush was a gun was reasonable. Judge Jones said, 'He acted under an honest and reasonable belief that a terrorist was going to shoot him from close range. He had little time to think'. He accepted McKeown's statement that he had shouted a warning. He accepted that Michael McCartan was shot in the back and that 'that does not contradict the accused's account and I see how this happened as the men turned to face each other'. During his judgement he said, 'Some people may question how a paint brush could be mistaken for a gun. But I think you have to consider the setting. It was a night of some tension and the light was poor.'

Taken from my account in the pamphlet Michael McCartan *(1980).*

Danny Barrett, killed by a British army sniper, 9 July 1981

On 9 July 1981 Danny Barrett, aged 15 years, of Havana Court, Ard-oyne, Belfast, was shot dead by the British army about 9.30pm.

On the afternoon of 9 July his friend, George McErlean, aged 16, called for Danny at his home in Havana Court. They went over to the Pool Hut at the bottom of Brompton Park between 6.30pm and 7.00pm and came back about 7.15pm. They called for a few minutes at Joseph Brown's house at Havana Court. He was watching 'Top of the Pops' so they left and came to Danny's house. There they watched 'Top of the Pops' until about 8pm. They went out and met the rest of their friends at Brompton. There had been a Black Flag March, not an un-common thing during the Hunger Strike at H Blocks, and there was a crowd there. They did not stand around so they went to the club at Herbert Street to go to the disco. There were four or five of them. There was no crowd at the disco so Danny, George, and Kevin Mullen returned to Danny's house. There was rioting down at the waste ground beside Holy Cross School. They watched and then heard a couple of shots. They went back to Danny's house.

James Barrett, Danny's father, recounts that, despite some rioting at the bottom of Brompton Park, all was quiet at Havana Court. Havana Court is a small square of newly-built red brick houses. There is a main entrance from Flax Street. The high building tower of Ewart's Mill, on top of which is a British army camera and sentry post visible to the eye, dominates the area and gives a clear visionary line right down the little front gardens of the row of houses where Danny lived. These small front gardens are surrounded by low brick walls about two feet high. A number of plastic bullets were fired at the rioters who were mainly children. The children threw stones; then ran to retrieve the plastic bullets. James Barrett also heard a number of shots fired but did not know from where or from whom. The shooting, he thought, seemed to come from the direction of Brompton Park. When Danny heard the first shots, he rushed into the house along with the other children. There was a short lull and Danny walked out to the front

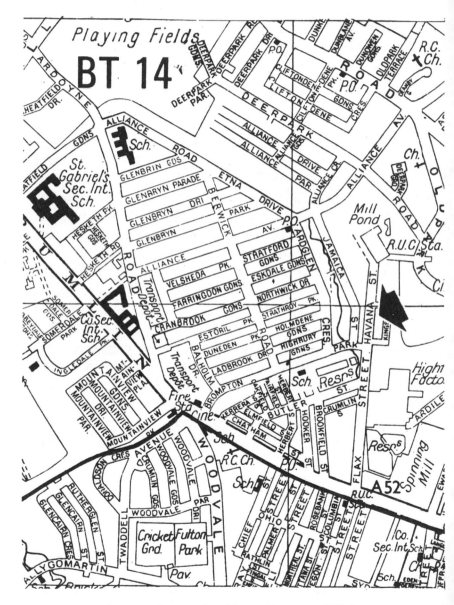

Arrow marks spot where Danny Barrett was killed

again and James went with him. James stood at the door. Danny sat on the low wall at right angles to the house and was facing towards Flax Street. George McErlean was standing in the hall of Danny's house. Joseph Foster, aged 16, had been at the Pool Hut and had come over to Havana Court by himself. He sat down on the wall beside Danny. Kevin Mullen was standing further down the path to the house. Gerry Ferguson was standing between James Barrett and Danny. Then there was a further number of shots. Joe Foster said to Danny, 'Get down!' Danny said, 'Ach, it's all right'. Then there was a single shot and Danny fell back over the wall. James saw Danny fall back over the wall. He thought at first Danny had thrown himself back to get down for cover. Gerry Ferguson got up. James looked over the wall and saw his son lying bleeding. He thought he had hit his head when he fell over. He jumped over the wall and saw he was losing a lot of blood. He knew then Danny had been shot. He was unconscious and appeared to be dead. He said an Act of Contrition in his ear and held him in his arms. He took off his shirt and tried to stem the flow of blood. An ambulance was called.

When Danny was shot, there was panic among the children and neighbours who had been drawn to the doors by the rioting and shooting. There had been some running to and fro by parents to bring children away from Brompton Park. When Danny was shot, some others in hysteria thought they had been shot too. Some ran into Mrs Veronica Clarke's house next to Barrett's. Some were screaming.

Patrick Clarke, husband of Veronica, says that on 9 July he went to the local disco at around 8.45pm to bring home his eight-year old son. On his way home he saw two RUC land-rovers driving up Butler Street. A third land-rover was further down the street. He reached the junction of Butler Street/Flax Street at the same time as the land-rovers. He heard shots being fired from the direction of Etna Drive/ Brompton Park at the land-rovers. He grabbed his son and ran back to the old houses at Butler Street. The third land-rover came racing past him to join up with the other two. He heard a second number of shots which sounded different from the first firing and he assumed this was the RUC returning fire. The RUC land-rovers went into Ardoyne Avenue. Patrick crossed the waste ground and went home. He heard a lot of people shouting that a child had been shot. He saw young Danny Barrett lying on the ground; some neighbours were beside him; they were waiting for an ambulance. When it came, he went with Danny to the Mater Hospital. He realised that Danny was dead. Halfway down Flax Street, they were stopped by the British army. He was questioned as to who Danny was and all the details. This took about three minutes. At the bottom of Flax Street, they were again stopped by the British army who wanted to know details. The ambulance crew protested at the delay. They had to give all the information again and this took three minutes. The soldiers then said they would escort the ambulance to the hospital. One hundred and fifty yards down the Crumlin Road they were stopped by the RUC. The soldiers, who were in front of the ambulance, drove on. They had to give the RUC the same information again. The RUC went with them to the hospital. When they reached the Mater Hospital, the doctors were waiting at the gates. They came into the ambulance and pronounced Danny dead. The RUC asked Patrick to identify Danny. He did that and then they went to the morgue.

At the time of the shooting, Danny's mother, Mrs Margaret Barrett, was visiting her friend Lily Canavan at Strathroy Park, Ardoyne. James went to the house to tell her. He was pale and shocked. Mrs Barrett was sitting with her back to the window. Lily Canavan said, 'Here's your Jimmy coming. There must be something wrong.' Mrs Barrett said, 'Jimmy, what's wrong? Is it our Danny?' He shook his head and she ran out and down the entry. He followed her and said, 'Danny was shot'. People were out of their homes. Mrs Barrett did not know Danny was dead. She saw the British soldiers and the RUC. She wanted to go to the hospital. She saw the priest at the hospital. She ran away. She knew he was bad. The priest told her he was dead and she came back home.

Immediately after the shooting, the RUC and the British army came on the scene and searched the Barrett home. They looked through Tina's schoolbooks. The officer in charge said they were looking for arms and not to go through trivial things. They searched through the yard, bin, coal-bunker and back-garden. They searched all the bedrooms and cupboards upstairs and down. They also searched Mickey Holland's home, Danny's chum. There was no one in the house at the time and they broke the back lock and window.

The next morning, 10 July, around 6am, the RUC, British army and forensic experts came to the outside of the house to examine a bullet hole in the next door neighbour's house. James Barrett went out and spoke to them. They were pointing in the direction of the high-rise building in Flax Street which is a British army base. There is an observation post on top of it. The forensic men told James that was the direction the shot came from.

Danny Barrett was buried after 10 o'clock Mass on 14 July 1981 from Holy Cross Church. Some statements have been made to the RUC but as yet there has been no inquest or any other development in the case.

Danny Barrett is another victim of the British/Irish conflict. His life reflects his own people, the oppressed Catholic nationalists of the north of Ireland. His father Jimmy Barrett was born and reared in Hooker Street. He married in June 1963. His wife came from Unity Flats. They bought a wee house in Hooker Street and were there during the whole 'troubles' until the 'peace line' went up. They went up to Gormanstown College in County Meath the night of internment but only stayed a night. During the years they were often kicked about just like their neighbours, sleeping in schools in bad times. They left Hooker Street in June 1980 and moved to Havana Court. Danny loved the new house because of the bathroom and plenty of room to bring all his chums. In all the 'troubles' he never got hurt. James Barrett, his father, is forty years of age, an unemployed crane-driver. There are three other children, Susan (17), Conn (12), Tina (7). Mrs Barrett was always terribly afraid for Danny because of his age and the hunger strike. She kept him home from school the whole week before Bobby Sands died. His school, St Gabriel's, is on the main Crumlin Road and she was afraid of any thing happening. Danny's favourite pastimes were playing pool, discos and playing records. He was a normal boisterous lad of his age, liked the girls and had plenty of friends. He and his sister were due to go on holiday to Bray arranged by Ardoyne Youth Club each year. Danny was a member of Ardoyne Youth Club and around thirty children were going on the trip.

On 19 May 1981, five British soldiers were killed by a land mine in Camlough, South Armagh. On that day, about 4pm, his mother was called to where some soldiers had stopped him. They were accusing him of having hijacked a car. Danny told his mother, 'The soldier is after saying to me – "You see the soldier in the observation post; if he identifies you as the one who hijacked the car from Brompton Park, you'll be sent away for a right spell."' It was from the same observation post Danny was shot. In July 1980, he was arrested with two others for alleged rioting. It went to court and the case was thrown out.

Who will take an interest in the case of Danny Barrett shot by the British army? Is he to join the 11 other completely innocent men, women and children killed by the British army and no justice follow? Are we silent too long?

I wrote this account in November 1981 for the pamphlet, Danny Barrett, *published by Mgr Denis Faul and myself in January 1982.*

State Killings in Northern Ireland, 1991–92

Amnesty International celebrated its thirtieth birthday in 1991. People involved in the campaign for human rights in Northern Ireland are grateful to them for their interest in the protection of citizens of the north from the illegal acts of those in charge of the law. One calls to mind their reports of February 1972 and June 1978 on ill-treatment of those detained under emergency laws in interrogation centres, and reports in 1988 and 1990 on Killings by Security Forces in Northern Ireland. In their report of 1991 entitled *United Kingdom: Human Rights Concerns* Amnesty International condemned British government secrecy in police and military investigations. It renewed its call for an independent judicial inquiry into disputed killings by security forces in Northern Ireland. The report said that Amnesty 'believes that such an inquiry is vital to help prevent future unlawful killings and to ensure that all disputed killings by security forces are promptly investigated and publicly clarified'.

The British government has held inquiries before, but it is clear that they do not want to reveal the truth. On 30 January 1972, in Derry,

British paratroopers shot dead 14 unarmed citizens in cold blood. Nevertheless, the inquiry under Lord Widgery into the events of Bloody Sunday did not fault the actions of the soldiers.

In May 1984, John Stalker, Deputy Chief Constable of the Manchester police force, was appointed by the Royal Ulster Constabulary (RUC) to investigate three incidents in 1982 when 6 unarmed people were killed by undercover policemen. This did not result in the uncovering of the full facts surrounding these murders. The administrative cover-up became known as the Stalker Affair. Stalker was digging too deep, discovering damaging new evidence. He was suspended from the police on trumped up charges and removed from the case. The Stalker Affair clearly indicated that the authorities have something sinister to hide.

In 1989 Cambridge Deputy Chief Constable John Stevens conducted an inquiry into collusion of security forces with loyalist paramilitaries. His report touched only the surface of the iceberg. Its scope was deliberately limited.

ABUSE OF LAW

Harassment, brutality, ill-treatment, torture, internment, severe prison conditions sanctioned or tolerated by the state have for 20 years distorted the face of Northern Ireland. The non-jury Diplock Courts, the acceptance by these courts of fictitious verbal statements, the use of supergrasses, the blackmailing of young people by the security forces, semi-official assassinations, the widespread and deadly use of plastic bullets and official shoot-to-kill policies have eroded confidence in law. The argument for this abuse of law is that the end justifies the means. Faced with the atrocities of the IRA and INLA the illegitimacy of the action of the security forces is blurred by public statements and pleading from the RUC, British army and British government that such counter-insurgency is justified in a warlike situation.

UNJUST KILLINGS

From the deaths of Samuel Devenney and John Gallagher in 1969 at the hands of the RUC to the shooting dead of Peter Mc Bride in Belfast by the British army in 1992, one can list some 150 direct administrative killings, many unjust killings and scores of indirect killings manipulated by the British Intelligence system.

In August 1992 the death-toll in Northern Ireland officially reached 3,000. Other compilations gave the figure as 3,022. I would regard the following killings in 1991–92 as unjust:– Colm Marks shot dead by the RUC in Downpatrick; Pete Ryan, Tony Doris and Lawrence McNally ambushed and shot dead by the SAS at Coagh, County Tyrone; Kevin McGovern shot dead by the RUC in Cookstown; Gerald Maginn shot dead by RUC in Belfast; Kevin Barry O'Donnell, Seán O'Farrell, Peter Clancy and Patrick Vincent ambushed and shot dead by the British army at Clonoe, County Tyrone; Peter Mc Bride shot dead by the British army in Belfast.

The forces of the state have been responsible for unjust killings, direct murder and indirect unjust killings and murder by collusion with loyalist paramilitaries. Mr Ed Moloney in an article in the *Sunday Tribune*, 9 June 1991, stated that since the 1982 killings investigated by John Stalker 67 civilians and paramilitaries had been shot dead in 'Shoot-to-Kill' operations. Twenty of these were civilians and 47 paramilitaries, of whom only two were loyalists. He wrote then :

'A large proportion of the victims were unarmed when they were killed. Twenty-six, or 39%, had no weapon when shot, while four were carrying imitation handguns or rifles. Of the 37 who had access to arms there were claims afterwards that nine were in no position to use the weapons, mostly because they were on their way to arms dumps when killed'.

BLACK PROPAGANDA

After the security forces kill people they seize the initiative by gaining a first story in the media. This is very hard to counteract. For example, when the British army shot dead an innocent young man, Daniel Rooney, in Belfast in September 1972 the commanding officer said he was a gunman, that he was engaged in a shooting incident at the time he was shot, that he got his just deserts. All these assertions were untrue. Even children killed by plastic bullets have been slandered. Now there is a distinct pattern – when the British army and RUC execute armed or unarmed IRA men, when they could have arrested them, they issue statements giving unsubstantiated and lurid potted biographies recounting the notoriety of the dead men and list the number of murders attributable to the weapons found on the scene. The idea is to show that they deserved to die, to divert attention from their own violation of the law, and to intimidate churchmen and politicians from criticising their action of shooting them.

FOUR CATEGORIES OF KILLINGS

There are four categories of killings carried out by the security forces:

1. A 'bad' soldier or 'bad' policeman who kills from a motive of revenge, hatred, bigotry, racism. He can prove to be an embarrassment to the senior people in the army, police and government, but because of the policy not to injure the morale of the forces the crime will be covered up and he will receive protection.

2. Murders and unjust killings by front-line regiments like the marines or paratroopers who do not relish the rôle of 'peace-keepers'. They are eager for trouble. From the beginning of their tour of duty they harass, abuse, beat and threaten civilians. The senior district police-men do not deter them. On their rota these soldiers usually assure themselves of a kill. Their harassment inevitably ends in tragedy. Knowing that, the government still retains the paratroopers and marines on the rota tours of duty of British regiments in Northern Ireland. When they kill innocent civilians they are most often than not protected by the authorities.

3. Civilians executed in error by the SAS, other undercover soldiers, or the RUC when they enter an ambush. This is also an embarrassment but it is covered up.

4. Cold blooded ambushes of republican paramilitaries. No challenge, no arrest contemplated. These murders have the official backing of the British government. It is administrative policy. The Gibraltar murders are an example of that. The government will go to great pains to cover up the truth. The Prime Minister and cabinet ministers will lie publicly.

SAS DEATH SQUADS

In November 1990 I published *The SAS in Ireland*. It may seem a narrow focus, a fraction of the state killings, but I wanted it to be symbolic of all the state killings. The SAS is an assassination squad, like the South American death squads, and it is acting outside the law. They kill persons when they have opportunities of arresting them and they are well known for shooting wounded and incapacitated persons lying helpless on the ground. Such actions are contrary to the moral law, the law of the land and the rules of war. There is no declared war in Northern Ireland between recognised insurgents and state forces. The law therefore is eminent and dominant and must be obeyed by every body including the forces of the law. The SAS are not therefore justified in killing civilians or IRA members in planned ambushes.

JUSTICE PERVERTED

The state perverts justice by attempting to solve its dilemma following these killings by inquests with limited powers and political decisions not to prosecute members of the security forces for murder. If, for example, all the killings carried out by the SAS, and I list 45 fatal shootings in the book, are examined in a continuous account a pattern of defence on the part of the SAS at inquests emerges:– they intended to make arrests; there was a threat to life and limb; the other party 'fired first'. There are cases where forensic and medical evidence, and the evidence of witnesses, do not seem to have prevailed against the word of security forces.

The inquest system is inadequate. The Amnesty International report *United Kingdom: Human Rights Concerns,* June 1991, outlined its worries on the restrictions on inquests in Northern Ireland, in particular that the coroner's court cannot make the finding of an unlawful killing by a named or an unnamed person as is possible in England and Wales. The unfairness of the inquest system is outlined in a pamphlet *Inquests and Disputed Killings in Northern Ireland* issued by the Committee on the Administration of Justice in January 1992. Are citizens not entitled to fair institutions in matters of law?

What about the prosecution of security forces in matters of murder and unjust killing? Security forces are not subject to the same interrogation procedures as others and impartiality and persistence in cases involving police and army are in doubt. The DPP is not independent and the attorney-general is on record on restricting justice for reasons of public interest and national security. Are not political considerations and danger to morale of security forces prevailing over legal justice?

The Amnesty Report of 1991 noted:

'There have been 21 prosecutions since 1969 of the security forces for using firearms while on duty in Northern Ireland (not including sectarian killings). Nineteen of these were found not guilty. One was convicted of manslaughter and given a suspended sentence. Just one – a soldier – was convicted of murder and released after serving two years and three months of his sentence and had been reinstated in the army. A total of 339 people have been killed by the security forces during the same period. Most of those killed were from the Catholic population and many were unarmed; many were killed in disputed circumstances.'

In the past decade 10 'joyriders' have been killed by the British army in west Belfast. On 31 July 1991 six members of the Parachute Regiment were charged with the fatal shooting of two teenagers and the wounding of a third in West Belfast in 1990. The charges followed a BBC Panorama programme on 'Shoot-to-Kill' which highlighted this shooting. It is highly unlikely that any soldier would have been charged with the murder of Fergal Caraher and the wounding of his brother on 30 December 1990 by marines if the Cullyhanna people had not organised an unofficial international inquiry to shame the British government into action.

One would like to know from those persons who run the High Court why soldiers or RUC men charged with murder or brutality have the good fortune to find such sympathetic judges. The few that are charged are acquitted in circumstances that are weird. It is almost impossible to have a British soldier convicted of murder in the courts of Northern Ireland. This is in direct contrast with the inordinate judicial revenge in the form of wholesale doubtful convictions against some forty people for the murder of two undercover British soldiers in Casement Park.

Catholics despair of getting fair treatment in human rights from the British government. Its image of keeping the peace between war-like factions is felt to be propaganda. It is beside the point when it comes to the forces of the state doing its share of unjust killing and murder. Catholics do not trust the RUC and the British army and they regard the UDR as a sectarian force. If the main motive and objective is to save human life it seems fruitless to inform the RUC who themselves pursue a 'Shoot-to-Kill' policy and allow the British army to take human life with impunity. The anger aroused in people when the security forces of the state engage in ill-treatment or killing outside the law, and then protect themselves by lies, can lead people into using violence with disastrous results for themselves and the whole community.

The government of the United Kingdom is deaf to pleas for justice and fair play. In its report of June 1991 Amnesty International called for an independent inquiry which should look into the legislation and regulations governing the use of lethal force, as well as into the procedures used to investigate disputed incidents. The government of the United Kingdom has constantly refused to do this.

SECTARIAN MURDER – SECRET SERVICE RÔLE
In the past 20 years sectarian assassinations of Catholics have been carried out by loyalist paramilitaries and pseudo-gangs tolerated and often directed by the British secret service. The purpose of the 500 murders of the 1970s was to break the nerve and sap the morale of the Catholic population, weaken its powers of resistance and draw off support for the IRA. This included British intelligence support for the Ulster Workers' Strike in May 1974 (which brought down the power-sharing executive government in Northern Ireland), the two Dublin bombings, 1 December 1972 and 17 May 1974, and other bombings in the Irish Republic, and cross-border assassinations and kidnappings. So close has been the collusion between the state and one loyalist paramilitary group, the Ulster Defence Association, that it took twenty years to proscribe them, even though this group has murdered more than 500 innocent Catholics, men, women and children.

The Stevens inquiry was set up in 1989 to investigate the collusion of police and army with the loyalist murder gangs. Collusion, however, has gone on for twenty years. The UDA has been switched on and off as a 'third force'. The Nelson Affair gave the public a glimpse of this underground murder campaign on the part of the British secret service. The manipulation was noticeable after the murder of Airey Neave and the Brighton bombing atrocity. It continues in east Tyrone and south Derry where in the past two years 19 Catholics have been murdered and no one made amenable. At political high-points, too, when indications are that Catholics might have a share in power the loyalist gangs are switched on. The 'taking out' of Sinn Féin councillors and members is systematic. In October 1991 a combination of loyalists groups, UVF and UDA, conducted an assassination campaign which resulted in the murder of 8 Catholics. The campaign was believed to be aimed at forcing Britain to adopt a more conciliatory attitude towards unionism in the pre-election period.

There are three main areas where the killing of Catholics takes place – north Belfast, south Derry/east Tyrone, and the Craigavon area extending into Lisburn. Murders of Catholics in these three areas have taken place in the past few years. Let us take the Derry/Tyrone area as an example. Since January 1989 21 Catholics have been murdered there by loyalist paramilitaries and security forces. The UDA under its cover name UFF shot dead Danny Cassidy a Sinn Féin election worker on 2 April 1992. He was hit seven times in the day time. His widow claimed that he had been constantly harassed by the DMSU – the District Mobile Support Unit of the RUC. At his funeral Mass Bishop Edward Daly said that a factor in his killing was the 'undue attention paid to him by some units of police'. The bishop told the congregation that Mr Cassidy had suffered constant cruel and public harassment from some members of the RUC. 'In a society such as ours,' he said, 'with more than its share of sectarian murders, it is unjust, irresponsible and wrong for police officers to pick out and highlight individuals in this public manner, thus putting their lives in mortal danger. This activity is wrong and unjust and it must stop.' Bishop Daly said that a week before Danny Cassidy was murdered a complaint was made by a local representative to a senior RUC officer about the way he was mistreated.

Prosecutions for these crimes are nil. There have been few arrests. Only one person has been prosecuted for indirect involvement. This must be the worst record for any police force in the world. Catholics believe there is collusion between the RUC, the UDR and the loyalist paramilitaries. They come from the same background and are politically hostile to nationalists. The feeling of the people of south Derry is stronger than the words of Bishop Daly. They think that the RUC through collusion were responsible for Danny Cassidy's murder.

The same pattern occurs in many of these killings. There is a presence of security forces before the shooting, then they disappear, the loyalist gunmen carry out the shooting, the UDR appear on the roads laughing and mock and harass Catholics. The RUC in most cases do not inform the relatives of the shooting or they do so in a cruel callous manner (like a phone call to Mrs Mc Govern in the early hours of the morning – 'Your son is in the morgue'). They rarely take statements from the relatives as to recent events in the life of the deceased and his movements on the day of the shooting. It is almost impossible for relatives to have an interview with the investigating detectives.

Here is a list of the Derry/Tyrone killings of Catholics since January 1989. Unless otherwise stated these killings were carried out by the UVF:–

14 February 1989. John Joe Davey, Sinn Féin Councillor. Car ambushed near home.

29 November 1989. Liam Ryan and Michael Devlin. Shot dead in public house, Ardboe.

26 October 1990. Tommy Casey. Member of Sinn Féin. Shot dead at house, Cookstown.

3 March 1991. John Quinn, Dwayne O'Donnell, Malcolm Nugent, Thomas Armstrong. Shot outside pub in Cappagh.

3 June 1991. Three IRA men, Pete Ryan, Tony Doris, Lawrence McNally, ambushed by SAS at Coagh.

12 August 1991. Pádraig Ó Seanacháin. Member of Sinn Féin. Van ambushed.

16 August 1991. Thomas Donaghy. Kilrea. Shot outside work.

16 September 1991. Bernard O'Hagan. Member of Sinn Féin. Shot outside work at Magherafelt.

29 September 1991. Kevin McGovern shot by RUC in Cookstown.

25 October 1991. Seán Anderson shot outside his home in Pomeroy.

3 January 1992. Kevin McKearney shot dead in the family butcher shop, Moy. His uncle Jack McKearney wounded in the shooting died some months later.

6 September 1992 Charlie and Theresa Fox were shot dead near the Moy.

In revenge for loyalist killings in this area and in the absence of RUC detection of the killers the IRA on 17 January 1992 murdered by a landmine seven Protestant workers at Teebane near Cookstown with the 'excuse' that they worked for the security forces – William Bleeks, David Harkness, James Caldwell, Robert Dunseith, John McConnell, Nigel McKee, Robert Irons. An eighth man – Oswald Gilchrist died on 21 January 1992 from injuries. There was a further repercussion to this slaughter when the UDA murdered five Catholics in a betting shop in Belfast on 5 February 1992 – James Kennedy, Peter Magee, Christy Doherty, William McManus, Jack Duffin.

As regards the shooting dead of Thomas Donaghy on 16 August 1991 as he arrived for work at Portna Eel Fishery, an area covered by the Ballymoney UDR, there is some background information which leads relatives and friends to suspect collusion. Thomas Donaghy was an ex-prisoner who left the IRA several years before his release from prison and did not become re-involved. The RUC harassed and tormented him non-stop from the three years from his release to his death.

In the same area Gerry Casey was shot dead in his home on 4 April 1989 by a gang who smashed in his door minutes after he went to bed. The police had already drawn a plan of the bedrooms of his house on a previous raid. His murder came only weeks after two men with a sledge-hammer were stopped at a checkpoint on their way to kill a Dunloy man a few miles from where the Caseys lived. In the same area of Kilrea, John O'Kane survived a booby-trap attempt on his life, 5 March 1988; another man with him, Stephen Kennedy, received head and eye injuries. The UDR had been in the vicinity on the previous night. There was a second booby trap attempt on O'Kane's life the following year 1989. A similar type of booby trap was used when a man was injured in an explosion at Kilrea GAA Club Rooms. Other ex-prisoners in this area are constantly harassed by the RUC, particularly by the District Mobile Support Unit. The RUC have told some of these men that their files are missing from Antrim RUC station.

I would suggest that international human rights organisations, besides carrying out *post factum* investigations and reports, should set up a 'Red Adair' type emergency team of lawyers, forensic experts, photographers, engineers, and doctors to fly immediately to the aid of families after they have a member shot dead by the security forces. Vital information may be lost through a cover-up. One no longer has full confidence in forensic evidence gathered by the authorities. It is important that the families have independent autopsies and that as much evidence as possible is gathered in statements from witnesses. Photography and mapping are also important. The legal experts should then attend the inquests and trials that may emerge. Those who dare to challenge the British authorities, such as solicitors, also are in danger of assassination. On 17 January 1989, Douglas Hogg, a junior government Home Office minister stated in Westminster that 'there are in Northern Ireland a number of solicitors who are unduly sympathetic to the cause of the IRA'. This statement was interpreted as a warning to solicitors not to contest too vigorously cases against British government institutions. Three weeks later, as though to underline this point, Pat Finucane, one of the leading human rights' lawyers in Northern Ireland, who had been particularly active in a number of the cases investigated by John Stalker, was murdered by the UDA in front of his family.

Amnesty International in its recent report focuses on this murder:

'A year before his death Amnesty International had heard from a former detainee that during interrogation at Castlereagh the police had said his lawyer, Pat Finucane, would be killed ... Loyalist sources claimed that prior to the killing UDA members detained at Castlereagh had been told by detectives that Mr Finucane and a few other solicitors were IRA members and implied that they should be shot. Although some of them were later arrested by the Stevens team, apparently none of them were questioned about these allegations. Furthermore it was reported that Brian Nelson, the alleged (British) army and UDA intelligence officer questioned by the inquiry, knew that Patrick Finucane would be shot, and indeed had been involved in providing intelligence which led to the lawyer's killing'.

All the information that has been disclosed about Pat Finucane's murder would suggest that the decision to kill him was taken by British Intelligence agents. It is clear that the use of UDA death squads has and is being employed by the British authorities for their own sinister purposes.

One welcomes the recent proscribing of the UDA.

The present inquest system in the north of Ireland is inadequate. It is not a large demand to ask for instant reform. It would show some goodwill on the part of the British government in the matter of law and justice. Bereaved relatives are denied elementary standards of justice.

The DPP should give reasons for decisions not to prosecute in cases involving the security forces. He should be answerable to the citizens of the state.

Fewer than 8% of the large RUC force is Catholic. The police force needs restructuring to include nationalists and republicans who are strong elements in the society of Northern Ireland. One suspects that the violation of human rights on the part of the state is linked to this scandalous situation.

One would like an official explanation of 'detention in military custody' which is practised when soldiers are remanded pending trial.

Submission to Initiative '92 and the Opsahl Commission. An abbreviated form was published by Relatives for Justice in 1991.

Relatives for Justice Meeting with Northern Ireland Office Representatives, 23 January 1992

Relatives of those killed unjustly and murdered directly by security forces, and those killed indirectly by the state through collusion (witness the Nelson affair) wish to communicate their feeling that justice is formerly and officially perverted.

1. Callous attitude towards the victims. The RUC either never inform the relatives of the deaths of those killed unjustly or murdered by security forces or they act in a cruel manner. Examples – Leo Norney, Anthony Hughes, Kevin McGovern.

The relatives of these victims are targeted for consistent harassment by RUC, UDR and British army.

2. There is no urgent and vigorous investigation of these killings. Security forces are not subject to the same interrogation procedure as others. There is suspicion of lack of impartiality and persistence in the investigations.

3. The DPP is shrouded in secrecy. He should be responsible to the citizens of the state. He should give reasons for decisions not to prosecute. His independence in 'state' killings is flawed since killings involving the security forces are discussed with the attorney general.

4. Inquests in Northern Ireland are inadequate and designed not to reveal the truth. At least in Britain there is a verdict and the killers would have to appear at the inquest. Legal aid should be provided both in Northern Ireland and Britain.

5. Collusion in the name of the 'fight against terrorists' has lead to murder on the part of British Intelligence and security forces. The administrative bodies share guilt. Confidence in the administration of justice is eroded. Nationalists feel that collusion is indicated in the lack of prosecution of loyalist murderers in south Derry/east Tyrone, Craigavon and north Belfast; this ultimately leads to 'revenge killings'.

SIMPLE DEMANDS

1. Would the Northern Ireland Office supply reasons why there has not been prosecution in this category of killings if given a sample list of cases?

2. Demands for a public inquiry into these cases have always been turned down by the authorities. Necessity for a public international inquiry.

3. Change of law regarding (a) DPP (b) Inquests (c) use of legal force (d) provision of autopsy report as of right (e) independent forensic and autopsy.

The Violation of the Right to Life

On 23 January 1997 I submitted a report on human rights in Northern Ireland to Chairman Benjamin A. Gilman, House Committee on International Relations, United States House of Representatives, Washington, DC. In the report I included two examples of unjust killings to illustrate the violation of the right to life. The shooting of a civilian, Aidan McAnespie, on 21 February 1988, when walking by a British army post at Aughnacloy, County Tyrone, is here related by his sister, Eilish. I give an account of the Gibraltar shootings of unarmed IRA members by the SAS on 6 March 1988. It is written by Niall Farrell, the brother of Mairéad, one of the victims. He is secretary of Relatives for Justice.

THE SHOOTING OF AIDAN MCANESPIE

It is of paramount importance that the killing of my brother, Aidan McAnespie, on 21 February 1988, is not viewed as an isolated incident but rather as the result of systematic and routine victimisation for several years by British crown forces. These include members of the Royal Ulster Constabulary, the Ulster Defence Regiment and the British army.

My brother, Aidan McAnespie, was the youngest of a family of six children. He was born in Aughnacloy, a predominantly loyalist

village on the border with the Republic of Ireland. The area historically had a high unemployment rate, that is, for those nationalists
living there. As a consequence, Aidan looked for work across the border and was fortunate enough to get a job in a poultry processing plant
in Monaghan town, in the Republic of Ireland, some ten miles south
of Aughnacloy. To go to work each day, Aidan had to pass through a
permanent British army checkpoint at the southern side of the village.
As a result, the security forces became familiar with him and often
asked him to remove his car from the road for what was termed a
'routine search'. They would then take the car apart, removing door
panels and wheels. They would also search through his lunch with
their bare hands saying, 'You'll be late for work today Aidan'. Aidan
made complaints to his trade union about these incidents and they
made representations on his behalf, but the harassment continued un-
abated. On other occasions they would ask him to remove his coat,
shoes and socks in the rain. When he refused, they would put him on
the ground and one soldier stood on his throat while another pulled
off his shoes and socks. Aidan made complaints to the local RUC
station.

It was not unusual for Aidan to be taken into the British army
base for a vehicle search two or three times a week and the car pulled
apart. The harassment got so bad that he stopped driving through the
checkpoint; instead he would drive to the filling station just south of
the checkpoint and would phone my mother. She would then cycle
down through the town and out past the checkpoint and walk back
through with Aidan. On one occasion a soldier shouted after them,
'Are you trying to protect your son Mrs McAnespie?'

Aidan contacted newspapers seeking the protection that publicity
might have given him and one national newspaper carried a story de-
scribing him as the most harassed person in Ireland. He could have
wallpapered his room with official complaints made to the RUC both
through solicitors and the local parish priest. Aidan's life revolved
around the continual threat of harassment and physical violence at
best and the real threat of being killed at worst. A soldier stopped my
father a year before the shooting and asked, 'Are you Aidan's father?'
When he said he was the soldier said, 'We have a bullet here for him'.

On 21 February 1988, Aidan parked his car at the northern side of the checkpoint and walked towards the local GAA pitch, which was just south of the checkpoint. He had only walked three hundred yards when a single bullet from a heavy calibre machine-gun cut him down, in the prime of his life, on a lovely sunny afternoon, while on his way to a Gaelic football match. Aidan's life was taken, his killer watched him walk towards the football pitch, aimed and fired to kill. This is the view of our family and many community and church leaders. The then Primate of All Ireland, Cardinal Tomás Ó Fiaich, described the killing as murder.

In stark contrast the British army described the incident as a tragic accident. They claimed, firstly, that the gun used was being passed from one soldier to another when it was accidentally discharged. This account later changed to one of accidental discharge when the gun was in the process of being cleaned. Because the Northern Ireland office's statement of what happened supported this version, all subsequent investigations carried out by the RUC were mobilised to support this explanation of events. In actual fact, the security force explanation was so incredible that they had to create evidence to support their claim. For example, eye-witnesses saw a man coming out of a sanger from which Aidan was shot, wearing casual clothes and sports shoes. The next day the British army had a number of their people painting the checkpoint dressed in casual clothing. Aidan's car was parked close to the checkpoint in a nationalist housing estate. On the day of the funeral eye-witnesses saw a man remove it. Our family phoned the local RUC station to report it missing. They said they knew nothing about it but to try CID (Criminal Investigation Department) in Dungannon. CID in Dungannon were not aware of the missing car. We then phoned the local police to report the stolen car. The press got to hear about the missing car and shortly after speaking to the local police, a local journalist could tell the family that the car was removed by police for its safety. It seems incredible that of all the cars parked in the housing estate this was the only car in some kind of danger.

In addition, the army claimed, that due to the accidental discharge of the weapon, three shots were fired, one of which ricocheted off the road hitting Aidan. Local people living nearby say the army reconstructed this account of things when, as darkness fell, a flashing light was placed at the spot where Aidan was shot and three shots were heard fired. It is widely believed that the army fired the shots to mark the road to support their ricochet theory. When challenged by the press, the army claimed that they came under fire from terrorists, a claim denied by the IRA and local people nearby who say no attack of any kind took place.

A soldier, David J. Holden, was charged with unlawful killing. While on this charge he was allowed to go home to his family in England. Approximately six months later all charges were dropped.

At Aidan's inquest, the coroner, Roger McLernon, said the death was a cause of 'profound regret' and 'was avoidable and should have been avoided'. The RUC stated at the inquest, and it was repeated by the coroner, that there was no suggestion that Aidan had ever been involved in any form of illegal activity. Guardsman Holden was not compelled to attend the inquest. The coroner advised the jury that, although the soldier was entitled under law not to attend, his unsworn statement should be treated with caution. The only other soldier in the sanger when the fatal shot was fired was conveniently absent without leave for the six months previous to the inquest. The coroner said this was 'amazing' and of 'profound concern'.

Our family was not present at this inquest because we had no faith in its ability to discover the truth. We have a series of unanswered questions: Why did the gun that killed Aidan have 'a live round in its breach while being cleaned'? Why was it cocked? Why was the safety catch off? How could David Holden's hands still be slippery and wet ten minutes after he finished washing sanger walls? Is it possible to accidentally exert nine pounds of pressure on a weapon's trigger, pulling it backwards and upwards? Why was Holden out of uniform, wearing what appeared to be a track suit when he left the sanger under police escort after the shooting? How could the Northern Ireland Office release a definitive statement of the shooting less than an hour after it had taken place? Was this a rigorous investigation?

It must be remembered that this is in no way the only incident of its type. The SAS, the British army and the RUC have been involved in the killing of many nationalists in controversial circumstances. On the day of Aidan's funeral the only serving member of the British army, Private Ian Thain, convicted for the murder of an Irish person, Kidso

Reilly, was set free after serving just over two years of a life sentence. He returned to active service (in fact he was never discharged from the British army). Holden was subsequently released and was charged before a military tribunal with not taking proper care of a weapon and was disciplined. He was later discharged on medical grounds and is a free man.

THE GIBRALTAR MURDERS

Introduction

On 6 March 1988 Mairéad Farrell, Dan McCann and Seán Savage were shot dead in Gibraltar by members of the British army's elite regiment, the SAS. While all three were members of the IRA they were all unarmed and could have been arrested. Indeed, independent witnesses stated that Mairéad, who was shot eight times, and Dan, shot five times, had their hands up in surrender when shot. Witnesses to Seán's killing – he was shot sixteen times – said he was given no chance to surrender and was shot as he lay on the ground. In all three instances the scientific evidence pointed to the fact that all three were finished off on the ground.

These killings had all the hallmarks of other Shoot-to-Kill deaths carried out by the British security forces in Northern Ireland. The families of the dead decided to challenge these killings through the courts. Justice was not forthcoming through the British legal system, so seven long years later their case was heard by the European Court of Human Rights in Strasbourg, France.

The court in a landmark decision found that Mairéad Farrell, Dan McCann and Seán Savage had been unlawfully killed, that the British government was guilty of having breached Article 2 of the European Convention of Human Rights, the Right to Life. In its judgement the court stated that the actions of the authorities lacked 'the degree of caution in the use of firearms to be expected from law enforcement personnel in a democratic society'.[1]

The British government responded angrily to the verdict. The Deputy Prime Minister, Mr Michael Heseltine stated: 'If we were faced with similar circumstances as those in Gibraltar, I have not the slightest doubt the same decisions would be taken again'.[2]

There is an eerie postscript to this case. Exactly a year later a young Irishman, Diarmuid O'Neill, was shot dead by the British security forces in a house in London. He too was unarmed and the authorities employed the same excuses for his death as they did when they murdered the three in Gibraltar. Within Relatives For Justice we firmly believe that the British government carried out the O'Neill killing with pre-meditation, as a bloody act of defiance against the highest human rights court in Europe, the European Court of Human Rights.

The Gibraltar Killings

On Sunday the sixth of March 1988 at 3.41pm my sister Mairéad Farrell and a companion Dan McCann were shot dead in Gibraltar. Seconds later, Seán Savage who was approximately 100 metres behind them was also gunned down. The killings were carried out by members of the British army's elite regiment, the SAS.

While all three were on active service for the IRA at the time of their deaths they were, however, all unarmed. They were in Gibraltar planning an attack against British army personnel. Since November of the previous year, both the British and Spanish authorities had been aware that such an attack was being planned. And on 6 March the three had been closely followed by the Spanish police as they travelled in two separate vehicles to Gibraltar from Marbella.

The Spanish police have stated since the killings that they informed their British counterparts that all three were unarmed and were not in possession of any explosive devices. It is worth noting that the day following the killings the British government in parliament thanked the Spanish for their co-operation.

The Actual Killings

At 12.30pm Seán Savage drove into Gibraltar in a white Renault 5 car. Indeed, he entered the colony using a passport in the name of Coyne, which was known to the authorities. He parked the car in a parking area where on the following Tuesday a British army band was to assemble. He did all this under the watchful eye of the British military.

My sister and Dan McCann crossed the border at 2.30pm and met Seán Savage near the parked car. They then set out to return to Spain with Dan McCann and Mairéad walking together. Seán Savage, who was following behind them, turned at a road junction and walked back again in the direction of the town centre, away from the border.

As the pair passed a petrol station a police siren sounded and they turned to see at least two armed SAS soldiers in plain clothes approach them. According to one of the principal independent witnesses, Carmen Proetta, who lives in a flat overlooking the garage, both Dan and Mairéad raised their hands in surrender. Despite that the soldiers opened fired.

Carmen Proetta was discovered not by the police but by a researcher working for Thames Television which was making a programme on the shootings entitled *Death on the Rock*. The researcher believed Ms Proetta's evidence because it coincided with another account she had received from a person who did not wish to come forward publicly.[3]

Ms Proetta told Thames television, 'They [security forces] didn't do anything ... they just went and shot these people. That's all. They didn't say anything, they didn't scream, they didn't shout, they didn't do anything. These people were turning their heads back to see what was happening, and when they saw these men had guns in their hands they put their hands up. It looked like the man was protecting the girl because he stood in front of her, but there was no chance. I mean they went to the floor immediately, they dropped'.[4]

Another independent witness Stephen Bullock who was 150 yards from the shooting saw Dan McCann falling backwards with his hands at shoulder height. The gunman was about four feet away. At the inquest into the killings Mr Bullock, a lawyer by profession, stated, 'I think with one step he could have actually touched the person he was shooting'.[5]

Both Carmen Proetta and Stephen Bullock gave further evidence, along with a third witness Josie Celecia, whose flat faces the petrol station, that the soldiers fired on Dan McCann and my sister as they lay on the ground.

The scientific evidence presented by the pathologist Professor Alan Watson at the inquest corroborated this evidence. Mairéad had been killed by three bullets fired into her back – at a distance of a few feet according to the forensic evidence – all of the wounds were within two and a half inches of each other. The upward trajectory of the bullets meant that the gunman was either kneeling and shooting upwards or that my sister was on the ground or close to it when these shots were fired. These three shots were the fatal ones. Mairéad had died from gunshot wounds to the heart and liver. She had also head wounds, but these were superficial. Professor Watson believed she had first been shot in the face and then in the back. In other words, even after initially shooting Mairéad in the face she was still alive and could have been arrested. In total she was shot eight times.

The pathologist further believed that Dan McCann had been first shot in the jaw. This had stunned him and then the lethal shots 'when he was down or very far down' were fired. Dan had two entry bullet wounds in his back which were again close together. The trajectory of the bullets were also upward. He had an entry bullet wound at the top left back of his head, which also strongly suggests he was on the ground when this shot was fired.

The Killing of Seán Savage

At the time Mairéad and Dan were shot Seán Savage was walking in the opposite direction towards the town centre. He was being followed by two members of the SAS (referred to as Soldiers C and D at the inquest) who said they were only five or six feet behind Seán when the shots that killed Mairéad and Dan rang out. According to the soldiers Seán spun round at this point and one of the soldiers claimed to shout a warning and then proceeded to open fire; the second soldier then followed suit.

There were three independent witnesses to this shooting. Diana Treacy told the inquest that she saw two men running towards her. After she was passed by the first one, who was Seán Savage, the second man who had a gun opened fire. She saw this same gunman fire up to five shots into Seán as he lay on the ground.

Another independent witness was a British holiday-maker, Mr Robyn Mordue. In the commotion of the shooting he was knocked to the ground when a woman on a bicycle collided with him. He thought there was a madman on the rampage, as he saw a man who had been walking towards him being shot again and again. He got up and ran behind a car where he was sick. He then looked back at the death scene, but what he saw is not clear. Mr Mordue was a very nervous witness. He had reason to be nervous. Before the inquest his identity was only known by the authorities. Nevertheless, in the weeks leading up to the inquest he received a number of threatening phone calls, 'Bastard ... stay away'. Mr Mordue's telephone number is ex-directory.

Kenneth Asquez was the third witness to this killing. He had alleged in two statements – one hand-written and the other before a lawyer but all unsigned in order to hide his identity – to Thames television that he saw a man with his foot on Seán Savage's chest, firing at him at point blank range. Up until the inquest he had remained anonymous, but he decided to retract this statement. However, Asquez's retraction must be treated with scepticism. As the handwritten statement said, the man with his foot on Seán's chest was wearing a black beret and the shooting was prefaced by the shout 'Stop, it's okay it's the police.' In fact, one of the soldiers who shot Seán had donned a black beret and the shooting had been prefaced with these words. But until the inquest these two facts had not been publicised. At the inquest many observers believed that Kenneth Asquez had also been put under pressure by those who feared the truth. Mr Asquez must surely have feared being vilified by the British gutter press the same way Carmen Proetta had been for telling exactly what she saw. In fact, the Windlesham/Rampton Report records that 'local people were afraid to speak about what they might have seen'[6] to Thames television researchers and that was before Carmen Proetta was slandered.

The scientific evidence produced by Professor Watson was damning. Seán had twenty-nine wounds in what the pathologist described as 'a frenzied attack'. He believed that between 16 and 18 bullets had hit Seán. He had seven head wounds, five of them were presumed to be entry wounds. Our lawyer, Mr Paddy McGrory, showed Professor Watson at the inquest a photograph taken by the police of four circled strike marks within the outline of Seán's head. This was the first time the pathologist had seen this photograph. He was asked by our lawyer whether it seemed as though these four shots had been fired into Seán's head as he lay on the ground. Professor Watson replied: 'Yes, that would be reasonable.'

The rôle of the police in investigating these three killings must be questioned. In the case of witnesses to Seán Savage's death the inquest was told that there were some thirty people who saw the shooting. However, there were only three independent witnesses found and two of them were discovered by the media. The same was true for witnesses to the shooting of my sister and Dan McCann. The police failed, for example, to set up the customary incidents' centres in the vicinity of the killings.

There is in police methodology a universal principle known as the preservation of the scene of the crime. It was applied sparingly in Gibraltar on that day. Within minutes of the killings, the police had ensured that it would be extremely difficult to reconstruct the killings. Spent cartridges were collected without first marking where they had been found. The bodies were removed without first photographing them *in situ*. The bodies of Mairéad and Dan McCann were not chalked around. The killers were not interviewed by the police until two weeks afterwards.

Normal police practice was disregarded just as it was in 1982 when six unarmed civilians were killed in County Armagh, Northern Ireland by an SAS-trained RUC team. There the police, too, failed to preserve the scenes of the shootings. As a result valuable evidence was tampered with and lost. Also the RUC, just like their Gibraltar counterparts, were recalcitrant in the search for eye-witnesses; they too failed to set up the customary incidents' centres in the vicinity of the killings. The similarities between these killings would suggest a set plan for the execution of unarmed dissidents.

In the Gibraltar case the positive obstruction of the establishment of the facts concerning the shootings continued. The pathologist, Professor Watson, was not given the normal co-operation. The hospital had an X-ray machine, which he would need to trace the track of the bullets through the bodies, but it was not put at his disposal. The clothing had already been removed; torn fabric can help determine entry and exit wounds, while the spread of blood stains could indicate whether the three were upright or prone when they were shot. The photographs taken in the morgue were inadequate, the police photographer not being under Professor Watson's supervision at the time.

He was not supplied with surgical assistance. Subsequently he was not given any copies of the ballistic and forensic reports, nor the reports on the blood samples he had submitted in London on his return to Britain. The systematic disruption of routine procedures parallels exactly the persistent refusal to arrest the three suspects at numerous opportunities.

The forensic scientist, David Pryor of the London Metropolitan Police, had also been hampered in his work. The blood soaked clothes had been sent to him in bags. 'The clothing was in such a condition when I received it,' said Pryor, 'that accurate determination of which was an entry site and which an exit was very difficult.'

Another peculiar feature was the fact that the evidence of the pathologist and the forensic scientist, although complementary, did not directly follow one another at the inquest. Instead, Professor Watson testified on 8 September 1988 and Mr Pryor on 27 September, with the result that the significance of the combined evidence was deliberately blurred. What Pryor's evidence did make clear is that the powder marks found on Mairéad's jacket and Seán Savage's shirt indicated the gun that killed Mairéad was fired at her from a distance of three feet, and the gun fired at Seán's chest was at a distance of four to six feet. In other words, the obvious question arising from the scientific evidence, too, was: why were these three unarmed people not arrested rather than killed?

THE BRITISH VERSION

By the time the inquest was held, six months after the killings, the British government had prepared what they saw as a credible story. Despite having publicly praised in the House of Commons the rôle of the Spanish police in the surveillance of the three, the British authorities began to claim that the Spanish had in fact lost track of the three on 6 March 1988 and that their appearance in Gibraltar took the British security forces by surprise. The British authorities believed, the story goes, that the Renault 5 driven into Gibraltar by Seán Savage – supposedly unnoticed – was packed with explosives. On top of that, the security forces were convinced that the bomb was to be detonated by remote control. The soldiers in their testimony claimed that the movements of the three seemed to indicate that they were about to use a 'button job', as they described it in tabloid-speak, and therefore had to be shot to death.

To back up the claim that the Spanish police had lost the three the Gibraltar police tried to present a copy of an alleged statement from a Spanish police inspector, Rayo Valenzuela, supporting this line. Our lawyer objected to its admissibility as the police inspector, who supposedly made it, would not be attending the inquest and therefore would not be available for cross-examination. It now transpires that this document is totally fraudulent. Not only was the statement unsworn, but the English translation delivered to the coroner was even unsigned.

However, a sworn statement does exist and was sent to the Gibraltar authorities. On 11 April 1990 the Spanish Minister of the Interior told the Spanish Senate that a Spanish police officer made a statement for the inquest, which was sworn before a judge. This statement was never presented to the inquest.

Any attempt by our solicitor, Paddy McGrory, to probe into the surveillance operation was made impossible with the issuing of a Public Interest Immunity Certificate by the British government. Nevertheless, this aspect of the official story was exposed when the head of Gibraltar's Special Branch, Detective Chief Inspector Joseph Ullger, gave evidence. He admitted that the authorities had deliberately allowed the three to enter Gibraltar in order to gather evidence for a subsequent trial. It also became apparent that on 6 March a member of the Gibraltar police was present on the Spanish side of passport control with the aliases and passport numbers of the three. So when Seán Savage crossed the border using the known pseudonym in the name of Coyne he was immediately identifiable.

The British gave no real evidence to back-up their claim that the notional bomb in the white Renault would be detonated by remote control. The only fact presented by Mr O, a senior British intelligence officer, was that an alleged IRA arms cache had been uncovered in Belgium and it had contained a remote control device. This had supposedly led the authorities to believe that the Gibraltar bomb would also be detonated in such a way. This has since been shown to have been a lie, because what made the Belgian police believe they had discovered an IRA cache was the fact that the devices for detonating the semtex were not of a remote control variety. The remote control detonating theory totally contradicted what 'official sources' told the BBC on the evening of Sunday 6 March 1988, which referred to a bomb that was 'timed' to kill British army bandsmen on the Tuesday. The following day the Minister of State for the Armed Forces, Mr Ian Stewart, repeated this point on the BBC's *Today* programme.

The other argument put forward by Mr O to explain the flawed remote control theory was that the IRA by employing this device wanted to ensure that there was not a repeat of the Enniskillen bombing in which many civilians were killed. This argument contradicts the view instilled into the SAS soldiers who carried out the killings. They told the inquest that the three at all costs had to be prevented from using the remote control detonator. If the IRA did not want to incur civilian casualties why would they detonate this notional bomb in the Renault 5 car on a Sunday afternoon when only civilians would be injured? Besides, it was scientifically proven at the inquest that the three could never have detonated any bomb supposedly in the Renault from where they were killed. If the authorities were so certain that there was a bomb in the car, why then did it take them several hours to make the area 'safe'? The probable answer to this question is that they simply did not think there was a bomb at all. Soldier G at the inquest testified that he thought there was a bomb in the car. Further information supplied by the British press since the inquest suggests he was accompanied on that day by two better qualified personnel who disagreed with his opinion. Their presence was concealed from the inquest. This suggestion has never been discounted by the authorities.

Nevertheless, according to the four killers, these three people, who were unarmed and did not have a bomb or possess any detonating devices, made threatening movements when they were approached by armed men. Why should they do such a foolish thing? The true answer to this question is that they didn't make any threatening movements. This was revealed to Roger Boulton, the editor of the Thames television programme *Death on the Rock*, by a senior Conservative politician who said: 'Of course there was a Shoot-to-Kill policy in Gibraltar just as we had in the Far East and in Aden'.[7]

In the days immediately following the killings, as we waited for the remains of our loved ones to be brought home, the families had to endure considerable harassment and intimidation from the RUC. For example, on 8 March I was spotted by the police leaving my parents' home by car with my sister's boyfriend. For no reason other than to insult us the RUC stopped my car and began to make obscene sexual remarks about Mairéad. All the other families were to experience similar harassment throughout this period and, in fact, the McCann family continue to this day to be harassed.

The McCanns own a butcher's shop on Belfast's Falls Road and British soldiers regularly shout obscene remarks in at the parents. Dan's brother almost on a daily basis is stopped and abused by British soldiers while escorting his child to school.

But in the days leading up to the funeral the families were visited by an RUC officer who threatened us with dire consequences if we fulfilled the wishes of our loved ones to be buried as members of the IRA.

The remains of Mairéad, Seán and Dan were flown from Gibraltar to Dublin and from there they were to be brought by road to Belfast. From the moment we crossed the border into Northern Ireland the remains were literally kidnapped by the RUC. As we followed behind the RUC jeeps, it was noticeable how they deliberately slowed down when we passed hostile crowds making us easy targets for missiles. When we reached the M1, some ten miles from Belfast, an RUC road-block prevented the relatives from following the cortège. The remains of the three were not brought to their homes until much later.

After approximately 30 minutes, the relatives who were in three cars were allowed to proceed onto the motorway, while the other mourners were made to take another route. On the motorway, we were stopped by the RUC again and held for at least two hours. Many of the relatives were subjected to considerable abuse. Two aunts had accompanied me to meet the remains in Dublin and they stated afterwards that this period, stuck on the M1 surrounded by hundreds of RUC men, was without doubt the most frightening experience of the aftermath, including the gun and grenade attack on the actual funeral.

The actions of the RUC throughout this whole period underlined time and again how sectarian a force it is. It exposed the nonsense of the Dublin government who considered it a breakthrough when they got the assurance of the British authorities that RUC men would accompany the Ulster Defence Regiment, another sectarian body, when on patrol.

Once the remains arrived home only the McCann's household was subject to intense harassment. Their home was literally surrounded back, front and side by British army saracens. Only on the morning of the funeral, 16 March, did they withdraw.

Quite unusual for the funeral of IRA members there was no British army or RUC presence, despite the fact that the families had been threatened with a repeat of what happened at Lawrence Marley's funeral when the RUC saturated the area and had refused to allow the remains to leave the Marley home until the Irish tricolour was removed from the coffin.

Many believe that the absence of the police and the attack carried out by a grenade-wielding gunman in the cemetery was no coincidence. In this attack three mourners were murdered. The killer made his retreat towards the motorway, which runs beside the cemetery. Parked on the motorway was a Ford transit van, and it seemed as though this was the killer's accomplices waiting to help make good his escape. When the killer was overpowered near the motorway, the van quickly left the scene. It was claimed later that this was an undercover RUC van. A number of questions arise: why didn't they intervene to halt the slaughter of mourners and how did the sectarian killer know that there would not be the usual police presence? Many believe that there was direct collusion between the so-called security forces and this murderer.

THE INQUEST
Five independent civil liberty organisations, the International Association of Democratic Lawyers, Inquest, the National Council for Civil Liberties (London), the International League for Human Rights (New York) and Amnesty International – all of which had observers at the inquest – have criticised many aspects of the proceedings and have called for further inquiries into the killings in Gibraltar.

The Amnesty International report stated that the inquest failed to answer 'the fundamental issue ... whether the fatal shootings were caused by what happened in the street, or whether the authorities planned in advance for the three to be shot dead'.[8]

The inquiry by its very nature was not equipped to determine the truth. The British authorities, which might have had an interest in concealing aspects of the truth, had access prior to the inquest and during it to identities of witnesses, their statements or possible statements and were to some extent able, on grounds of availability, to dictate the order of calling some witnesses.

In contrast, our legal advisers had virtually no information except one ballistics' report and a pathologist's report.

Amnesty International in its report expressed its concern 'that the legal representatives of the deceased's families were significantly and unfairly disadvantaged in comparison with the representatives for the other interested parties. The system is inherently weighted against the deceased's families in preparing for cross-examination'. Our lawyer, Mr Paddy McGrory, received the other forensic reports after the inquest began. He did not receive any of the witnesses' statements in advance, and even during the inquest he did not receive the statements made by security force personnel shortly after the incident. Without access to these statements in advance he was not able to cross-examine witnesses on the basis of what other witnesses, who testified at a later stage, said about the same incident. Thus, for example, he was not able to question the soldiers, who testified in the second week of the inquest, about information which was presented in later weeks by police officers and civilian eye-witnesses. He also did not have witnesses' earlier statements to compare with their court testimony.[9]

Our lawyer faced numerous obstacles including for example the price of the court's daily transcripts being increased from 50p to £5 per page. Because the price was so prohibitive our lawyer could not avail of them – not so the British Ministry of Defence.

The use by the British government of Public Immunity Certificates prevented Mr McGrory, our lawyer, inquiring into many matters such as the planning of the operation, including the rôle of the 'accessories before the fact'.

Finally there was the coroner's summing up of the evidence to the jury, in which he told them to avoid an open verdict. By doing this he unduly influenced these eleven men. This is especially true as after six hours of discussion the jury was deadlocked, divided 7 to 4 in favour of a 'lawful killing' verdict. In normal circumstances an open verdict would have been a likely compromise, but this had been ruled out. The coroner then recalled the jury and gave them what seemed like an ultimatum to return a verdict. Two hours later they returned stating that they found, by 9 to 2 – the smallest majority allowed – the killings lawful.

Despite all the disadvantages faced by our solicitor, Paddy Mc-Grory, a man with lifelong experience as a lawyer, he firmly believed that the verdict went against the weight of the evidence, that it was a 'perverse verdict'.

SEVEN YEAR QUEST FOR JUSTICE

The United Kingdom government insisted that the Gibraltar Inquest, despite its fundamental flaws, was the final word on these controversial killings. It consistently thwarted through the use of Public Interest Immunity Certificates any attempt by our families to have our case examined in the Northern Ireland courts.

Eventually we brought our case first to the European Commission of Human Rights and then in February 1995 to the European Court of Human Rights in Strasbourg, France. On 27 September 1995 – seven years and six months after the actual killings – the court found the British government guilty of having unlawfully killed our loved ones. It was a landmark decision, it being the first time that a signatory to the European Convention of Human Rights was found guilty of breaching Article 2 of the Convention, the Right to Life.

The British government said it would 'ignore' the verdict. The Deputy Prime Minister went as far as to say that the government would do the same again. Almost exactly a year after the verdict a young Irishman, Diarmuid O'Neill, was shot dead in very similar circumstances in a house in London.

The stance of the British government must be viewed as quite unacceptable. If Britain continues to refuse to operate within the constraints of law, both national and international, if it continues to refuse to meet its specific obligations with regard to the 'right to life' under the United Nations International Covenant on Civil and Political Rights and the European Convention for the Protection of Human Rights and Fundamental Freedoms, then it must be ostracised and no longer treated as being part of the democratic family of nations.

1 European Court of Human Rights, Judgement, paragraph 212, Strasbourg, France, 27 September 1995.
2 *The Guardian*, 28 September 1995.
3 *The Windlesham/Rampton Report on Death on the Rock*, p. 92, paragraph 85, Faber & Faber, London 1989.
4 *Op. cit.*, p. 53.
5 *Op. cit.*, p. 55.
6 *Op. cit.*, p. 92, paragraph 86.
7 Roger Boulton, *Death on the Rock and Other Stories*, p. 305, W. H. Allen Optomen, London, 1990.
8 *United Kingdom: Investigating Lethal Shootings: The Gibraltar Inquest: Summary*, p. iii. Amnesty International, April 1989.
9 *Ibid.*

Desmond Grew and Martin McCaughey shot by the SAS, 9 October 1990

The phone call shattered the silence of my bedroom. Pieces of sound seemed to shower down around me. To get a call in the night when you are on priestly duty always brings a sense of foreboding of tragedy. Almost in one action I pulled the light-string and lifted the phone. The quiet voice, so quiet, contrasted with the clamour of the phone. 'This is the police. There has been a shooting. A priest is needed. Go out the Moy Road until you come to Trainors' pub. Turn right and go on a mile until you come to a school. There is a road to the right opposite it. Turn down the road and go on until you come to a two-storey white house. There will be police there with a red light. Then you will be brought to the scene of the shooting'. I said I would go immediately.

I looked at the clock. It was a quarter to three. I dressed hurriedly and took the holy oils and blessed sacrament with me.

As I drove out the Moy Road, the silence of the night pressed against me. There was no traffic. Only the heavy stillness of night. I had asked no questions. I thought to myself: Is somebody wounded? Is somebody dead? Who could it be? Then a sudden thought, quickly dismissed, 'Is this a trap? Was it really the police who phoned?'

I followed the directions. I met no car or person. Then as I turned right at the school, a red car halted at the junction coming from the other direction. A man in civilian clothes, but obviously a policeman, called out to me that I was on the right road. The white house soon showed up in the dark and then the waving blood-red light. I was directed by gestures to park my car. A group of uniformed police stood in the shadows. Nobody spoke. There was white tape, familiar sign of an incident, across a lane leading down by another house. A policeman came forward from the other side of the tape and introduced himself to me as an inspector. He was polite and friendly, so different from the sullen phalanx of uniforms I had just passed through. He guided me to the scene, past a farmhouse to an open yard. He told me two men were dead and that one of them was Desmond Grew. There was an open empty mushroom shed, of the old arc-shaped type. It had no frontage. A light was shining inside and there was a white car in it. In front of the shed was an apron yard of concrete. In the half-light I looked down at the black forms of two bodies lying on the ground. The inspector then directed his flash lamp on to them. The two men were lying within a few yards of one another, sprawled out. Beyond their heads, lying on the ground, were two Kalashnikov rifles. I said the Act of Contrition, gave them conditional absolution and anointed them. I recognised Dessie Grew. He was very badly shot in the head. The blood from the heads of the two men was thick and clotted and the dark intestinal-looking brain matter shone slightly red in the poor light. They were dressed in casual denim-like clothes, unmasked. The butt of a pistol protruded from a trouser pocket of Martin McCaughey. All was silence. I prayed at length. The bodies looked so small and thin and even vulnerable in death. We seemed to stand towering over them like giants. Such an impression I have experienced before at scenes of fatal accidents. Perhaps it is psychological, the power of life lording it over death.

I never asked any questions while I was there. I was on a spiritual mission. Anyhow, I knew I would not get answers. I learned, however, that they had been shot at mid-night. What happened? From my experience of writing a book on the SAS, I would ask: Were the weapons discovered and were they staked out? Did the two men come to move the weapons only or to pick them up for an IRA action? Could they have been taken prisoner, considering the soldiers were in a strong superior position? Were they shot without warning, with or without the rifles? Were they shot in cold blood and were the guns then planted beside them? To date, 1997, there has been no inquest and no explanation given. Only the police and soldiers who were present at the shooting know the full truth. Will they tell it?

On my way home my thoughts strayed to a lovely sunny autumn day in 1969. I was visiting the house of the Grew family who then lived in Knockaconey in my parish, a short distance as the crow flies from the scene of this shooting. Mrs Grew was peeling apples at the table. The front door was lying open. Suddenly two schoolboys ran in and pitched their schoolbags in the corner. They seemed delighted to see the priest. They wanted someone on whom they could bounce their ideas and questions. A running commentary on current politics, particularly that of the People's Democracy, flowed from them. I can still see their eager excited faces. Little did I imagine that the same two boys would be shot dead some years later in the 'troubles' which were then just beginning. Séamus was shot dead along with Roddy Carroll on 2 December 1980 in one of the County Armagh 'Shoot-to-Kill' killings that were the subject of the Stalker Report. Both men were unarmed. Desmond was shot dead by the SAS on the night of 9 October 1990.

Memorial to Fergal Caraher, 30 December 1991

On 30 December 1990 Fergal Caraher was shot dead by the British army in his native village of Cullyhanna, County Armagh. His brother Mícheál was severely injured in the same incident. He was twenty years of age, was happily married to his wife Margaret and was the father of a one-year old son, Brendan. His father Peter John, a local farmer, and his mother, headmistress at the local primary school, are highly respected people in Cullyhanna. The nationalist population regarded the killing as part of the Shoot-to-Kill policy of the British government in Northern Ireland. The killing so affected the local community that they formed the Cullyhanna Justice Group in March 1991. With the aid of the Irish National Congress and other groups they organised an inquiry into the shooting. The inquiry, held in Cullyhanna, was made up of five international jurists chaired by Michael Mansfield, QC. Its aim was to inquire into the fatal shooting and wounding and also look at the Shoot-to-Kill policy. Four jurists found that there was ample evidence to charge the soldiers with murder and all the jurists raised questions about the Shoot-to-Kill policy. Mr Mansfield withheld his findings because of news he received from the office of the Director of Public Prosecutions. Twelve days after the launch of the jurists' report two Royal Marines, L. Cpl Richard Elkington (25) and Marine Andrew Callaghan (21), were charged on 5 February 1992 with the murder of Fergal Caraher and with attempting to murder Mícheál Caraher and causing him grievous bodily harm. On 23 December 1992 the two soldiers were acquitted. The soldiers from 45 Commando claimed they fired twenty shots at the brothers' car at a checkpoint to save another soldier they believed was being dragged away on the bonnet of the car driven by Mícheál Caraher. The Lord Chief Justice, Sir Brian Hutton, said he could not rely on the accounts given by the civilian witnesses for the defence or on those given by the accused and Marine B. He said the scientific evidence gave some support to the claim that the soldiers opened fire because the car hit Marine B and carried him off on the bonnet. He said he had to acquit them because he had a reasonable doubt of their guilt.

Reporting on their work over two years, before the trial, the Cullyhanna Justice Group, published the following account of the incident:

'On Sunday 30 December 1990, the car of Dr Donal O'Hanlon broke down in the South Armagh village of Cullyhanna. As he tried to fix it, two locals, Liam Murphy and Mícheál Caraher, drove past and, seeing him in difficulty, stopped and assisted him in trying to restart the car. Oliver McArdle, a qualified mechanic, arrived and succeeded in fixing the car. Oliver and the doctor then left.

'As they drove off, Mícheál's brother Fergal drove up in his white Rover. He got out to pass the time of day to his friend and brother. A patrol, consisting of four member of the British army, appeared and began questioning the three. They asked their names and addresses and checked the registration number of both cars. The patrol then left.

'After a brief discussion the three agreed to go to Dundalk in Liam Murphy's car. Fergal decided to leave his car in the car park of the local bar, the "Lite 'n' Easy".

'As Liam followed behind he remembered that he was to leave his car with his wife who was in the local shop a few hundred yards past the car park. He explained the problem to Mícheál. He told him he would drop him off at the car park where he could tell Fergal that they would take the white Rover and he himself would meet them further down the road. Approaching the car park, both cars were waved through a British army checkpoint.

'When he parked his car Fergal was approached by a soldier. Mícheál then arrived to tell his brother of the new arrangements. Fergal asked the soldier, 'Are we right?' The soldier nodded. Mícheál decided to drive the car. He pulled out of the car park. Several of the soldiers then opened fire on them without warning. Both brothers were hit within seconds of each other. Mícheál, seeing the condition of his brother, continued driving in an effort to find a doctor. Liam Murphy and Jimmy Quinn, who had heard the shots, followed the car and found it about half a mile down the road.

'Fergal Caraher was pronounced dead at 4.20pm on arrival at Daisy Hill Hospital, Newry. Mícheál was rushed to the Royal Victoria Hospital, Belfast, where he underwent emergency surgery.

'That night the British army, through the RUC, released a statement implying that the car had failed to stop at the checkpoint and that two members of the British army patrol had been knocked down, one of whom was carried some distance by the car.

'The next day several eye-witnesses made statements to a local solicitor contradicting the British army's statement of events. At the funeral of Fergal, his father made a public statement that the family was not satisfied with the statement from the authorities. He called for an independent public inquiry'.

Unveiling of Memorial to Fergal Caraher, Fr Raymond Murray, 30 December 1991

This evening we have gathered together to remember, in a loving and spiritual way, Fergal Caraher aged 20 years shot dead by the British army Royal Marines Regiment a year ago today. In the same shooting his brother Mícheál was severely injured. Tragedies come to us as they came to God's own Son unbidden and unwanted. A tragedy is an occasion for deep and anguished faith. In the past year Fergal's parents, wife and brothers and sisters have had to offer to God a weight of grief and tears. Our prayer for them throughout the year has been that the Spirit of God's consolation would enfold them in his loving arms and strengthen their faith in the immense happiness, glory light and joy that surrounds Fergal in the everlasting life. May eternal light shine upon him.

Whilst we tread our pilgrim way here on earth we must live in charity, truth and justice. The great torch light procession we have seen here tonight not only reflects the 345 people killed by security forces but all the deaths. The death of any human person diminishes us all. We are all aware of the great mountain of suffering of all bereaved people in this sad and too long a conflict. There is an emphasis, however, this evening on this category of deaths by government forces because the tight control of media by the British government authorities attempts to hide the truth that more than half of these 345 deaths were unjust killings and sometimes murder. There has been no redress or justice for the families of victims of government killings. The cover-up not only includes senior officers in their forces but also civil servants, judiciary bodies and elements in the British cabinet.

On the night of 14 August 1969 John Gallagher was shot dead by 'B' Specials in Armagh. The Scarman Tribunal was able to unravel the facts relating to this fatal shooting. Justice was not done. Twenty-two years later no one has been charged with this unjust killing. The rot set in then and the government has followed a policy of lies and cover-up in similar shootings. It is my belief that there is a government policy not to injure the morale of their security forces and so the crimes of army and police are covered up and they receive protection. The only time they weaken in their resolution is when the media shames them into cosmetic action by the sheer weight of facts. Would six members of the Parachute Regiment have been charged with the killing of two teenagers and the wounding of a third a year after the incident if a BBC *Panorama* programme had not highlighted the facts to the public? Seventeen people including eight children have been killed by rubber and plastic bullets fired by lethal weapons and over 100 have been seriously injured. Any other government would hang its head in shame at these unnecessary and tragic criminal acts and would withdraw the use of these death-dealing missiles. The plastic bullet gun has never been used in riots in Britain. This underlines the contempt the British government has for the Irish people.

The Irish people should strongly urge that front-line regiments like the marines and paratroopers should not be sent in the rota of British forces service in Ireland. The build-up to the shooting of Fergal Caragher was a litany of harassment, verbal abuse, beatings and threats to the lives of citizens. This was tolerated by RUC authorities. Inevitably it ended in tragedy. The same scenario of pre-killing harassment was evident in the run-up to the shooting by the paratroopers of unarmed people like Brian Smith in Belfast and the teenage joyriders in 1990.

British forces have shot armed people when arrests could have made due to control of a situation. This happened for example at Coagh, Loughgall, and Drumnakilly.

There is a long list of men, women and children, unarmed persons who have been unjustly killed and some murdered.

Most sinister are the shootings of Catholics by loyalists acting in collusion with security forces like Loughlin Maginn and Pat Finucane. In the past two years 14 people have been murdered in the south Derry/east Tyrone region by loyalists. Collusion is suspected. The success rate of the RUC in charging people for these murders is nil. That must be the worst statistic for vigorous investigation of any police force in the world. The murders of Catholics by loyalists in the Craigavon region and the absence of prosecutions there tells a similar story.

Add to these deaths the killings by the SAS, an assassination squad acting outside the law and the vulgarity of praise bestowed on them by government ministers for their bloody deeds.

Public opinion should call on the British government as a democratic right to have the law changed so that the Deputy for Public

Prosecutions should give his reasons for his decisions not to prosecute in cases of disputed killings. We must be able to see behind the scenes what is going on. This is a matter of charity, truth and justice so that we can bring peace to our country.

The serious problem that the police force in Northern Ireland is drawn from only one section of the community must be faced. London and Dublin should set about setting up a second level police force which will also draw from the nationalist community; it is up to them to work out a solution to the complexities involved.

In the absence of fair play at home we must seek international help on the occasion of every fatal shooting carried out by the security forces. In that line the Cullyhanna community has to be commended for bringing Fergal Caraher's death to the attention of the world. Their new-found expertise will be welcomed in other areas of the north. Furthermore we must encourage the non-governmental human rights' bodies to set up teams of experts – legal, medical and forensic who will fly quickly to emergency situations here and give immediate help to local communities in their investigations, since they have no trust that the RUC vigorously and urgently carry out investigations into the shootings of people by the security forces.

The system of coroners' inquests must be urgently reformed. They are unfair. Bereaved relatives are denied elementary standards of justice. The families should have access to legal aid to secure proper legal representation. They are unable to penetrate the veil of secrecy surrounding information on how their loved ones came to die. Because the outcome can influence subsequent civil or criminal proceedings the government authorities make sure they have a strong legal team. The dice is loaded against the relatives. A campaign to reform the system of inquests is necessary in the name of justice so that the public can have an idea for themselves that proper investigations are taking place and chances of a cover-up can be avoided. For bereaved families inquests in the north of Ireland lead to distrust and give minimum satisfaction.

Shoot-to-Kill and Collusion, 1990–94

This is an extract from the pamphlet *Collusion 1990–1994: Loyalist Paramilitary Murders in North of Ireland* published by Relatives for Justice, 1995. It lists murders committed by loyalist paramilitaries 1990–1994 and specifies those caused by South African weaponry.

For twenty-five years the counter-insurgency methods of the British government in Northern Ireland has involved a Shoot-to-Kill policy, in direct ambushes when both innocent victims and suspects have been shot dead without warning, and in a sinister indirect campaign of murder which involves manipulation of loyalist paramilitaries who are provided with security information and who then kill with the knowledge that they are free from prosecution. This policy is pursued by small groups of RUC personnel and British army and the secret intelligence network of MI5 and MI6. A section of the Northern Ireland administration is aware of this policy, protects it by withholding information, insincere cosmetic investigation, non-prosecution and curbing of inquests. The families and friends of the victims not only suffer the insult of cover-up and lies but they often become targets for harassment and abuse from the British army and the RUC. They seek redress in publicising the truth to the world and will not cease to bring their grievances before governments and international human rights' bodies.

This Shoot-to-Kill policy has already been outlined in *The SAS in Ireland 1969–1989* (Raymond Murray) and in a pamphlet entitled *State Killings* (Raymond Murray) published by Relatives for Justice. The policy became a virtual campaign in the 1980s.

From the time of Sam Marshall's death in Lurgan on 7 March 1990 until John O'Hanlon's death on 1 September 1994, loyalist paramilitaries have killed 185 people (3 others not in these figures were killed by an RUC member in a Sinn Féin office in Belfast in 1992). Of the 185 killings 168 of them were sectarian or political in motive. The remaining 17 deaths were internal and non-sectarian. There were also over 300 attempted killings and other attacks during the same period. In 103 of the sectarian/political type killings there is evidence of some form of collusion between loyalist paramilitaries and the security forces.

The RUC informed some of the victims that their personal details, contained in official British Intelligence files, were in the hands of loyalist paramilitaries. Some victims were killed by loyalist gangs with members of the security forces in their ranks. Some were killed by weapons reportedly stolen from members of the security forces before their deaths. Some were killed by weaponry acquired by loyalist paramilitaries with the assistance of a number of British Intelligence agents, Brian Nelson being the best known of these. Nelson, when he appeared in court in January 1992, was suspected to have played a vital rôle in 10 murders and the targeting of a further 16 people who were later murdered or wounded. An apparent deal was made and he was convicted of less serious offences.

Brian Nelson received a 10-year sentence in February 1992 for his rôle in loyalist violence. He was a British military agent. He was also the UDA's intelligence officer, responsible for setting up people to be killed. He had unlimited access to security forces intelligence documents on nationalists and republicans. Such information was supplied to the UDA by himself or by security forces sympathetic to loyalist paramilitaries. The effects of Nelson's work in refining the UDA's intelligence department is still being felt.

'The legacy is that since Nelson's arrest another 6 people have been killed and 3 injured. These people's names were among the 369 found in Nelson's possession at the time of his arrest'. (BBC Panorama Programme *The Dirty War 1992.*)

The rôle of Nelson and other British agents in assisting loyalist paramilitaries to acquire an arms shipment from South Africa has had a great impact on loyalist violence. The significance of the South African weaponry to loyalist death squads, and how they acquired it, was exposed in a report on BBC's *Insight Ulster* on 28 January 1993. British intelligence services alleged a breakdown of their own intelligence and surveillance. The shipment, it was reported, had been monitored by British Intelligence from South Africa to the north of Ireland, but a breakdown occurred when it arrived and they lost trace of it. The report pointed out how the South African weapons have enhanced the killing capacity of loyalist paramilitaries, revealing that before the arrival of such sophisticated weapons loyalist killers were more likely to have used home-made machine-guns, sawn-off shotguns and old revolvers.

The murders in Cappagh, at the mobile shop in Craigavon, the Hyster factory in Lurgan, the Ormeau Road and Oldpark 'bookies', and Castlerock, the pub massacres at Greysteel and Loughinisland, were all carried out by loyalists using weaponry imported from South Africa. They also used them in many individual killings. In fact from the Milltown killings in March 1988 to the slaughter of six men watching a football match on television in a public house at Loughinisland, County Down, in June 1994, all loyalist multiple killings have been carried out with South African weaponry.

Note the following comparison. In the six years before the arrival of these weapons, from January 1982 to December 1987, loyalist paramilitaries murdered 71 people of whom 49 were sectarian/political. In the six years following, from January 1988 to 1 September 1994, loyalists murdered 229 people, of whom 207 were sectarian/political.

Brian Nelson was arrested in January 1990, following the investigation of Cambridgeshire Chief Constable John Stevens into the leaking of security forces' intelligence files. The UFF had boasted that they used security forces' intelligence files in the murder of Loughlin Maginn in August 1989. Stevens ended his inquiry in May 1990. In his report he was able to conclude 'that members of the security forces have passed on information to paramilitaries' and that 'there was no organised campaign of leaks'.

But, if his recommendations were introduced, he said, 'then there is every hope that future collusion between the security forces and paramilitary groups will be eradicated'.

Among the 83 recommendations of John Stevens were the blurring of copies of files when files were photocopied and a system to identify user access to computer records on suspects. Amnesty International in a statement following the release of people charged with possession of leaked files in October 1990 said, 'It is obvious from all the evidence that collusion remains a fact of life and that the government is not prepared to confront it'.

The belief of Amnesty International that the Stevens inquiry was a failure can be seen in the continuing evidence of security forces' intelligence files going missing and ending up in the hands of loyalist paramilitaries.

The continuing flow of security forces' intelligence files to loyalist paramilitaries led to the return of (now Northumbria) Chief Constable John Stevens to Northern Ireland in August 1993. As in September 1989, the content of his investigation was not disclosed. A report on the second investigation was sent to the Director of Public Prosecutions (DPP) in February 1994. In July 1994 the DPP asked Mr Stevens to make further inquiries. The DPP's request, it was reported, was made following an examination of the findings of Mr Stevens' recent inquiry. To date there has been no indication of charges being brought.

Amnesty International in reports published in 1993 and 1994 again criticised the British government and the RUC for their handling of the collusion issue and for their failure to establish an independent inquiry.

The Nelson case focused on another suspicion of the nationalist community, namely, that British troops patrolling nationalist areas have had on occasions a rôle in loyalist attacks. In the murders of Gerard Slane and Terence McDaid in 1988, both of whom were set up by Nelson, relatives claimed there was suspicious activity by the security forces near their homes prior to the loyalist attacks. Gerard Slane's home was raided by the security forces two weeks before his death. Both families believed the activity of the security forces was a reconnaissance in preparation for the loyalist killings.

The most common accusations of collusion concern the removal of checkpoints, some of which were in place before loyalist attacks. Some areas where loyalist attacks have taken place have witnessed saturation levels of security forces patrolling and searching prior to attacks. The suspicion of collusion was supported in January 1993 by remarks made by their commanding officer in the north, Sir John Wilsey. When asked what was his attitude to employing agents like Nelson and the morality thereof, he replied that he was 'certainly not ashamed of Nelson's rôle'.

Information and weaponry are not the only forms of collusion between the security forces and loyalist paramilitaries. During the period covered by this article, 51 serving and former security forces' members were charged or convicted of terrorist-related offences rang-ing from illegal possession of arms to murder.

Political and clerical leaders in the Catholic community and their local press have criticised the security forces' lack of response to appeals for adequate protection. Loyalist death squads have used the same routes again and again to enter nationalist areas and to flee after murders. Lanark Way off the Springfield Road in West Belfast was opened in the summer of 1986 and, despite it being used as an escape route by loyalists in eight murders and numerous attempted killings, it was not closed until the murder of Philomena Hanna in April 1992. She was the ninth victim of loyalist violence. North Howard Street, Rosapenna Street and the Donegall Road are other examples where persistent pleas for closure of thoroughfares used by loyalist death squads have been ignored.

A recent example of security forces ignoring requests by Catholics for protection occurred on the night of 27 April 1994 in west Belfast. Paul Thompson and a friend were in a car and were making a U-turn at the bottom of Springfield Park, which is a cul de sac. Unknown to both men, loyalist gunmen had gained access to the street through a hole in the pallisade fencing which was part of the 'peace line'. The gunmen opened fire on the vehicle killing Paul Thompson and wounding his friend who saved his life by driving away. One of the first on the scene was a woman resident of Springfield Park. She had noticed the hole in the fencing earlier that day and, realising the danger (there had been at least 16 murder attempts in the Upper Springfield Road area in the previous three and a half years), telephoned the RUC and the Northern Ireland Office immediately. She was told by those who received the calls that the matter would be looked into and resolved as soon as possible. But the fence was neither repaired nor security in the area increased. Several hours after her plea, as she stood at the front door, she witnessed what she feared might happen, the murder of an innocent person. ·

This inadequacy of the security forces in protecting nationalists was revealed again in the failure of British army and RUC bases, despite sophisticated surveillance equipment, to detect, deter or arrest loyalist murder gangs. The murders of Sam Marshall in Lurgan and Thomas Hughes, Martin O'Prey, James Carson, Kieran Abrams, Joseph McCloskey and Seán Monaghan in Belfast, are examples where the gangs responsible could have been observed by security forces in their bases. There are other examples of this situation in a number of attempted killings.

Another persistent complaint of nationalists concerns the failure of the security forces to respond promptly to some killings and attempted killings by loyalists. When they arrive on the scene their reaction has been misdirected. It is often nationalist areas which feel the brunt of follow-up operations rather than the areas to which the killers escaped. There have been murders and attempted murders where there have been no follow-up operations. Relatives and friends of the victims of loyalist violence have complained about the bad behaviour of security forces arriving in the aftermath of a murder or attempted murder. Their conduct at the scene of the Sinn Féin office killings, the Peter McTasney killing in Bawnmore estate, the Seán Anderson murder near Pomeroy, and the murder of Theresa Clinton in Belfast was insulting and oppressive. Funerals of some of the victims of loyalist violence have been disrupted by an undue heavy force of RUC and British army presence either around the family home while the body was waked or at church and graveyard. Mourners have been stopped, searched and on occasions abused. Mourners at the funerals of Thomas Donaghy, Kilrea, Kevin McKearney, Moy, and Conor Maguire and Mark Rodgers in Belfast were severely harassed.

RUC forensic teams investigating killings and attempted killings have sometimes failed to remove all relevant material from the scene of the incident. The bag, with spent shells inside, used by the RUC member who murdered three people in the Sinn Féin office on the Falls Road, was found in the office after the forensic team left the scene. Similarly, after the forensic team left the home of teenager Gerard O'Hara, having spent a number of hours in the house, bullets fired by the gunmen were found in the living-room where the young man was killed. One of the bullets had blood on it.

RUC forensic teams have been reluctant to disclose the ballistic history of weapons used by loyalists. In the mid-Ulster and north Armagh areas demands for this information by nationalist politicians and others have been ignored. When information has been released, it has tended to be general rather than specific. For example, following the murder of four men in Cappagh, County Tyrone, on 3 March

1991, the RUC confirmed that the weapons had been used before in seven killings in two years in the Lurgan, Stewartstown and Cookstown areas, but they did not specify which killings. 'It is not our policy to give the history of firearms for evidential reasons' was how an RUC spokesman responded to a demand for information on the weapons used to kill Tommy Casey in October 1990 near Cookstown. This attitude contrasts with the release of the ballistic history of weapons used by republican groups. The most recent example followed the shooting of Jimmy Brown in Belfast by the IPLO in August 1992. Within hours of his death the media had a full record of the weapon used to kill Brown and previous victims.

Catholic complaints about the British army and the RUC in regard to their attitude to loyalist violence may be summarised as follows:

1. Failure to respond to nationalist demands for protection.
2. How do RUC and British army bases fail to detect or deter loyalist murder gangs when they enter Catholic areas since they are equipped with sophisticated surveillance apparatus?
3. The response of the RUC after loyalist attacks is slow and complacent.
4. Injury is added to injury when the RUC and British army oppress Catholic areas following loyalist attacks. They do not direct their attention to the areas into which the loyalists have escaped.
5. There have been incidents when there have been no follow-up operation of the RUC.
6. British army and RUC have sometimes insulted and abused the families of the victims and have beaten and insulted mourners at funerals of their murdered relatives even when the funerals have had no paramilitary trappings.
7. RUC forensic teams have been wilfully negligent or incompetent in gathering evidence at the scene of murders carried out by loyalists paramilitaries.
8. The RUC is selective in releasing ballistic information in regard to killings. Prior to court cases it releases the history of weapons used by republican paramilitaries but withholds such information in regard to loyalist paramilitaries and of course state forces.

Collusion Unveiled

On 20 March 1998 investigative journalists John Ware and Geoff Seed, with Alasdair Palmer, published an article in *The Sunday Telegraph* unveiling documntary evidence that the British army colluded in murder with Brian Nelson. They called it assassination by proxy. A combination of Nelson's diaries and the British army's records show in their estimation that Nelson was involved in 15 murders, 15 attempted murders and 62 conspiracies to murder. Secret files provide evidence that the British army's Force Research Unit (FRU), a branch of Military Intelligence responsible for running agents in Northern Ireland, was associated with murders carried out by the UDA between 1987 and 1990. The documents are secret records of meetings between FRU and Nelson, commonly known as 'contact records'. The theme of the article is that British army handlers planted Nelson in the UDA, provided him with detailed profiles of republicans, and directed him to refine the UDA's wide target of 'any Catholic will do' to 'taking out' republicans. This was a return to the tactics of the 1970s when army intelligence under the name of the Military Reaction Force had recruited 'pseudo gangs' to assasinate 'republicans'. The return to such a risky course of action followed the thwarting of the 'Shoot-to-Kill' policy by the Stalker report. The journalists claim that Nelson was paid £28,000 a year by the British army. In the article they highlighted the attempted murder of Alex Maskey, Sinn Féin councillor, and the murders of Gerard Slane at 4.15am on 23 September 1988 and of Terence McDaid on 10 May 1998. Nelson organised and planned Slane's murder, providing the assassins with his address, picture and logistics of surveillance. Slane was suspected by the UDA of having links with a republican paramilitary group. The evidence was flimsy. Nelson checked out Slane's photograph with people who witnessed the murder of a UDA associate, William Quee. Two of these said he might have been the gunman but they were not sure. This was one of the killings which prompted Nelson's British army handler to write, 'his targeting information is already of a high quality and recent attacks have proved this accurate'.

Nelson also suggested Declan McDaid as a target to a UDA assassin called 'Winkie' Dodds. He believed he had a republican link. He provided Dodds with a photograph but mistakenly gave the address of McDaid's brother Terence. The UDA murdered Terence McDaid who had absolutely no association with the IRA. The army handler placated Nelson when he discovered his mistake by telling him that Terence McDaid had been 'traced as Provisional IRA.'

The journalists expand on Nelson's background. He was born in 1947 and grew up on the Shankill Road, Belfast. He joined the Black Watch regiment when he was seventeen. Within five years he was discharged, officially on medical grounds but, as they say, 'he had been absent without leave and was known to be wild and reckless'. He joined the UDA in the early 1970s. He was sentenced to seven years imprisonment in 1974 after his conviction of kidnapping and torturing a partially-sighted Catholic. After his imprisonment he rejoined the UDA but at the same time offered to work for British army Intelligence. He went to work in Germany in 1985 after being involved in shootings. In 1987 Colonel J of the Force Research Unit asked him to return. He was then planted in the UDA once more to target IRA activists. Naturally he became their chief intelligence officer since he had access to security files. The journalists speculate that there had been a 'battle between the army and M15 as to who was to secure his services'. Of course M15 was fully aware of Nelson's trip to South Africa to ship arms to the loyalists in January 1988.

In 1992 the BBC *Panorama* team in a programme drew on a 90,000 word account which Nelson wrote on his work for the military Force Research Unit.

It was the UDA themselves who laid Nelson open to discovery when they could not resist boasting of the excellence of their intelligence following the murder of Loughlin Maginn at his home in Rathfriland, County Down, on 25 August 1989. They published a confidential security force file on Maginn. Public opinion forced the RUC to hold an inquiry. It was led by the Deputy Chief Constable in Cambridgeshire, John Stevens. The army warned Nelson not to reveal to the inquiry that he worked for them. They called in Nelson's entire collection of intelligence 'P cards' which they had helped to compile lest he should hand them over to the inquiry. Stevens first report concluded that the leakage of intelligence was occasional material available to every policeman and soldier. Then Nelson's fingerprints, traceable from his criminal records, were found on confiscated leaked documents. The inquiry team planned to arrest him on 11 January 1990. Nelson, obviously tipped off, fled to England the evening before. That same night, by an extraordinary coincidence, many of the inquiry team's statements and documents were destroyed by fire in their office within a secure area of Carrickfergus RUC complex. On his return to Belfast, Nelson was arrested. He revealed that he was an army agent. It was only when Stevens's deputy, Detective Chief Superintendent Vincent McFadden, threatened to arrest senior army officers on a charge of obstruction of justice that the 'Contact Forms' written by Nelson's handlers were handed over. Colonel J, head of FRU, told the inquiry that the policy was to use Nelson to persuade the UDA to target republicans rather than just Catholics. He indicated that the protracted time it would take the UDA to gain intelligence could give the army enough time to warn the RUC Special Branch who was at risk and thus save lives. 730 intelligence reports, he said, which identified threats to 217 individuals, had been passed to the RUC. The RUC denied the value of this information. One Special Branch superintendent testified that, 'I have been asked if I can name an individual whose life was saved as a result of Nelson's information and I cannot'. Special Branch officers testified that only two cases received from FRU were specific enough to anticipate an attack and put preventive measures into action. One of these intended victims was Gerry Adams. Notes of Nelson's army handlers show that in at least 92 cases FRU knew who the UDA was going to murder.

The Stevens team compiled a second report. It was never published. John Ware and his associates wrote, 'In that report, it set out the evidence that the army's Force Research Unit had colluded with the UDA in targeting members of the Provisional IRA. The file was passed to the DPP, Northern Ireland. In consultation with Sir Patrick Mayhew, then the attorney general, it was decided not to prosecute Colonel J or any of Nelson's army handlers: only Brian Nelson was to be charged. In the event, there was no trial. Nelson was persuaded to plead guilty to five charges of conspiracy to murder. In a hearing in 1992 before a judge on the length of his sentence, Colonel J once again stressed that he believed that Nelson's intelligence had enabled his unit to pass on to Special Branch reports that identified 217 individuals. The judge at the hearing accepted this. In sentencing Nelson he said that he gave special weight to the fact that he passed on what was possibly life-saving information in respect of 217 individuals.

Nelson was sentenced to ten years imprisonment. He was released in 1997. The article continues, '(He) is now believed to be living with financial assistance from the army. But his legacy continues. Nelson distributed his "P" cards to several other Protestant paramilitary groups, which may have used them in the planning of assassinations. Colonel J was awarded the OBE. Some of Nelson's handlers have been promoted and given medals. One went on to give lectures on "agent handling" to Military Intelligence.'

The *Sunday Telegraph* says that the Force Research Unit, set up for the sole purpose of running agents in Northern Ireland, had no authority to mount such an operation. It consisted of around 50 officers and soldiers and ran more than 100 agents. It was disbanded in 1990 after Stevens' second report. It suggests that it was reconstituted under another name.

The editorial in the paper on 29 March 1998 was critical of the British army 'No less than the police or the judiciary in Northern Ireland, the army has always been expected to observe the due process of law: soldiers face trial for murder if they fail to follow the procedures laid down for the lawful use of lethal force. Indeed, it is this belief in legality which has helped draw a completely unambiguous distinction between the necessary use of force by soldiers and the murderous violence of the terrorist gangs. It is this basic distinction which army intelligence jeopardised by colluding with loyalist paramilitaries and taking sides in the conflict. Those officers involved demeaned the moral authority of the crown. Their defence was little more than a moral fig-leaf: that, since the UDA was going to kill people anyway, it should kill identifiable republican terrorists, rather than randomly selected Catholics. But even judged by their own supposedly military criteria, Nelson's handlers failed abysmally.'

The Death Toll caused by South African Weaponry, 1988–94

The consignment of illegal weapons that British agents and UDA Intelligence Officer, Brian Nelson, had been instrumental in acquiring from South Africa arrived in the north of Ireland in January 1988. It consisted of 200 AK47 automatic rifles, 90 Browning 9mm pistols, c.500 fragmentation grenades, 30,000 rounds of ammunition, a dozen ROG7 rocket launchers and an unknown number of warheads. Because of Nelson's position within the UDA, he also knew the storage locations of the weapons. On 8 January 1988, 60 AK 47 automatic rifles, 31 pistols, 150 grenades and 11,000 rounds of ammunition were recovered near Tandragee from the UDA. On 5 February 1988, 38 automatic rifles, 15 pistols, 100 grenades, one RPG7 rocket launcher, 26 warheads and 40,000 rounds of ammunition were recovered on the northern outskirts of Belfast from the UVF.

Since 1988, over 30 AK47 rifles, 3 RPG7 rocket launchers and a number of grenades have been recovered in other finds, including some from the Ulster Resistance Movement. Some of these weapons had already been used by loyalists to kill nationalists. Loyalist paramilitaries, therefore, still possess a significant amount of the initial consignment. BBC's *Insight Ulster* programme on 28 January 1993, dealing with the South African weapon consignment, reported that British Intelligence services attributed the fact that loyalist paramilitaries had received the weapons to a breakdown of their own intelligence and surveillance services. The weapons shipment, the report continued, had been monitored by British Intelligence from South Africa to the north of Ireland, but a breakdown occurred when it arrived in the north. They lost trace of it.

Speakers from South Africa made a deep impression on the delegates at a conference held in Belfast, 6–8 June 1995, entitled Reconciliation and Community: The Future of Peace in Northern Ireland. Members of Relatives for Justice held discussions with Mr Dullah Omar, the South African Justice Minister during his visit. Mr Peter Madden, legal representative of Relatives for Justice, travelled to South

Africa in June 1995 to present a submission on their behalf to the Cameron Commission on arms trade. I went to South Africa in November 1995 and met with Dr Alex Boraine, Justice in Transition Minister, to seek details of the Truth and Reconciliation Commission in South Africa and explore the possibility of the murders from South African weaponry in Northern Ireland being included also under that commission. Mr Martin Finucane followed up the South African contacts with a visit to South Africa in March 1998.

The Relatives for Justice submission was made at the same time as a Sinn Féin submission presented by Brian Currin (Lawyers for Human Rights) and Gregg Nott (Bell Dewyer and Hall, Johannesburg). The submissions were made in week two of the hearings which related specifically to 'procedures' which were under consideration for application to any future domestic arms trade policy which might be introduced by the government. The submissions were well received. Both were the only submissions from outside the country made orally.

The use of South African arms by loyalists in Northern Ireland to murder Catholics between 1988 and 1994 was sanctioned by the British government.

The pamphlet Collusion 1990–1994: Loyalist Paramilitary Murders in the North of Ireland *contained a list of killings that can be attributed to imported weaponry from South Africa. I am indebted to Arthur Fegan for his research.*

Submission of Relatives for Justice to the Cameron Commission

Submission to Cameron Enquiry into Alleged Arms Transactions between Armscor and one Eli Wazan and other related matters appointed by President Mandela on 14 October 1994.

The submission is made by a number of families of those persons who were murdered by weapons allegedly shipped from South Africa to Northern Ireland by loyalists in 1988.

We are concerned that the 1988 shipment may have been only the first of a number of shipments made and that further shipments may have been made between 1988 and 1994 (See our pamphlet *Collusion 1990–1994* enclosed herewith). Details of arms shipments from South Africa to Northern Ireland were disclosed by several investigative journalists. Shortly after the weapons arrived in Northern Ireland in 1988 there was a clear upsurge in the use of weapons allegedly supplied from South Africa.

According to the investigative journalist Ed Moloney of the Dublin-based newspaper *The Sunday Tribune,* Brian Nelson, a British soldier working undercover in Northern Ireland, established links in 1985 with South Africa to set up an arms deal involving the purchase and shipment of a large supply of arms and ammunition for use in the murders of Catholics in Northern Ireland.

At the time Nelson was both a member of the British army under direct command of an officer of colonel rank and a senior intelligence officer in the UDA (Ulster Defence Association, the main loyalist group) [see *The Sunday Tribune* 26 January 1992].

A plan to forge links with loyalists and the South African government was established in order to transport weaponry originating from Armscor to loyalists in exchange for missile technology from the north of Ireland. The plan was that the South African government would obtain the technology for use in its wars with neighbouring African states and the loyalists would receive an arms arsenal of modern weaponry for its war against the IRA (Irish Republican Army) and the republican movement and for its ongoing terrorist campaign against the general Catholic population in Northern Ireland. It is suspected that, since the British government could not be seen to supply the loyalist groups directly, they used the South African arms industry and its international arms dealing policy to sanction the supplies of weapons to loyalist groups in Northern Ireland.

In April 1989 three loyalists and a South African government official were arrested in Paris along with an international arms dealer. It was alleged in the press that they were all involved in a conspiracy to exchange missile technology being developed in Belfast for arms shipments from South Africa. As a result of this, it is our concern that arms shipments were made subsequent to 1988.

In September 1989, as a result of a public outcry about collusion between British security forces and the loyalists, the British government set up an enquiry into collusion headed by John Stevens who was then deputy chief constable of the Cambridge constabulary. Stevens submitted a report of which only a part was made public.

Nelson was arrested in Belfast in January 1990 by police officers working for Stevens and was charged with the murder of Catholics and plotting to murder political opponents of the British government.

Two investigative journalists, John Ware and Geoffrey Seed, revealed that Nelson had spoken to them before and after his arrest. Both journalists obtained a 'jail diary' from Nelson and spoke to him at length about his rôle as a member of the British army and as a member of the UDA group responsible for hundreds of murders in the north of Ireland. Ware and Seed produced the BBC *Panorama* programme on collusion which was broadcast in February 1990, after Nelson's arrest but researched in 1989.

Ware and Seed wrote an article for the London newspaper *The Independent* in January 1992, shortly before Nelson's trial, in which they indicated that Nelson would disclose his actual rôle as both British soldier and UDA intelligence officer as part of his defence (see *The Independent* 9 January 1992).

At Nelson's trial in Belfast, in February 1992, he plea-bargained a ten-year prison sentence in return for the dropping of the murder charges. A plea in mitigation was entered and it was not necessary for him to give evidence. It was admitted by the British attorney general's counsel that Nelson was an important link between the British army and the UDA, since he was a member of both organisations at the same time.

It was further admitted that he was responsible for the selection and targeting of republicans and Catholics but had not supplied information to his superiors about many of the plots. This formed the substance of the charges against him.

The British attorney general, through the British army colonel who was Nelson's superior officer and who was called as a witness at his trial, attempted to convince the court and the public that Nelson's rôle was one of supplying information to his superiors so that steps could be taken to save lives. But Nelson's rôle, both as undercover soldier and UDA intelligence officer, raised suspicions in Northern Ireland that he was not put in place in Northern Ireland by the British authorities to prevent murders of Catholics by the UDA but to set up and murder those persons who were considered enemies of the state by the British. The use of the UDA to murder military and political opponents of the British as well as random Catholics in a reign of terror was a clever tactic which made it difficult to blame the British directly for the murders. No documentary evidence was presented to the court to prove that Nelson's rôle was benevolent.

Nelson was responsible for the murder of Patrick Finucane, a leading civil rights lawyer in Northern Ireland. Patrick Finucane was shot dead by the UDA in February 1989. He was murdered with a British army owned Browning pistol.

Pat Finucane represented many people who had been bereaved as a result of the use of lethal force by the British security forces. He also represented the families of those persons murdered by loyalists where there was evidence of collusion. He represented many families who are members of Relatives for Justice and who instructed him to get redress from the British government. He represented families at inquests and initiated legal proceedings to recover compensation for the bereaved families. He attempted to get the truth surrounding the murders of many people who were murdered by loyalists where there was widespread belief that the RUC (Royal Ulster Constabulary) were colluding in those murders by supplying information and arranging safe passage for the loyalist assassins. He also represented the families of many people who were murdered directly by the British security forces.

For upwards of a year before his murder members of the RUC threatened that he would be shot dead by loyalists.

Three weeks before Patrick Finucane's murder, the British government minister Douglas Hogg said in the British House of Commons on 17 January 1989: 'there are in Northern Ireland a number of solicitors who are unduly sympathetic to the cause of the IRA' and he went on to say ... 'I state it on the basis of advice that I have received, guidance that I have been given by people who are dealing in these matters ...'

Nelson detailed his involvement in the murder of Patrick Finucane at his trial and gave more details to Ware and Seed.

It is suspected by many people in Ireland and abroad that Patrick

Finucane was murdered on the direct order of the British government and that the order was conveyed to Brian Nelson who carried it out.

The British government has so far refused to hold an enquiry into the death of Patrick Finucane even though they have been accused of complicity and a large number of distinguished individuals and organisations have called for a full judicial enquiry into his death. (See the report of the New York based Lawyers Committee for Human Rights, *Human Rights and Legal Defence in Northern Ireland: The Intimidation of Defence Lawyers, The Murder of Pat Finucane*).

As far as the remit of your enquiry is concerned we would ask you to investigate the area relating to arms shipments from South Africa, particularly those shipments having their origin at Armscor for the period 1988 to date.

We suggest that there is at least a *prima facie* case that arms from South Africa were used to murder Catholics in Northern Ireland from at least 1988 and that there may be a current arrangement to supply arms whenever required by loyalists. Catholics have been murdered by these weapons as lately as 1994.

There are a number of lines of enquiry which we suggest could be initiated in South Africa:

1. Enquiries could be made to determine if Brian Nelson entered South Africa in 1985 or at any time between then and 1990. Were there any official or unofficial contacts with him by the South African authorities? Was his visit to South Africa the subject of South African government surveillance? Is there any official record of his visit?

2. The records of arms shipments in 1988 could be checked to determine if a shipment similar to that described by Mr Moloney in *The Sunday Tribune* left South Africa during that year for any destination, i.e., 200 AK47 rifles, scores of Browning pistols, 500 splinter grenades, rocket launchers and tens of thousands of bullets.

3. Enquiries could be made about the persons named in the Sinn Féin pamphlet *Brian Nelson & the Re-arming of the Loyalist Death Squads* (enclosed herewith) as to their alleged rôle in the affair.

There are a number of lines of enquiry which could be initiated in Northern Ireland and Britain:

1. The British government authorities could be asked for details of all weaponry captured or used in attacks against Catholics which have a South African origin or which fit the description of the weapons described by Mr Moloney. Even weapons of a foreign manufacture could have been purchased in South Africa. Those details will be retained by the RUC.

2. British government documents could be supplied to your commission to determine the extent of the connection between Brian Nelson and his rôle in the South African arms shipments from military documents from his superior officers.

3. The RUC could be directed to supply your enquiry with ballistics and other forensic reports in certain specific cases (see *Collusion 1980-1994* by Relatives for Justice enclosed herewith).

4. Those parts of the secret Stevens report which relate to a South African connection between loyalist collusion with British security forces and the South African arms suppliers could be revealed to your enquiry.

5. The families of those murdered by South African weaponry could be consulted to obtain more detail of inquest and other court documents.

6. The journalists who have reported on the affair could be consulted to obtain further details and any documents in their possession could be examined.

Court records in Belfast and Paris could be inspected to determine the extent of the conspiracy. We are asking that your commission carry out a proper detailed investigation into this very serious matter in an attempt to bring those involved to justice and to set up procedures to ensure that there are safeguards in place to prevent as far as possible a recurrence of any link between South African arms and the murder of Catholics in Northern Ireland.

We think that we are entitled to enquire if arms from your country were used to murder our loved ones. We think we are entitled to know if the British government through Brian Nelson was involved either directly or indirectly in those murders.

We are confident that with the new spirit of truth and reconciliation which now prevails in South Africa that our submission will not go unheard. We too are part of a country in transition. We seek the truth in these matter so that no one, not even those in high places in sovereign governments, can escape liability for human rights abuses. Only when all parties to a conflict can accept their own share of responsibility for that conflict, can true healing and lasting reconciliation take place.

Representatives of the Relatives for Justice are willing to attend any hearing in South Africa to expand on this submission if necessary and to meet any members of your commission which may travel to Northern Ireland if it is considered necessary to gather evidence material to the investigation.

Enclosed with this submission:

1. *Human Rights and Legal Defence in Northern Ireland: The Intimidation of Defence Lawyers, The Murder of Pat Finucane*: Lawyers Committee for Human Rights (New York).

2. *Collusion 1990–1994*, Relatives for Justice.

3. *Brian Nelson & the Re-arming of the Loyalist Death Squads* (Sinn Féin, Belfast).

4. *The Independent*, extract 9 January 1992.

5. *The Sunday Tribune*, extract 26 January 1992.

6. *The Sunday Tribune*, extract 9 February 1992.

FURTHER SUBMISSION TO THE CAMERON COMMISSION OF ENQUIRY BY RELATIVES FOR JUSTICE, BELFAST, NORTHERN IRELAND
We understand that a hearing into proposed procedures for the implementation of government policy in relation to international arms dealings will be held in Capetown later this month.

We refer specifically to page 10 of our previous submission sent on 5 June 1995.

We cannot and would not attempt to dictate policy to the South African government in relation to any of its affairs.

We express no view as to the moral or ethical questions arising from the manufacture and international trade in arms.

We are only concerned to ensure that innocent people are not murdered due to the unlawful purchase and transportation of those arms.

There is a widespread belief in Northern Ireland and beyond that

South African arms have been used in the past to murder innocent people in Northern Ireland. We have set this out in our first submission. Although there is at present a cease-fire in force in our country, no proper negotiations have yet taken place between the parties to our conflict. The weapons referred to in our first submission remain in the hands of loyalist armed groups. We are hopeful that the question of removing these and all other weapons from those involved in the conflict will be addressed in future negotiations.

If there is any basis for our belief that the arms in question originated in South Africa, and that may be a matter for investigation or enquiry under a different remit, then we would implore the South African government to establish safeguards to ensure that arms transactions are conducted according to law and that international standards are applied.

We know that you are in a period of transition and that you have a difficult task to perform, but we only want to ensure that our people are protected in any future policy which may be implemented by your government.

We know that the majority of your people deplore the use of South African arms for the murder of innocent people.

We know that you are aware, as we are, that those who have no regard for the law or for the right of a people to live in peace without threat will ride roughshod over constitutions, laws, regulations and procedures to accommodate their own political expediency and they will find weaknesses in any system of control or supervision.

It is for that reason that we ask that particular care is taken to ensure that procedures will be established which will prevent as much as possible any future unauthorised transactions by unauthorised persons. We ask that such weaponry, if sold and transported, is carefully regulated and monitored to ensure that it arrives at their authorised destination and that proper identifying marks are applied to ensure that if allegations of improper dealings are made, then meaningful enquiries can be undertaken to establish the validity of any such allegations.

We know that our plea will not go unheard by your people and we wish you well in your very difficult task of formulating policies which accommodate the views of all your people and which must also comply with the basic requirements of human rights so that a harmonious and peaceful society emerges.

List of Murders by Loyalists Attributed to South African Weapons

From January 1988 until 13 October 1994, the date of the loyalist paramilitaries' ceasefire, loyalist death squads have carried out 207 sectarian murders.

The following list of fatalities are some of the killings that can be attributed to weaponry imported from South Africa.

16 March 1988. Thomas McErlean (20), John Murray (26), and Caoimhín Mac Brádaigh (30). Milltown Cemetery, Belfast. Browning 9 mm pistols and grenades. UDA/UFF.

15 May 1988. Damian Devlin (24), Paul McBride (27), Stephen McGahon (27). Shot in pub, Union Street, Belfast. AK47 rifles. UVF.

25 July 1988. Brendan Davison (33). In his home, Markets, Belfast. AK47 rifles. UVF.

8 August 1988. Séamas Morris (18) and Peter Dolan (25). On street, Ardoyne, Belfast. AK47 rifle. UVF.

24 November 1988. Phelim McNally (20). In brother's home, Coagh, Co. Tyrone. AK47 rifle. UVF.

14 February 1989. John Davey (61). Near home, Gulladuff, Co. Derry. AK47. UVF.

10 March 1989. Jim McCartney (38). Springfield Road, Belfast. AK47. UVF.

19 March 1989. David Braniff (63). In home, Alliance Ave, Belfast. AK47. UVF.

29 November 1989. Liam Ryan (39), Michael Devlin (33). Public house, Ardboe, Co. Tyrone. AK47. UVF.

7 March 1990. Samuel Marshall (31). In Kilmaine Street, Lurgan, Co.

Armagh. AK47. UVF.

25 April 1990. Brian McKimm (22). In Limehill Grove, Ligoniel, Belfast. AK47. UDA/ UFF.

4 June 1990. Patrick Boyle (60). In home, Annaghmore, Co. Armagh. AK47. UVF.

26 October 1990. Thomas Casey (60). Kildress, Cookstown, Co. Tyrone. AK47. UVF.

8 November 1990. Malachy McIvor (43). In garage, Stewartstown, Co. Tyrone. AK47. UVF.

5 January 1991. Gervase Lynch (26). In home, Magheralin, Co. Armagh. AK47. UVF.

27 January 1991. Seán Rafferty (44). In home, Rosapenna Court, Belfast. Browning 9 mm pistol. UDA/UFF.

3 March 1991. John Quinn (23), Dwayne O'Donnell (17), Malcolm Nugent (20), Thomas Armstrong (50). Cappagh, Co. Tyrone. AK47 rifles. UVF.

4 March 1991. Michael Lenaghan (46). Found shot in taxi, Heather Street, Shankill, Belfast. Browning 9 mm pistol. UVF.

28 March 1991. Eileen Duffy (19), Caitríona Rennie (16), Brian Frizelle (29). Near mobile shop, Craigavon, Co. Armagh. Browning 9 mm pistol. UVF.

17 April 1991. John O'Hara (41). In taxi, Dunluce Ave, off Lisburn Road, Belfast. Browning 9 mm pistol. UDA/ UFF.

25 May 1991. Eddie Fullerton (56). In home, Buncrana, Donegal. Browning 9 mm pistol. UDA/UFF.

12 August 1991. Pádraig Ó Seanacháin (33). In cab of van, Killen, Castlederg. AK47. UDA/UFF.

16 August 1991. Martin O'Prey (28). In home, Lower Falls, Belfast. Browning 9 mm pistols. UVF.

13 September 1991 Kevin Flood (31). In street, Ligoniel Road, Belfast. Browning 9 mm pistol. UVF.

25 October 1991. Seán Anderson (32). Near home, Pomeroy, Co. Tyrone. AK47 rifle. UVF.

14 November 1991. Desmond Rogers (54), Fergus Magee (28), John Lavery (27). Coming from work, Lurgan, Co. Armagh. AK47 rifle. UVF.

22 December 1991. Aidan Wallace. In public house, Finaghy Road

North, Belfast. Browning 9 mm pistol. UDA/UFF.

3 January 1992. Kevin McKearney (32), killed, Jack McKearney (69), wounded. In shop, Moy, Co. Tyrone. Jack McKearney died of wounds 4 April 1992. Browning 9mm pistol. UVF.

9 January 1992. Philip Campbell (28). In mobile chip shop, Moira, Co. Down. Browning 9 mm pistol. UDA/UFF.

5 February 1992. Peter Magee (18), James Kennedy (15), Jack Duffin (66), William McManus (54), Christy Doherty (52). In betting shop, Ormeau Road, Belfast. AK47 rifle and Browning 9 mm pistol. UDA/UFF.

4 March 1992. James Gray (39). In cab of his lorry, Portadown. AK47 rifle. UVF.

29 March 1992. Terence McConville (43). In home, Barn Street, Portadown. Browning 9 mm pistol. UVF

29 April 1992. Conor Maguire (22). At work, Ligoniel, Belfast. AK47 rifle. UVF.

6 September 1992. Charlie Fox (63) and Theresa Fox (53). In home, Moy, Co. Tyrone. AK47 rifle, Browning 9 mm pistol. UVF.

27 September 1992. Gerard O'Hara (18). In home, North Queen Street, Belfast. Browning 9 mm pistol. UDA/UFF.

14 November 1992. John Lovett (72), Frank Burns (62), Peter Orderly (50). In betting shop, Oldpark, Belfast. AK47 rifle and grenades. UDA/UFF.

19 November 1992. Peter McCormack (42). In public house, Kilcoo, Castlewellan, Co. Down. Browning 9 mm pistol. UVF.

20 December 1992. Martin Lavery. In home, Upper Crumlin Road, Belfast. Browning 9 mm pistol. UVF.

3 January 1993. Patrick Shields (51) and Diarmuid Shields (20). In home near Dungannon. Browning 9 mm pistol. UVF.

28 January 1993. Martin McNamee (25). At work, Kildress, Cookstown, Co. Tyrone. Grenade booby trap. UVF.

11 February 1993 Thomas Molloy (32). In home, near Loughgall, Co. Armagh. AK47 rifle. UVF.

24 March 1993. Peter Gallagher (44). At work, Grosvenor Road, Belfast. Browning 9 mm pistol. UDA/UFF.

25 March 1993. James McKenna (52), James Kelly (25), Gerard Dalrymple (52), Noel O'Kane (20). At work, Castlerock, Co. Derry.

Browning 9mm pistol. UDA/UFF.

25 March 1993. Damian Walsh (17). At work, Twinbrook, Belfast. Browning 9 mm pistols. UDA/UFF.

1 May 1993. Alan Lundy (39). In street, Andersonstown, Belfast. AK47 rifle. UDA/UFF.

2 June 1993 Brendan McKenna (29). In cab of lorry, near Comber, Co. Down. AK47 rifle. UDA/UFF.

8 August 1993. Seán Lavery (21). In home, Lr Antrim Road, Belfast. AK47 rifle. UDA/ UFF.

1 September 1993. James Bell (49). In street, Short Strand, Belfast. Browning 9 mm pistols. UVF.

12 October 1993. Joseph Reynolds (40). In workmen's bus, east Belfast. Browning 9 mm pistols. UVF.

26 October 1993. James Cameron (54) and Mark Rodgers (58). Killed in place of work, Andersonstown, Belfast. AK47 rifle and Browning 9 mm pistol. UDA/UFF.

30 October 1993. James Moore (81), Karen Thompson (19), Steven Mullan (20), Joseph McDermott (60), Moira Duddy (59), John Moyne (50), John Burns (54), and from injuries received Samuel Montgomery (76) in April 1994. In public house, Greysteel, Co. Derry. AK47 rifle and Browning 9 mm pistol. UDA/UFF.

5 December 1993. Brian Duffy (15), John Todd (31). In taxi cab, Ligoniel, Belfast. AK47 and shot-gun. UDA/UFF.

14 April 1994. Theresa Clinton (33). In home, Lr Ormeau Road, Belfast. AK47 rifle. UDA/UFF.

26 April 1994. Joseph McCloskey (53). Killed in home, New Lodge Road, Belfast. Browning 9 mm pistols. UDA/UFF.

27 April 1994. Paul Thompson (25). In friend's car, Springfield Park, Belfast. AK47 rifle. UDA/UFF.

8 May 1994. Rose Ann Mallon (70). In sister's home near Dungannon. AK47 rifle. UVF.

17 May 1994. Éamon Fox (40), Gary Convey (24). At place of work, North Queen Street, Belfast. AK47 rifle. UVF.

17 June 1994. Cecil Dougherty (30), William Corrigan (32). At place of work, Rathcoole, Belfast. AK47 rifles. UDA/UFF

18 June 1994. Barney Greene (87), Éamon Byrne (39), Patrick O'Hare (35), Adrian Rogan (34), Don McCreaner (59), Malcolm Jenkin-

son (52). In public house, Loughinisland, Co. Down. AK47 rifles. UVF.

10 August 1994. Harry O'Neill (60). In place of work, off Castlereagh Road, Belfast. Browning 9 mm pistol.

There have also been many attempted killings using such weaponry which have resulted in serious injuries.

The Search for Truth, 1994

Preliminary thoughts on a Campaign for the Right to Truth, 1994

We are now in a period of transition, if we accept the permanency of the present cease-fires. Such transition has parallels in South American countries, South Africa and post-communist régimes.

The transition period here is called the peace process. It may be useful to accept that peace is founded on truth, justice and charity. Commissions for Truth were established with some success in some other countries during a period of transition. A Commission for Truth in a transition period must not delay in making investigations. It has to be independent and credible. It would demand considerable talent and resources. Secondly, will effective urgent investigations, prosecution and sentencing continue in the likelihood of an 'amnesty'?

It will be in the interest of the three warring parties in the conflict, republicans, loyalists and the state, to draw a line through the violations of human rights of the past twenty-five years, including killings and murders. There will probably be a *de facto* undeclared amnesty. This will be connected with phased demilitarisation on all sides, the release of prisoners, no serious investigation or prosecution of those linked with killings in the past twenty-five years, the return to the north of those on the 'wanted' list, the delivering up of missing bodies. Immunity to further prosecution will include not only those responsible for casualties of war (members of state forces, paramilitaries and innocents caught in shootings and bombings) but also those who carried out blatant sectarian murders.

There is no hope, I think, of a powerful Commission for Truth unless it is agreed on by the Irish and British governments and the political parties who sit around the negotiation table. But paramilitaries and the state excuse the crimes they commit themselves – all maintain a high moral ground, the state, of course, the highest. It will be in the interest of all political sides to agree on an unspoken amnesty. A Commission for Truth goes against that.

Even though it is highly improbable that the negotiators will even contemplate such a commission, the proposal to set one up should be put in writing to the two governments and the proposal published. At least that establishes publicly the principle that concerned citizens do not want a cover-up. In the absence of a Commission for Truth, is there a substitute?

1. The very question of the necessity for the search for truth should at least be put before the public. The pursuit of truth re events of the last twenty-five years is something positive. Truth helps a peace process and has healing effects; in countries where this has not happened trauma remained and serious difficult political situations followed.

2. Justice and truth groups should attempt to put on record in the next few years the many violations of human rights that occurred here.

(a) In 1973 Penguin books published *Political Murder in Northern Ireland* by Martin Dillon and Denis Lehane. Malcolm Sutton has recently written *An Index of Deaths from the Conflict in Ireland 1969–1993*. It would be helpful to have a combination of the type of material in these two books, an expansion on the 'index' giving more details of the deaths and whether or not prosecutions took place. Besides information in newspapers, magazines, books already published and radio and television documentaries, there is a wealth of information to be gathered from the victims' families, from living witnesses and from solicitors' papers; if these sources are not tapped in the next few years, vital evidence will be lost.

(b) Individual books or in-depth studies on Bloody Sunday and many other killings by the state forces should be published. The Relatives for Justice hope to record in picture and story the deaths of all the children in the 'Troubles'. A lot of writing has still to be done on collusion; at some time in the future members of the secret British forces will break rank and give part of the inside story. A detailed study has still to be written on the failed system of inquests in Northern Ireland.

(c) Even though, as I believe, there will be an unspoken but *de facto* amnesty, organisations and individual families should still pursue cases of state killings and sectarian killings of obviously innocent people in their homes and places of work. If, despite pressure, the police do not carry out vigorous investigation, it may be necessary for solicitors to have recourse to civilian actions and international bodies.

(d) Although the urgency in the transition period is to deal with truth, a new civil rights movement will be necessary to work for justice in the long term: justice re security, legal justice, social justice, equality of treatment, parity of esteem. Part of this campaign should be the revoking of all emergency laws, the establishment of a restructured police force, strict regulations re the appointment of judges, magistrates and coroners.

In October 1994, awaiting the setting up of a governmental Commission for Truth, a Campaign for the Right to Truth was initiated after consultation with and support of the following bodies:

1. Relatives for Justice
2. United Campaign against Plastic Bullets
3. Bloody Sunday Justice Group
4. Cullyhanna Justice Group
5. Casement Accused
6. Voice of the Innocent – Ballymurphy Seven
7. The Pat Finucane Centre, Derry
8. The Dublin–Monaghan Justice Group.

THE AIMS AND OBJECTIVES OF THE CAMPAIGN FOR THE RIGHT TO TRUTH

Introduction
At a time when people are engaged in a process of healing and understanding, we believe that peace must be based on truth, justice and

charity. Without these, political agreement will almost certainly be impossible. We note that whereas paramilitary organisations and political parties associated with them in Ireland have indicated their regret and remorse over their contribution to the deaths and suffering of innocent people, the British government refuses to acknowledge or apologise for the deaths and suffering of innocent people it has caused.

The Campaign for the Right to Truth seeks to win an acknowledgement by the British government that over the past twenty-five years it acted unlawfully and unjustly on many occasions.

We believe that victims of state violence and the public have the right to know the truth about the actions of the state and its agencies. We believe such an acknowledgement will have enormous moral power and help secure a better future for ourselves and our children. We believe that as victims and as citizens we have the right to know fully what injustices were done by the state and its representatives. Only when we know the truth can we identify the remedies needed to secure that these things never happen again.

We believe that the right to truth is:

(a) the inalienable right of all citizens.

(b) historically and ethically necessary for every society.

(c) necessary for the emotional healing of our people and the process of building a just society.

(d) essential for full freedom of expression for both the individual and the media.

(e) necessary to maintain the dignity and identity of the dead and of those who have suffered.

OBJECTIVES

The Objectives of the Campaign for the Right to Truth are:

1. A full, public, comprehensive and binding acknowledgement by the British government that many of the activities carried out by the state and its representatives were unlawful. In particular this includes murder, collusion with paramilitary organisations to commit unlawful acts, including murder, the unlawful imprisonment and detention of those innocent of any crime, and the use of violence, torture, inhuman and degrading treatment.

2. A full identification of those responsible for authorising and carrying out such unlawful acts.

3. The right of access to all information concerning unlawful acts carried out by the state and its representatives.

4. A complete independent investigation into all unlawful acts by the state and its agents.

On 11 April 1995 the Campaign for the Right to Truth made oral submissions to the Forum for Peace and Reconciliation in Dublin Castle, 11 April 1995. Those who made the submissions were: Fr Raymond Murray (Introduction), Mrs Emma Groves (Plastic and Rubber Bullets), Tommy Carroll (The Armagh Killings), Eilish McAnespie (The Execution of Aidan McAnespie), Alice O'Brien (Collusion: The Dublin and Monaghan Bombings), Martin Finucane (The Murder of the Human Rights Lawyer Pat Finucane), Jim Kelly (Miscarriages of Justice: The Casement Accused).

The following is the submission of Martin Finucane.

The Murder of the Human Rights Lawyer Pat Finucane

This submission is based on the proposition that the reconciliation between the people of Ireland will not be possible until issues relating to the abuse of basic human rights are addressed by both governments in their search for political agreement between unionists and nationalists as to the future structure of government of the island as a whole.

Pat Finucane was the Catholic solicitor who was shot dead in front of his wife and three children on 12 February 1989. He was born on the Falls Road in Belfast in 1949 and was a student at Trinity College Dublin in 1969 when his family in Belfast was forced out of their home by loyalists at the start of the present 'troubles'. He pursued his studies at Trinity and, upon completion of his degree, returned to Belfast and commenced his study of law, eventually qualifying as a solicitor. He began to practice in 1979.

Throughout his short career he represented many people, Protestants and Catholics and anyone who requested his services. He turned no one away. He was known, however, for his fearless representation of nationalists and republicans in seeking the protection of law and establishing their rights in a hostile political system which discriminated against such clients since the establishment of the state itself. There is no doubt that his fearless representation caused resentment to the authorities who were attempting to paint a picture to the outside world that any complaints of human rights abuses in the north of Ireland were not only unfounded but were in fact part of a widespread propaganda campaign by those intent on destabilising the state. Pat Finucane was murdered on 12 February 1989 by the loyalist paramilitary group the UFF (UDA) directed by the British army agent Brian Nelson. Brian Nelson was also a member of the British army.

Pat's murder followed shortly after the remark made by Douglas Hogg in the House of Commons on 17 January 1989. Hogg said, 'There are in Northern Ireland a number of solicitors who are unduly sympathetic to the cause of the IRA' and he went on to say, 'I state it on the basis of advice that I have received, guidance that I have been given by people who are dealing in these matters.'

The murder was passed off by British government officials as just another sectarian killing carried out by lawless thugs. Tom King, the Northern Ireland Secretary of State at the time, said that Pat Finucane was murdered by 'the other side', implying that loyalists had attacked a republican in the on-going sectarian 'troubles'. In February 1993, the New York based Lawyers Committee for Human Rights, published *Human Rights and Legal Defence in Northern Ireland: The Intimidation of Defence Lawyers, The Murder of Pat Finucane*. It states that the 'Lawyers Committee mission found credible evidence suggesting collusion between elements within the security forces and loyalist paramilitaries in the Finucane murder.'

Pat Finucane's murder was no 'ordinary' sectarian murder. Pat Finucane was murdered because he defended those who were seen as enemies of the state. He was murdered because he was successful in many challenges to British authority in the north.

The British government was at war with the IRA and the republican movement. The loyalist paramilitaries were allies of the British government in this war. They carried out attacks against those enemies of the state as well as against ordinary Catholics. The work of Pat Finu-

241

cane encapsulated the widespread abuses of British rule in the north of Ireland during the present 'troubles'.

Loyalists undoubtedly murdered Pat Finucane. But was the murder sanctioned by the British government?

Was it planned by the British military and carried out as directed by British soldier, Brian Nelson?

Why did Douglas Hogg make his statement in the House of Commons on 17 January 1989, three weeks before Pat's murder?

Why did he refuse to give any further details when pressed to do so?

Who were the advisers he referred to? Did the RUC, whose officers threatened to have Pat Finucane murdered by loyalists, advise Douglas Hogg?

In short, what is the connection between RUC death threats to Pat Finucane, Douglas Hogg's statement, Brian Nelson's rôle in the British army and the murder of Pat Finucane?

Is the fact that he was murdered with a British army gun just a coincidence? Is there a connection?

Why does the British government refuse to hold a public judicial inquiry into the murder of Pat Finucane when there is great public concern both in Ireland and abroad about their rôle in his murder?

Why does the British government refuse to give reasons for refusing to hold such an inquiry?

Are Douglas Hogg and his advisers and Brian Nelson and his superiors reluctant to give evidence at such an inquiry?

Are they reluctant to submit to cross-examination?

In order to achieve lasting peace in Ireland, reconciliation between the two traditions on the island is essential. Loyalists must sit down with republicans eventually. Unionists must sit down with nationalists eventually. A framework for the future government of the island of Ireland must be agreed between the two traditions eventually, otherwise the conflict will never be resolved. However, there are unresolved deaths of civilians caused by British soldiers and policemen which require satisfaction.

The compliance with internationally recognised documents enshrining fundamental rights and freedoms is a matter for governments. The right to life is the most important right of all and the investigation of deaths involving government agents must also be carried out in compliance with internationally recognised norms.

The British government must address the issues raised as it is obliged to do. It must answer questions asked and investigate properly any death which the public at large attributes to them or to their servants or agents. No satisfactory resolution of the conflict can be achieved until all these matters are dealt with satisfactorily.

POSTSCRIPT: In October 1997 Mr Dato Param Cumaraswamy, the United Nations special reporter on the independence of judges and lawyers, paid a ten-day visit to Britain and the north of Ireland to investigate complaints and to look into the killing of Pat Finucane. At the end of his visit he said there 'seemed to be truth' to the allegations by defence lawyers in the north that they had been subjected to harassment and intimidation by police officers and that the RUC made threats through the lawyers' clients while they were in RUC interrogation centres. Mr Cumaraswamy accused the RUC of not treating the situation seriously. He called for an independent inquiry into Pat Finucane's murder. Suspicion of security force involvement had 'not been allayed'. There were serious suspicions that the state knew the lawyer was a target and did not fulfil its duty to protect him. He said his final report would be submitted to the UN Commissioner on Human Rights in 1998.

Cumaraswamy's report on Northern Ireland, published as an addendum to his fourth annual report (98 paragraphs) on 5 March 1998, called for an independent judicial inquiry into Pat Finucane's killing which he details at some length. He also called for an independent and impartial investigation of all threats to legal counsel in Northern Ireland.

In paragraph 21 of his report he writes, 'The Chief Constable (Ronnie Flanagan) alluded to an agenda in which paramilitary organisations ensured that detainees remain silent and alleged that solicitors may be involved in conveying this message to the detainees. Further he stated that there is in fact a political divide in Northern Ireland and part of the political agenda is to portray the RUC as part of the unionist tradition. These allegations concerning police intimidation and harassment of solicitors is part and parcel of this agenda. The

Assistant Chief Constable also admitted that during the course of an interrogation an officer may express the view that the solicitor is providing bad advice to the client and not acting in his interest, for instance, by advising the client to remain silent.'

Cumaraswany says that Brian Nelson claims in his prison diary that as early as December 1988 he informed the Force Research Unit of British Military Intelligence that Pat Finucane was targeted. Nelson provided the murderers with a 'P-card' three days before they killed him. The RUC denied that any information regarding the planned murder of Finucane was passed on to them. Stevens has publicly stated that he knows 'absolutely' who killed Pat Finucane. Cumaraswamy wrote to Stevens on 27 November 1997 asking whether the military knew that the killing of Finucane was planned by the loyalists and if so, did the military inform the RUC. If they did not tell the RUC, then why not, and why did the military not warn Finucane/or provide protection for him? If the RUC was told, why was Finucane not provided with police protection or warned of the threat?

Stevens replied on 14 January 1998: 'As you will be aware the reports submitted by me are the property of the Secretary of State for Northern Ireland and the Chief Constable of the RUC. I am therefore not in a position to release the reports or indeed divulge any of the contents. The reports are highly classified and the authority of the above persons will be required before information is released'.

3,171 VICTIMS IN NORTHERN IRELAND;
14 AUGUST 1969 TO 31 DECEMBER 1994

Deaths due to Republican activity (excluding 1ac, 2ac, 8ac)

	Cath	Prot	Total
3a Civilians killed in explosions	76	106	182
4a Civilians killed in cross-fire and accidents	47	16	63
6a Civilians assassinated by Republicans	161	382	543
9a Civilians killed in riot situations	0	12	12
	284	**516**	**800**

Deaths due to Loyalist activity (excluding 1bc, 7bc, 8bc)

	Cath	Prot	Total
3b Civilians killed in explosions	100	18	118
4b Civilians killed in cross-fire and accidents	2	4	6
6b Civilians assassinated by Loyalists	614	173	787
9b Civilians killed in riot situations	30	4	34
	746	**199**	**945**

Innocent Victims of Security Forces

	Cath	Prot	Total
4c Non-involved people killed accidentally	5	3	8
5c Non-involved people killed deliberately	111	19	130
	116	**22**	**138**

Deaths due to military/paramilitary activity
(Included: Republicans v. Security Forces
   Loyalists v. Security Forces
Republicans and Loyalists killed by their own
   activity, killed in premature explosions or
   killed accidentally trying to escape)
(Excluded: Republicans v. Loyalists, and internal
   feuds – these are all included in 6a and 6b)

	Cath	Prot	Total
1ac Security Forces killed by Republicans	116	803	919
2ac Republicans killed by Security Forces	133	0	133
8ac Republicans killed by their own activity	118	1	119
1bc Security Forces killed by Loyalists	2	12	14
7bc Loyalists killed by Security Forces	0	15	15
8bc Loyalists killed by their own activity	0	28	28
	369	**859**	**1228**
Others (unclassified or uncertain)	**36**	**24**	**60**
TOTALS	**1,551**	**1,620**	**3,171**

Formal Cease-fires
IRA from Thursday 1 September 1994.
Ended 9 February 1996. Renewed 20 July 1997.
INLA declared a cease-fire on 22 August 1998.
Combined Loyalist Military Command from Friday 14 October 1994.
The Loyalist Volunteer Force (LVF), centred in mid-Ulster, continued a campaign of murder until its cease-fire on 15 May 1998.
IRA dissidents the 'Real IRA' suspended all military operations from midnight 18–19 August 1998 following the Omagh bombing atrocity on 15 August and declared a cease-fire on 8 September 1998. Another dissident group the 'Continuity IRA' has yet to declare a cease-fire.

I am indebted to Very Rev. Seán Clerkin, Glaslough, for the recording and classification of these deaths. There is also a detailed analysis of deaths in Malcolm Sutton, An Index of Deaths from the Conflict in Northern Ireland 1969–1993 *(1994). In this period he gives a total of 357 killed by British forces. The British army was responsible for 294 of the total.*

EPILOGUE

Peace in a Transition Period, 1997

We are now in a period of transition in Northern Ireland and indeed there is a constant fluidity in the relations between Ireland and Britain. The Anglo-Irish Agreement, the Downing Street Declaration and change within the European Union are part of an evolutionary process towards a settlement of conflict within the island of Ireland, within Northern Ireland and between Britain and Ireland.

In the past 28 years external influences have been very great. The consequences of the single common market have not yet had a chance to fructify to the full but they will, now that there is relative peace, and this, together with a good economy in the Irish Republic, is leading to an all-Ireland economic union. One notices the new flow of trade south from the north and the great number of men from the north working in the building trade in Dublin. The opening up of eastern Europe has ended the 700 year British self-interest in Ireland. In time of war with Spain, France and Germany, Ireland was looked upon as a backdoor to invasion. This danger led to the Tudor conquest of Ireland when England became a nation state competing with continental powers. This security consciousness ensured the partition of Ireland and, as in the matter of the Act of Union of 1800, the Protestants were conveniently used as a support to bring it about. Ireland as a security risk to Britain was a factor until recently in the western alliance against Russia and the communist block. It affected politics as late as the Thatcher/Reagan close relationship, and then it suddenly collapsed with the Berlin wall. The eastern European threat has disappeared. Russia and the eastern European block are now vitally needed to boost a population-depleted and economic weak Europe, a Europe now dwindling in the global economic and political power context. In this picture Northern Ireland is a nasty embarrassing nuisance. Continental Europe will want to see it settled quickly and Britain, now freed for the first time in hundreds of years from its strategic tie to Ireland, has publicly declared that she has no longer a selfish interest in Ireland

and will forego sovereignty if that is the will of the majority of people in Northern Ireland.

A century ago kith and kinship bound Britain to unionists in Ireland; there was a common strong Protestantism, a united Unionist-Conservatist party, an aura surrounding the royal family. This has diminished greatly and, what is more, there is a new post Second World War Britain, empireless, tied to Europe, and with a more pluralist society, including a million southern-born Irish. It is important to mention this greater picture; while people in the north fight and squabble, the world leaves them behind.

The internal situation in Northern Ireland is still sad and fearful. On the ground parades were in the news. The loyalist marching season, which has jumped from some hundreds of parades to nearly three thousand, is now spreading beyond July and August to cover a period from Easter to October. Besides the Orange Order, the Black Preceptory and the Apprentice Boys, a new separate marching element has emerged – the 'Kick the Pope' bands and their followers. Some members of the Orange Order are not happy with this new element. They feel they are mistakenly identified with them. Sadly, once the war in a sense ended, underlying sectarianism rose to the top again. It was lying latent.

We have a second IRA cease-fire but before it we had the murder of two soldiers and two policemen. The viciousness of these murders are set against a strategy which might be called 'to go out on a high'. There was no respect for the sacredness of human life. These murders shocked everybody and created a tremendous pathos in the Catholic communities at home and abroad. The mid-Ulster Loyalist Volunteer Force (LVF), a break-away from the Ulster Volunteer Force, are still active and in the past year have committed horrible gruesome murders. They murdered a girl lying on a bed, a teenager who took a lift, a GAA official locking up a pavilion and a young man walking home. In the case of the men and boy their faces were bashed in and they were horribly mutilated. The LVF has a perverse religious foundation: they will batter any Catholic to death; to them a Catholic boy or girl, woman or man, young or old, is evil in himself or herself. The INLA is always potentially dangerous but they have not killed recently; they say they will not strike first. The 'continuity IRA', another splinter group, exploded the hotel bomb in Fermanagh; they might gain some recruits as the republicans consolidate their political strength and grow into a constitutional party, leading logically to electoral pacts with the SDLP and perhaps ultimately merging with them into a single party.

The two governments are encouraging all sides to talk. This is welcome and of course the bright new words are dialogue and trust. The unionists have opened up dialogue with the Catholic Church. I praise them for that. All the political parties should now follow this example and go beyond their narrowed-minded selves and talk to representatives of the churches, the business people, the trade unions and the universities. The great charismatic leaders in South Africa, de Klerk and Mandela, could hardly have succeeded without the tremendous backing of the business people.

In my opinion the general population in the north at present want less party political activity. They just want a breathing space. People forty years of age have not known peace from their childhood. Most people are not over-anxious about an immediate political settlement; they want to hear less not more of entrenched politicians on the media. They would like direct rule to continue for a peaceful period for some years to allow healing and let good measures already taken to fructify. Nobody can see an agreement across a board from Ian Paisley to Gerry Adams in the Mitchell supervised talks. Realistically people know that the two governments will have to work out a settlement. The settlement, one hopes, will be a fair one. It will have to be based on a British dimension for unionists/loyalists and an Irish dimension for nationalists/republicans. No one of the two communities for the foreseeable future should be imprisoned within the absolute ruling authority of either Britain or Ireland. It was inevitable that the entrapped nationalists in the north would revolt against injustice. They did that in the 1960s when they had gained a little strength. The present solution will involve balancing change in the Irish constitution and the Government of Ireland Act. It will be joint sovereignty in fact if not in name. The stronger partner in the working out of this agreement will be Britain whose wielding authority is finance. Anything short of at least *de facto* joint sovereignty would ultimately undermine Adams' republicans and would lead to a renewal of violence in the next generation. For the moment people are war weary. If the present deal turns out to be radical but fair, there is a good chance of permanent peace and good will, and the final solution of the government of the island of Ireland will be left to a future generation.

The continuance of a form of direct rule for some years is important. It is more important that society changes and all the injustices end than that we have a bitter short-lived, hastily cobbled together, devolved government. Let devolution come later. By that time some politicians, who are themselves an obstacle to peace, may be rejected in the ballot box.

In the meantime what is the immediate priority for Catholics in Northern Ireland? – the radical reform and restructure of the RUC. It is the one remaining important imbalanced structure of state. The RUC was raised from some 3,000 in 1969 to the present 14,000, which includes reserves, and is 94% Protestant. It has to change. It is not a matter of tinkering with minor things here and there; a major radical change is necessary. Ms Mo Mowlam, the Secretary of State, has already said there will be reform but she has not spelled out how radical that reform will be. If a major change in the RUC comes, it will upset the Protestant Churches. The RUC has always been closely linked into the religious and cultural life of the Protestant Churches and they are naturally aggrieved that many policemen lost their lives and many were injured in the conflict. The RUC were pushed to the front during the Ulsterisation of the 1970s and were established very formally in their traditional rôle as a standing army to defend the state. It hasn't been easy for them to carry out normal policing as a secondary rôle. Catholics would welcome a Bill of Rights which would incorporate the United Nations 'International Covenant on Civil and Political Rights' into domestic law and this could be the basis of policing and leave its ranks open to all shades of political adherence.

On 19 August 1969 Prime Minister Harold Wilson issued the first Downing Street Declaration announcing an end to religious discrimination: 'Every citizen in Northern Ireland is entitled to the same equality of treatment and freedom from discrimination as obtains in the rest of the United Kingdom'. With one stroke of the pen, the Labour government then abolished the housing discrimination in Northern Ireland that had lasted for 50 years and which was tied into the political and unjust manoeuvring of the unionist monolithic state. This was one of the grievances that had led to the Civil Rights Movement. This reform changed the face of Northern Ireland; wherever you travel in the north you can view with pride the new sprawling suburbs built under direct rule. The Fair Employment Agency has also done great work under the scrupulous leadership of Mr Bob Cooper. Its powers, however, have not been draconian. Inequality still exists. Catholic men in the north are over 2.5 times as likely to be unemployed as Protestants and are more likely to suffer long term employment.

A change to a society based on equality has been very difficult for unionists; a situation of dominance for Protestants was created by government in the Stormont parliament and so a whittling away of power and privilege to face fair competition and merit has met with opposition. The consequences of fair play arouse all the old bitterness of the Reformation and Counter-Reformation. Equality means a challenge to power; it means power sharing in government. A sudden change in demography has heightened the fear of Protestants. Even though the Catholic birth rate has fallen, the more just direct rule and the change to housing according to need and fairer employment has meant a sharp growth in the Catholic population in the north. That is also seen as a threat. Nationalists' success in the recent local government elections underlined this new reality. The population is now 56% Protestant, 44% Catholic with an equal number of young people. It is a further argument for the inevitability of joint sovereignty. Can unionists face up to this fact? Many of them, heads in the sand, still talk pathetically in loaded words like 'minority', 'the democratic majority', 'the people of Ulster', 'the mainland', 'the British Isles'.

What is it like to live in Northern Ireland now? A lot better. Even the absence of checkpoints is a blessing. During the twenty-eight years of virtual war, and the emotional trauma that went with it, there were many times when people would have asked would the 'Troubles' ever come to an end. There was a mountain of suffering and a mountain of prayers for peace. People let loose their pent-up inner joy of relief when President Clinton visited Derry, Belfast and Dublin. You can imagine then the harm that murder, torture, destruction of property, and imprisonment did to human relationships. Generally speaking the two communities in Northern Ireland have always lived separately. They grew more apart following the partition of Ireland; they grew still farther apart physically and mentally during the last twenty-eight years.

One hopes for a vision of people who might some time in the next hundred years come to respect one another and live in peace. I reckon it will take at least three generations of goodwill to bring about a real friendship. We should talk about one community but, unfortunately, the fact is there are two. At present there is little or no deep friendship between the two halves. There are some tiny pockets of people who live reasonably well together as a mixed community; there is a token dialogue between the heads of the Churches; there are ecumenical services once a year; there are some mixed prayer groups of wonderful spiritual people; a few people of mixed religion work together and are good friends; there are mixed marriages and some mixed schools; there are many decent and good people who lead very quiet and private lives. Co-operation at local level has improved in local councils; conditions of cross-community promotion attached to funds has helped that. The local history societies have been doing wonderful work to help people realise that their traditions are not necessarily opposed to one another and that some aspects of traditions are mutually hostile and divisive. There are schemes of education for mutual understanding but these vary according to the depth of local prejudices. That is the good side but generally speaking the two communities live apart – the working class in every city and town are almost completely separated from one another. Even the well-to-do form into ghettos. This horrible war has brought about a polarisation. In some cases people simply were afraid following intimidation and murders and found security living in their religious background. Such polarisation affects trade and even simple things like greetings on the public street. I wonder do visitors sadly see us, who have only one life to lead, imprisoned in our minds and hearts.

Elsewhere in conflict situations we see a new emphasis on people and especially on the individual. So the importance of incorporating civil and political rights into domestic law in Northern Ireland. About a year ago, I attended a major seminar on reconciliation in Belfast; some countries from South America, the eastern bloc of Europe, South

Africa and Israel and Palestine were present. The delegates from El Salvador and South Africa were impressive. Why? Because of their honesty and humility; they had learned to admit crimes on all sides; they saw the importance of a commission for truth as an integral part of the healing process. Yes it is important for the republican paramilitaries to tell the truth about their murders and crimes and repatriate missing bodies. Yes it is necessary for the loyalist paramilitaries to tell the truth about their murders and atrocities. Yes it is necessary for the British government to acknowledge that over the past 28 years it acted unlawfully, immorally, and unjustly in the murders and unjust killings of innocent people, in ill-treatment in interrogation centres and in corruption of courts. If honesty prevails, all this is tied into the question of the decommissioning of arms. It may scare all the three perpetrators of violence, republican and loyalist paramilitaries and the state from pursuing the issue. South Africa and El Salvador bravely faced up to the problem; they set up truth commissions. They saw that this was necessary for the emotional healing of people and the process of building a just society. Why do we lack this honesty and humility?

Talk given at a Mass for Peace in St Paul's Church, Mullingar, 21 August 1997.

LITERATURE

Publications of Denis Faul and Raymond Murray

BOOKS AND PAMPHLETS

The Mailed Fist: A record of Army & Police Brutality from Aug. 9–Nov. 9, 1971. Issued by the Campaign for Social Justice in Northern Ireland in collaboration with the Association for Legal Justice.

British Army and Special Branch RUC Brutalities. December 1971–February 1972. First printed 1972. Reprinted 1972. Compiled by Fr Denis Faul, Dungannon, and Fr Raymond Murray, Armagh.

Whitelaw's Tribunals. Long Kesh Internment Camp, November 1972–February 1973. Compiled by Fr Denis Faul, Dungannon, and Fr Raymond Murray, Armagh.

The Hooded Men. British Torture in Ireland, August, October 1971. Fr Denis Faul, Dungannon, Fr Raymond Murray, Armagh. July 1974.

The Iniquity of Internment. Long Kesh, August 9th 1971–August 9th, 1974. Compiled by Fr Denis Faul, Dungannon, and Fr Raymond Murray, Armagh.

Corruption of Law. Memorandum to the Gardiner Committee on the Working of Emergency Legislation in Northern Ireland, from Fr Brian J. Brady, Belfast, Fr Denis Faul, Dungannon, Fr Raymond Murray, Armagh. September 1974.

Internment 1971–1975. By Fr Brian Brady, Fr Denis Faul, Fr Raymond Murray. 1975.

The Shame of Merlyn Rees. 4th Year of Internment in Ireland, Long Kesh 1974 – 1975. By Fr Denis Faul, Fr Raymond Murray. 1975.

The Flames of Long Kesh 15–16 October 1974. By Fr Denis Faul, Dungannon, Fr Raymond Murray, Armagh. December 1974.

The Triangle of Death. Sectarian Assassinations in the Dungannon–Moy– Portadown area. By Fr Denis Faul, Dungannon, Fr Raymond Murray, Armagh. Three separate editions with added material. 1975.

A British Army Murder. Leo Norney (17 years) killed by Black Watch regiment, 13 October 1975. By Fr Brian J. Brady, Fr Denis Faul, Fr Raymond Murray. September 1975.

The RUC: The Black and Blue Book. By Fr Denis Faul, Fr Raymond Murray. First published 1975. Reprinted 1983.

Majella O'Hare. Shot dead by the British Army 14 August 1976. By Fr Denis Faul and Fr Raymond Murray. September 1976.

British Army Terror. West Belfast, September, October 1976. (Brian Stewart).

By Fr Brian J. Brady, Fr Denis Faul, Fr Raymond Murray. 1976.

The Birmingham Framework. Six Innocent Men Framed for the Birmingham Bombings. By Fr Denis Faul, Fr Raymond Murray. 1977. Reprinted 1984.

SAS Terrorism – The Assassin's Glove. By Fr Denis Faul, Fr Raymond Murray. July 1976.

The Castlereagh File. Allegations of RUC Brutality 1976/1977. By Fr Denis Faul and Fr Raymond Murray. Printed 1978. Reprinted in USA 1979.

Violations of Human Rights in Northern Ireland 1968 – 1978. By Fr Denis Faul, Fr Raymond Murray. 1978.

The Sleeping Giant. Irish Americans and Human Rights in N. Ireland. By Fr Denis Faul, Fr Raymond Murray. 1978.

H Blocks. British Jail for Irish Political Prisoners. By Fr Denis Faul and Fr Raymond Murray. 1979.

Moment for Truth on Northern Ireland. By Denis Faul and Raymond Murray. 1980.

H Blocks and its Background. By Denis Faul and Raymond Murray. 1980.

Michael McCartan. An Innocent Catholic Boy Shot Dead by the RUC, 23 July 1980. By Fr Denis Faul, Fr Raymond Murray. September 1980.

The British Dimension. Brutality, Murder and Legal Duplicity in N. Ireland. By Fr Denis Faul and Fr Raymond Murray. 1980.

Hunger Strike. H Blocks, Long Kesh, Northern Ireland 27 October 1980. Published by a group of lawyers and priests.

Rubber & Plastic Bullets Kill & Maim. By Fr Denis Faul, Fr Raymond Murray. 1981.

Danny Barrett. A British Army Murder. By Fr Denis Faul, Fr Raymond Murray. 1982.

Plastic Bullets – Plastic Government. By Fr Denis Faul, Fr Raymond Murray. 1982.

The Sacredness of Human Life: An Invitation to Debate. By Denis Faul, Raymond Murray. October 1982.

The Stripping Naked of the Women Prisoners in Armagh Prison 1982–83. By Denis Faul. Published by Fr Denis Faul, Fr Raymond Murray. Easter 1983.

Angela D'Arcy. Irish Catholic Girl Shot Dead by a British Army Soldier in Enniskillen 25 November 1981. By Fr Denis Faul, Fr Raymond Murray. Published 1983.

The Alienation of Northern Catholics. By Denis Faul, Raymond Murray. February 1984.

Collusion 1990 –1994. Loyalist Paramilitary Murders in North of Ireland. By Arthur Fegan and Raymond Murray. Issued by Relatives for Justice, 1985.

The SAS in Ireland. By Raymond Murray. Mercier Press. First published November 1990. Sixth Printing 1997.

Hard Time: Armagh Gaol 1971–1986. By Raymond Murray. Mercier Press, 1998.

PRESS RELEASES

Whitelaw's Tribunals. Fr Denis Faul, Fr Raymond Murray. 1 June 1979.

The Hooded Men. Fr Denis Faul, Fr Raymond Murray. 1972.

The Shame of Merlyn Rees. Fr Raymond Murray, Fr Denis Faul. 9 August 1975.

The Birmingham Framework. Fr Fr Denis Faul, Fr Raymond Murray. 4 July 1977.

SAS Terrorism – The Assassin's Glove. Fr Denis Faul, Fr Raymond Murray. 6 July 1976.

The Black and Blue Book. Fr Denis Faul. Fr Raymond Murray. February 1975.

H-Blocks. 'British Jail for Irish Prisoners'. Fr Denis Faul, Fr Raymond Murray. 1979.

Michael McCartan. September 1980. Fr Denis Faul, Fr Raymond Murray.

LEAFLETS AND BROADSHEETS

THE LAW

Know Your Rights. Issued by Fr Denis Faul with NCCL (National Council for Civil Liberties) Abbey Printers (Cavan) Ltd. Undated (1975).

Legal Rights for Those Detained. Fr Denis Faul, Dungannon. Printed both in blue and black. Undated (1976).

Legal Rights for Those Detained. Fr Denis Faul. June 1977.

Legal Rights. Fr Denis Faul. Dungannon, 1/3/78.

Legal Rights for Those Detained. Fr Denis Faul. February 1979.

Legal Rights for Those Detained. Fr Denis Faul. January 1980.

Whitelaw Violates Article 6 of the European Convention on Human Rights. Repression of the Catholic Minority in Northern Ireland. Fr Denis Faul, Fr Raymond Murray. 1972.

The Courts. Repression of the Catholic Minority in Northern Ireland. Fr Denis Faul, Dungannon, Fr Raymond Murray, Armagh. 1972.

Anti-Catholic Bias in the Courts of Northern Ireland. A Sample Study March 1974. Association for Legal Justice.

Anti-Catholic Bias in the Courts of Northern Ireland. A Sample Study April 1974. Association for Legal Justice.

Anti-Catholic Bias in the Courts of Northern Ireland. A Sample Study May and June 1974. Association for Legal Justice.

Anti-Catholic Bias in the Courts of Northern Ireland. A Sample Study July to October 1974. Association for Legal Justice.

Anti-Catholic Bias in the Courts of Northern Ireland. A Sample Study November 1974 to June 1975. Association for Legal Justice.

Desert Labour. Issued by Fr Denis Faul, Dungannon, and Fr Raymond Murray, Armagh. Undated (1975).

The Law No Longer Protects Me. An Analysis of the Use of Supergrasses. Fr Denis Faul, Fr Raymond Murray. October 1983.

20 Points against Internment. Repression of the Catholic Minority in Northern Ireland. Issued by Fr Denis Faul, Dungannon. Undated (1972).

List of Injuries and Inhuman Treatment meted out to Political Remand Prisoners in Cage 8 – since 11th September, 1972. Repression of the Catholic Minority in Northern Ireland.

List of Injuries sustained by Remand Prisoners in Compound 6, Long Kesh, on Friday, 22nd September, 1972. Repression of the Catholic Minority in Northern Ireland. Fr T. Connolly, Fr Denis Faul, Fr Raymond Murray, Fr John McKean.

Long Kesh Internees. Patrick J. McClean. 1972.

Ill-treatment of Political Prisoners in Long Kesh, The Maze, July 4, 1973.

Selective Releases from Long Kesh Internment Camp – Christmas 1973. Association for Legal Justice.

Remember Long Kesh. May 20th, 1975. Fr Denis Faul, Dungannon.

Remember Long Kesh, No Negotiations under Duress. Issued by Fr Denis Faul and Fr Raymond Murray, Armagh. Undated (1975).

20 Reasons why an Amnesty should be given to all imprisoned because of alleged misdeeds committed because of a lack of security or justice in society. Issued by Fr Denis Faul, Dungannon. Undated (1975).

Amnesty. Holy year 1975. Fr Brian Brady, Fr Denis Faul, Fr Raymond Murray.

Five Reasons why Political Status – Special Category – is a Fact of Life in Northern Ireland. Published by Fr Denis Faul with some families of political prisoners. 1976. Arguments for Politcal Status (or AMNESTY). Lurgan relations 1976.

Maladministration of Prisons. Published by the families of political prisoners, Lurgan April 1976.

H-Blocks Protest. The No Washing, Non-Cooperation Phase. April 1978. By Fr Denis Faul and Fr Raymond Murray. Issued in blue and black.

H-Block. By Fr Denis Faul, Fr Raymond Murray. 1978.

H-Block. The Care and Welfare of Prisoners in Northern Ireland. Produced by Fr Denis Faul and Fr Raymond Murray. Easter 1978. Issued in black, red, green, blue, pink.

Die Politische Häftlinge in Nordirland. Eine Frage von Krieg oder Frieden. 1978.

Rapport Fra et Faengsel i Nordirland. 1978.

An Information Sheet. From the Relatives Action Committee of South Derry and West Antrim. September 1978.

H-Block. Christmas 1978. Fr Denis Faul, Fr Raymond Murray. Issued in red and blue.

Appeal to Irish Voters in Britain and Scotland. 1979.

Appeal to Irish Voters in Britain and Scotland. Issued by the County Tyrone and Armagh parents of families. Poster. 1979.

Remember H Block and Forget Labour. Parents of County Derry Prisoners in H

Blocks. 1979.

H-Blocks. A Letter Fr Denis Faul, Fr Raymond Murray. 1 June 1979.

H-Block. The Year of the Child. Issued by South Derry and South West Antrim Relatives for Action Committee, November 1979.

H-Blocks. A letter from a blanket man to the Association for Legal Justice. 1979.

H-Block. Christmas 1979. Fr Denis Faul, Fr Raymond Murray.

American Delegation to H-Blocks and Armagh Jail. Issued by Fr Denis Faul and Fr Raymond Murray. September 1980.

Remember H Blocks and Armagh Jail. Issued by South Derry and South West Antrim relatives Action Committee. Autumn 1980.

Hunger Strike 2. By Fr Denis Faul, Fr Raymond Murray. March 1981.

Hunger Strikes – The Search for Solutions. Fr Denis Faul, Fr Raymond Murray. May 1981.

Deputation of Anti-Unionist Councillors, Dungannon District Council, to Mr Michael Alison, Minister of State, on Tuesday 21st July 1981. Prisons.

Prison Problems and the Alienation of Catholics in N. Ireland. Statement of Help the Prisoners, 13 June 1984. Issued by Fr Denis Faul and Fr Raymond Murray.

Women in Jail in Northern Ireland. By Fr Denis Faul. July 1978.

Prevented from Going to Mass. Armagh Prison, Northern Ireland. Undated (1980).

Black February. Armagh Prison. Beating Women in Prison. Compiled by Fr Denis Faul. 1980.

Armagh Prison. The Parents Speak. Issued by Fr Denis Faul, Fr Raymond Murray. 1980.

The Stripping Naked of Women Prisoners in Armagh Gaol. November 1982 January 1984. The Shame of James Prior and Nicholas Scott. Fr Denis Faul.

Stripping Girls Naked in Armagh Prison. A Letter to Nicholas Scott. Minister for Prisons by Fr Raymond Murray. 11 January 1985. Published by Fr Denis Faul, Fr Raymond Murray, Armagh Social Acion Group.

Torture, Torture. Torture. Association for Legal Justice. November December 1973. (Forced feeding of Dolours Price, Marion Price, Hugh Feeney, Gerard Kelly, Roy Walsh). In English, French, German.

Brutality in Albany Prison, Isle of Wight. Repression of Irish Catholics in the Fourth World. Fr Denis Faul, Dungannon, Fr Raymond Murray, Armagh. 1976.

'In Prison in England'. Christmas 1977. Fr Denis Faul, Dungannon, and Fr Raymond Murray, Armagh, with the help of Sister Sarah Clarke, London.

The Birmingham Pub Bombing Case. Synopsis of the forensic evidence, presented by Fr Denis Faul and Fr Raymond Murray. February 1980.

Parole for Fr Patrick Fell. Fr Denis Faul, Fr Raymond Murray. March 1980.

The Need for Security. Treatment of Prisoners in Portlaoise. By Fr Denis Faul, Dungannon, and Fr Raymond Murray, Armagh. 1977.

Questions a Candidiate should Answer. Issued by the Relatives of Prisoners. Undated (1981).

Portlaoise Prison. By Fr Denis Faul, Dungannon, Fr Raymond Murray, Armagh. June 1984.

The Murrays. Must they hang in Dublin? Issued by Murray Defence Committee (Northern Ireland). Correspondence Secretary, Fr Denis Faul.

THE CATHOLIC COMMUNITY

Some Examples of Attacks on Catholic Church Property. Repression of the Catholic Minority in Northern Ireland. 1972.

The Plight of Catholics in Newtownabbey. 16th February 1974.

Short Brothers Limited, Belfast. A Case Study in Anti-Catholic Discrimination. By Rev. Brian J. Brady. Published by Irish National Caucus, Inc., Washington DC, April 1983. Reprinted by Fr Denis Faul, Fr Raymond Murray, July 1983.

Memorandum to Members of Parliament taking part in the Debate on Northern Ireland, Westminster. June 3–4, 1974. The Ulster Workers Council Strike. Repression of the Catholic Minority in Northern Ireland.

The Alienation of the Catholic/Nationalist People in N. Ireland. 20 Reasons for Alienation. Reply to the Northern Ireland Church of Ireland bishops. Issued by Fr Denis Faul, Dungannon, Fr Raymond Murray, Armagh, 30 November 1984.

THE RUC

25 Methods of Brutality by Military and Special Branch RUC, December 1971 – February 1972. Repression of the Catholic Minority in Northern Ireland. Fr Denis Faul, Fr Raymond Murray. 1972.

Ballykelly, RUC Special Branch Interrogation Centre. Fr Denis Faul, Dungannon, Fr Raymond Murray, Armagh. 1973.

20 Reasons Why Catholics Should Not Give General Support to the RUC. Repression of the Catholic Minority in Northern Ireland. Issued by Fr Denis Faul, Dungannon, November 1974.

Unacceptability of RUC in 1975. Repression of the Catholic Minority in Northern Ireland. Fr Denis Faul.

The Harassment of the Mulgrew Family. June to October 1976. Repression of the Catholic Minority in Northern Ireland. By Fr Brian Brady, Fr Denis Faul and Fr Raymond Murray.

Allegations of Brutality, Signing of False Statements and Threats of Assassination Made by Regional Crime Squad Members in the Strand Road RUC Station, Derry City, 22 – 25 November 1976. Issued by Fr Denis Faul, Dungannon, and Fr Raymond Murray, Armagh.

What Happened to Eddie Rooney on the Night of 28 February 1977? Oppression of the Catholic Minority in Northern Ireland. Issued by Fr Denis Faul, Dungannon, Fr Raymond Murray, Armagh.

Allegations of Brutality in Armagh RUC Station. March 1977. Catholic families in
   Co. Armagh complain of RUC ill-treatment. Printed on white and
   green paper.
*Serious Allegations of Ill-treatment in Omagh and Dungannon RUC Stations. April
   23rd – May 12th, 1977.* Issued by Fr Denis Faul, Dungannon, and Fr
   Raymond Murray, Armagh.
20 Methods of Brutality in Castlereagh and Other RUC Interrogation Centres. Re-
   pression of the Catholic Minority in Northern Ireland. Issued by Fr
   Denis Faul, Dungannon, and Fr Raymond Murray, Armagh. 1977/78.
   Printed in blue and black.
Ten Years On: Violations of Human Rights 1968 78. A Letter. 25 October 1978.
   Fr Denis Faul, Fr Raymond Murray.
Brutality against Persons Arrested under Emergency Powers. Fr Denis Faul. March
   22nd 1979.
*Second International Tribunal of Inquiry into Deaths and Injuries by Plastic Bullets,
   Belfast, N. Ireland, 16 October 1982.* Issued by Fr Denis Faul, Fr Ray-
   mond Murray
Plastic Bullets. Shootings that Shame the State. Raymond Murray, September 1985.
   Issued by Fr Denis Faul,, Fr Raymond Murray
RUC: Abuses of Law, 1985. Fr Denis Faul, Fr Raymond Murray.
An Alternative Police Force in Northern Ireland. By Fr Raymond Murray. Sub-
   mission to Initiative '92 and the Opsahl Commission. May 1993.

THE BRITISH ARMY
65 Priests Working in West Belfast issued the following statement on Monday
   20th November, 1972. Repression of the Catholic Minority in North-
   ern Ireland. Presented at a Press Conference in Belfast by Fr Desmond
   Wilson, Ballymurphy, Fr Brian Brady, Andersonstown, Fr A. Reid,
   Clonard.
*Statements by Luke McKiernan and Kevin Clancy of Derrygosh, Newtownbutler, Co.
   Fermanagh.* Repression of the Catholic Minority in Northern Ireland.
   August 1974. Issued by Fr Denis Faul.
The Amazing Dis-Grace of the Royal Scots Dragoon Guards at Eglish, Dungannon.
   Repression of the Catholic Minority in Northern Ireland. June 5–6th,
   1976. By Fr Denis Faul, Dungannon.
The Behaviour of the 3rd Parachute Regiment in South Armagh, June – July 1976.
   Repression of the Catholic Minority in Northern Ireland. June 5–6th,
   1976. Fr Denis Faul, Dungannon, Fr Raymond Murray, Armagh.
*The Behaviour of the Royal Marine Commandos in Crossmaglen on Tuesday evening,
   31st August 1976.* Fr Denis Faul, Dungannon, Fr Raymond Murray,
   Armagh.
*Terror Tactics of the British Army. Royal Marine Commandos at Crossmaglen. October,
   1976.* Repression of the Catholic Minority in Northern Ireland. By Fr
   Denis Faul, Fr Raymond Murray.

The Killing of Martin Malone. Catholic Youth of 18 Years shot dead by the Ulster Defence Regiment 30 July 1983. Published by Fr Denis Faul, Fr Raymond Murray.

Second International Tribunal of Inquiry into Deaths and Injuries by Plastic Bullets, Belfast, N. Ireland, 16 October 1982. Conclusion of the Tribunal. Issued by Fr Denis Faul, Fr Raymond Murray.

State Killings in Northern Ireland. By Fr Raymond Murray. Issued by Relatives for Justice. 1991.

Unveiling of Memorial to Fergal Caraher, Cullyhanna. Fr Raymond Murray. 30 December 1991.

INDEX

THE SAS IN IRELAND

RAYMOND MURRAY

The SAS in Ireland traces the history of the British Army Special Air Services Regiment, the SAS, in Ireland over the past twenty years. It details their activities – intelligence gathering and surveillance, their links with British Intelligence, notably MI5 and MI6, their connection with sectarian murders and many other deaths.

In this book Fr Raymond Murray analyses in detail the activities of the SAS and plain clothes soldiers in the six counties. His research leads him to the conclusion that in many instances the SAS engaged in a careful and organised shoot-to-kill policy.

HARD TIME
ARMAGH GAOL 1971–86

RAYMOND MURRAY

Raymond Murray was Catholic chaplin of Armagh Women's Gaol from 1971 to 1986. The number of women political prisoners increased from two in 1971 to more than one hundred in the 1972–76 period. Thirty-two of these women were imprisoned without trial. Most of the political prisoners in gaol were girls in their teenage years and one internee was in her sixties. In the 1972–76 period the prisoners had 'special category' or 'political' status.

Raymond Murray's reports became more hard-hitting as injustices increased and oppression grew. Some prisoners in Armagh Gaol alleged beatings by male officers, strip-searches, denial of access to toilets, denial of laundry, denial of visits from concerned persons, the use of 23-hour lock-up and other degrading practices.